PRAISE FOR

The JAVA EE
Architect's Handbook

"Derek Ashmore has assembled a 'must have' book for anyone working with Java and/or Java EE applications. Mr. Ashmore covers all the bases in this 'how to' approach to designing/developing/testing/and implementing Java EE applications using Java with frequent references to XML, JDBC libraries, SOAP, relational database access (using SQL), and references various useful tools when relevant. This book clearly illustrates Derek's expertise in the Java world. . . . Thank you for sharing your knowledge with the IT community with such a useful book."

DAN HOTKA, AUTHOR/INSTRUCTOR/ORACLE EXPERT

"This book is very well crafted and explains everything you really need to know in order to be a successful and productive Java EE architect. It is an excellent book, which offers a full and detailed coverage of the topic of Java EE architecture and can be used as a handbook by the novice or as a reference tool for the experienced architect. The straightforward writing style and good visuals make for a quick and comprehensive learning experience. If Java is your primary programming language, and you're currently working as a Java EE architect or considering it as a future career, this book should be in your library."

IAN ELLIS, VICE PRESIDENT AND CHIEF INFORMATION OFFICER, IESAbroad

"[Derek has written] an in-depth and comprehensive resource for the Java2 architect! The book provides a concise road map for real-world Java EE development. The approach is practical and straightforward, based on a wealth of experience. All aspects of project management, application and data design, and Java development are covered. This book avoids the 'dry style' and over-abstraction (over-simplification) common to so many books in this subject area. An awesome book, I keep it on my 'A' shelf!"

JIM ELLIOTT, CTO, WEST HAVEN SYSTEMS, INC.

"Clear reading and bridges the gap between professionals and professors. I've read many technical books in my thirty-year career where the author spends more time tossing around the current buzzwords and fails to get the point across. Derek's book really connects with the hard core developer. Practical, knowledgeable, excellent examples."

JOHN R MULL, PRESIDENT, SYSTECH SOFTWARE PRODUCTS, INC.

The JAVA EE
Architect's Handbook

SECOND EDITION

*How to Be a Successful Application Architect
for Java EE Applications*

DEREK C. ASHMORE

Publisher's Cataloging-in-Publication Data

Ashmore, Derek C.
    The Java EE architect's handbook : how to be a successful application architect for Java EE applications. —2nd ed. / Derek C. Ashmore.
        pages cm
    ISBN: 978-0-9729548-8-4 (pbk.)
    Includes bibliographical references and index.
    1. Java (Computer program language). 2. Application software—Development. 3. Web site development. 4. Internet programming.   I. Title.
QA76.73.J38 A84 2014
005.13`3—dc23

2013953828

Editor: Cathy Reed
Cover Design: The Roberts Group
Interior Design: The Roberts Group
Indexer: The Roberts Group

Published by:
DVT Press
Bolingbrook, IL
sales@dvtpress.com
http://www.dvtpress.com

The opinions and views expressed in this book are solely that of the author. This book does not necessarily represent the opinions and views of the technical reviewers or the firms that employ them.

TRADEMARKS: Java, Java EE, Java Development Kit are trademarks of Oracle Corporation, Inc. All other products or services mentioned in this book are the trademarks or service marks of their respective companies and organizations.

While every precaution has been taken in the preparation of this book, the author and publisher assume no responsibility for errors and omissions or for damages resulting from the use of the information contained herein.

ISBN: 978-0-9729548-8-4

Contents

Preface

The *Java EE Architect's Handbook* was written for application architects and senior developers tasked with designing and leading the development of Java EE applications. The objective of this book is to help you fulfill the application architect role in a Java EE project. If you are a senior developer needing to fill the role of an application architect for the first time, this book will help you succeed. If you are already an application architect, this book will empower you with additional skills so that you can improve your ability to fulfill that role. This book provides numerous strategies, guidelines, tips, tricks, and best practices to help the junior architect navigate the entire development process, from analysis through application deployment and support. To help you achieve success as a Java EE application architect, the book presents the following material:

- A basic framework for filling the role of application architect at every stage of the project life cycle
- Architect-level tips, tricks, and best practices at each stage of development
- Tips, tricks, and best practices for establishing coding standards to make code consistent and more maintainable
- Tips, tricks, and best practices for creating and communicating designs
- Estimation and project-planning material

This edition of the handbook concentrates on application architect *deliverables* at each stage of development. That is, the book describes discrete tasks typically performed by the application architect and provides tips and techniques for performing these tasks. As many learn best by example, this book will provide examples of your deliverables.

Readers of the first edition might be confused by the title change for the second edition. The first edition of the book was titled *The J2EE Architect's Handbook*. The term "J2EE" was deprecated in 2006 and replaced with the term Java Enterprise Edition or "Java EE" for short. Essentially, both terms refer to the same platform.

This book will *not* teach you how to program Java EE applications. While most application architects do code parts of the applications they support, they do so in their capacity of a *developer*, not in their capacity of application architect. The marketplace is replete with technical books that provide instruction on how to code Java EE applications. This book will complement, but not attempt to duplicate, that material. While there is sample code in the book, its purpose is to illustrate application architecture concepts; not to be a detailed instructional guide on how to write code.

This book is *not* a study guide for any of the certification exams for Java and Java EE technologies provided by the Oracle Corporation. Those exams concentrate purely on technical skills. While technical skills are necessary to be an effective application architect, they are not sufficient. The role of application architect transcends raw technical ability. Architects must be effective communicators, must work well with other team members, and must be able to understand the business aspects and requirements for the end user areas their applications support. None of these facets of being an effective application architect is measured by any of the certification exams.

Furthermore, the book is *not* for beginners. Readers should know Java syntax and basic Java EE concepts and have at least an intermediate programming skill set and basic experience with the following:

- Relational databases, SQL, JDBC, and a JPA implementation such as Hibernate
- JSPs, servlets, and experience with at least one web framework (e.g., Spring-MVC, Struts, Java Server Faces)
- Experience working with what are commonly open source projects such as Apache Commons, Spring, Hibernate, and many more
- Experience working with a development team
- Experience supporting applications not written by you

A common conception is that Java EE applications are incredibly complex. Authors of technical books and articles unintentionally support this conception by providing incredible technical depth on aspects of Java EE not commonly used. For example, many texts begin their discussions of enterprise beans by describing Java EE transaction capabilities in great detail; however, most Java EE applications make only limited use of Java EE transaction management capabilities. In this book, I strip away some of the complexity (aspects that the majority of developers rarely use) to reveal how relatively straightforward Java EE applications can be. Your time is too valuable to waste reading about features and concepts you'll rarely use in the marketplace.

HOW THE BOOK IS ORGANIZED

The first chapter of the book describes the role of the application architect in most organizations and explains how the project life cycle illustrated in this book fits in with Extreme Programming (XP), the Rational Unified Process (RUP), and other possible methodologies.

Section 1 details how to define the project objectives using use-case analysis. It also discusses how to define scope and create a preliminary project plan. The guidelines presented in this section will help you successfully complete these tasks that are critical to your project coming in on time and on budget. The most common reasons for project failures or cost overruns are poorly defined and managed objectives and scope, not technical problems.

Section 2 focuses on object-modeling and data-modeling activities, describing how detailed they need to be and illustrating common mistakes. In addition, you will learn how to architect interfaces with external systems and how to refine the project plan and associated estimates. The modeling skills presented in this section are critical to effectively communicating a design to developers.

Section 3 presents implementation tips and guidelines for all aspects of Java EE applications. You'll learn how to layer your application to minimize the impact of enhancements and changes. You'll also become acquainted with several open source libraries commonly used to streamline application code and the development process.

In addition, section 3 details application architecture decisions you'll need to make regarding testing, exception handling, logging, and threading, and you'll learn tips and techniques for implementing major sections of the design. The failure of an application architect to define implementation strategies and methodologies can slow down a project significantly and increase the number of bugs.

Section 4 offers tips and guidelines for developing testing procedures and process improvement. These suggestions are directed at making your applications more stable and maintainable. In addition, you'll learn the signs warning you that refactoring activities are necessary. Reading this section will enable you to make your future projects even more successful.

COMMON RESOURCES

This book makes frequent references to the following open source projects that are often used with many Java EE applications:

- Apache Commons Lang (http://commons.apache.org/lang/)
- Apache Commons Collections (http://commons.apache.org/collections/)

- Apache Commons BeanUtils (http://commons.apache.org/beanutils/)
- Apache Commons DbUtils (http://commons.apache.org/dbutils/)
- Apache Commons IO (http://commons.apache.org/io)
- Google Guava Core Libraries (https://code.google.com/p/guava-libraries/)
- Hibernate (http://www.hibernate.org/)

Another open source project on which this book relies is Admin4J. The author is the chief architect and a developer of Admin4J. Admin4J is used as an illustration for implementing the concepts presented in this book. Admin4J binaries and source can be downloaded at http://www.admin4j.net.

Errata, example source code, and other materials related to this book can be found at http://www.dvtpress.com/.

FEEDBACK

I'm always interested in reading comments and suggestions that will improve future editions of this book. Please send feedback directly to me at derek.ashmore@dvtconsulting.com. If your comment or suggestion is the first of its kind and is used in the next edition, I will gladly send you an autographed copy. Additionally, reader questions are sometimes selected and answered in entries in my blog at http://www.derekashmore.com/.

Acknowledgments

This book could not have been written without a large amount of assistance. Several colleagues helped tremendously to refine the book concept and edit the drafts, thus keeping me from mass marketing mediocrity. They have my undying gratitude and thanks. I could not have written the book without the assistance from the following people: Michael Lyons, D. Scott Wheeler, Todd Pagni, Haim Izrael, Ken Liu, Budi Kurniawan, Peeyush Maharshi, Mohit Gupta, Rick Miller, Shawn Racinto, Michael Spicuzza, Scott Kramer, Pradeep Sadhu, and Sauabh Gupta.

Many thanks to my editor, Cathy Reed, who painstakingly corrected my numerous grammar mistakes and graciously pointed out places where my verbiage was less than clear. Many thanks to Sherry and Tony Roberts and their colleagues at the Roberts Group for fantastic cover art, typesetting, indexing, and general wizardry that makes the book aesthetically pleasing.

Many thanks to my wife, Beth, and my children, Zachary and Morgan. They put up with music coming out of the office at all hours of the night while I was working on this. Beth routinely watched our children so that I could devote time to writing this book.

I retain responsibility for any and all errors that remain.

SECTION I

PLANNING JAVA EE APPLICATIONS

The application architect typically assists in planning Java EE applications by participating in analysis activities, defining scope, and estimating resources, among other activities. The architect's role in the planning stage varies greatly from company to company. Although I've taken the perspective that the architect leads and facilitates planning activities, your role at an individual company may be to assist rather than facilitate.

In this section, you will learn how to:

- Facilitate and document business analysis.
- Assist the project manager in defining project scope.
- Estimate needed time and resources.
- Define and design interfaces to external applications.

The skills you learn here will enable you to apply the design techniques discussed in section 2.

CHAPTER 1

PROJECT DEVELOPMENT TEAM AND PROJECT LIFE CYCLE

This chapter lays the foundation for building a successful first project, from inception to release. It begins by defining what an application architect is and does, and by summarizing how the architect works with other team members. The chapter continues with a look at a few alternative approaches to the development process. Still a subject of considerable debate, the definitive process for building a successful project does not yet exist, leading many companies to adopt a hybrid plan.

PROJECT DEVELOPMENT TEAM: ROLES AND RESPONSIBILITIES

All Java EE development teams need people with a wide variety of skills to fill numerous roles within the team. Among the many skill sets needed to make a Java EE project successful are:

- Application architect
- Product manager
- Project manager
- Business analyst
- Graphic designer
- Presentation-tier developer
- Business logic developer

- Data modeler
- Database administrator
- Data migration specialist
- Infrastructure specialist
- Testing specialist
- Test automation specialist

Although the book focuses on the role of the application architect, this section defines the roles and responsibilities of other major players on the Java EE development team and describes the responsibilities of the application architect with respect to those roles.

Some organizations use different labels for the roles. For instance, an infrastructure specialist may be called a system administrator; a testing specialist may be a tester; and some organizations may distinguish between a test team manager and individual testers. Regardless of the terms you attach to these skill sets, making all of them part of a development team greatly increases the team's chances of creating a successful Java EE project.

Further, it's possible for one person on the team to fill many roles and for one role to be co-owned by multiple people if the project is large enough. Some organizations combine the roles of application architect and project manager. Some organizations have a senior developer double as a database administrator or as an infrastructure specialist. And some have the same developers work on the presentation tier as well as the business layer. Here I'm not trying to recommend a particular team organization but merely to communicate what skill sets are necessary, however they are organized.

Application Architect

The application architect identifies the technologies that will be used for the project. In many organizations, some technology choices are made at an enterprise level. For instance, many organizations make hardware and operating system choices and some software choices (e.g., the Java EE container vendor) at an enterprise level. Commonly, choosing a language, such as Java, is an enterprise-level decision.

However, most applications have technical requirements that aren't explicitly provided in enterprise-level edicts. I make a distinction between technology choices made at an enterprise level and those made for individual applications. For example, a decision to use the Java language for all server-side programming might be made at an enterprise level, but a decision about which XML parser to use might be left to individual application architects. In many organizations, the people making enterprise-level technology choices make up a group separate from the Java EE development team.

The application architect is commonly responsible for identifying third-party packages or utilities that will be used for a project. For example, the architect might identify a need for a template-based generation engine and choose Apache's Velocity.

Increasingly, organizations are differentiating between enterprise architects and application architects. Enterprise architects assist with deciding which software products will be purchased and which will be built. An effective enterprise architect will ensure that software products in use are aligned with the business goals of the enterprise. Enterprise architecture is out of scope of this book; additional material on the role of enterprise architects can be found at the following URL: http://en.wikipedia.org/wiki/Enterprise_architect.

The application architect recommends the development methodologies and frameworks of the project. Typically, the architect makes these recommendations to the project manager. For example, a common recommendation is to document all analyses in use-case format and supplement with a prototype. Another common recommendation is to document the design in terms of an object model. Some organizations define the methodologies used at an enterprise level.

The application architect provides the overall design and structure of the application. Each developer brings to a project a unique set of preconceived opinions, habits, and preferences. Synthesizing the input of this sometimes widely divergent group, the application architect ensures that the work done by individual developers is complementary.

I liken the role of application architect to that of an orchestra conductor. All musicians have differing opinions about how to interpret a given work. The conductor provides the interpretation that will be used and works with the musicians to implement it. Depending on the development methodology, the design for each feature may not occur upfront. In this case, it is the architect's job to work with developers as feature development is occurring to assist with the design and ensure the implementation fits with the overall architecture.

The application architect ensures that the project is adequately defined. A project analysis must be detailed and consistent enough to form the basis for building an application. Typically, the application architect works with the project manager and business analyst to define the project.

The application architect ensures that the application design is adequately documented. Documenting the application design is a critical step in establishing sound communication with and among developers. The process of creating documentation forces the architect to think through issues thoroughly. The final document enables management to add or change developers to the project without adversely encroaching on the architect's time. For developers, documentation allows them to proceed if the application architect is absent from the project for a limited period, and it enables them to work through design inconsistencies on their own without consuming the time of other members of the development team. Documentation also helps to insulate the project against the effects of personnel turnover.

Often, the size and scope of the project indicates how extensive the design documentation needs to be. For example, a project containing less than 1,000 hours of work using two developers will require much less documentation than a project containing 100,000 hours of work requiring a fifty-person team. There is no objective rule that indicates an optimal amount for a given project.

I've seen many projects that were not documented, and this meant that adding a developer was a major chore because the architect had to verbally convey the design to the newcomer. Having to communicate the design verbally negates some of the benefits to bringing on additional developers.

It should be noted that there are tools that provide limited support for managing feature requests and work assigned to fulfill those requests. Examples of such products are JIRA (https://www.atlassian.com/software/jira) and Mingle (http://www.thoughtworks.com/products/mingle-agile-project-management). Such tools are of great value for larger shops where detailed history on certain changes is needed.

The application architect establishes coding guidelines. Because individual developers have coding preferences, coding standards need to be articulated so that the individual pieces are more easily brought together. The application architect is responsible for establishing project procedures and guidelines for topics like the following (which are covered in more depth later in the book):

- Exception handling
- Logging
- Testing
- Threading
- Caching
- Configuration

The application architect identifies implementation tasks for the project manager. This role is especially important for Java EE projects because they encompass a much wider range of technologies than do other types of systems projects. Out of practical necessity, the application architect also helps the project manager with project planning and estimates.

It's a good idea for application architects to at some point gain experience managing small projects. This helps them understand typical project management challenges faced by the person in the project manager role, and this understanding will enable them to provide better support for the project managers they work under.

The application architect mentors developers for difficult tasks. Typically, the architect is more experienced than the developers. In fact, it is not uncommon for application architects to also function as a senior developer for the projects they work on. When the developers run into a technical problem that slows them down, the architect is often the one who helps them create a solution. For many projects, the architect is more of a mentor than an implementer.

The application architect enforces compliance with coding guidelines. Being the one who establishes coding guidelines, the application architect is the most likely to recognize when the guidelines are not being followed and is therefore the logical choice to enforce them. A project manager, who typically is charged with enforcement tasks, often does not have the technical experience to recognize compliance.

Code reviews are an excellent enforcement mechanism. It is much harder for individual developers to privately skirt team coding standards if other team members examine the code. I also leverage source control to streamline my review of coding changes on a periodic basis. That is, most source control products provide a feature that will notify you of check-ins by e-mail. As a practical matter, the attention I pay to individual check-ins depends on the skill set of the developer doing the check-in. Over time, some developers will prove more reliable than others and require less oversight.

Code reviews are also an excellent learning tool for all members of the development team. The application architect discovers holes in the design, and all participants learn tips and tricks from the rest of the team. Typically the most experienced member of the team, the application architect often facilitates the code review. To be most useful, a code review should be held in a congenial, nonthreatening atmosphere.

It should be noted that there are source analysis tools, such as Checkstyle (http://checkstyle.sourceforge.net/), PMD (http://pmd.sourceforge.net/), and FindBugs (http://findbugs.sourceforge.net/) that provide automated review support. That is, they will examine your source and point out likely coding issues. Usually, I need to spend time configuring these tools (e.g., determining which rules to enforce) before formally incorporating them in the build.

The application architect assists the project manager in estimating project costs and benefits for management. Although this is usually the project manager's responsibility, most project managers are less experienced with Java EE technologies and may not be aware of everything that needs to be done. It's the application architect's responsibility to review the project plan and make sure the project manager hasn't forgotten any tasks. I often have the entire team review the project plan and I solicit feedback. It's harder for team members to complain about an inadequate or inaccurate project plan if they had the opportunity to review and critique it.

The application architect assists management in making personnel decisions for developer positions. While personnel decisions are often viewed as a management function, the application architect is in a good position to assess technical competence. Mistakes in personnel decisions can cause considerable damage to project timelines.

Product Manager

The product manager is responsible for the product and its requirements. For most organizations, this position is staffed by the business area that the application is meant to service. For organizations building software to market or sell to other organizations, the product manager is responsible for ensuring that the product is based on the needs of the market.

The application architect is responsible for providing technical advice and guidance to the product manager. The application architect works with the business analysts and the product manager(s) to help determine what features are feasible within the application or feasible for a specific release.

Project Manager

The project manager is responsible for coordinating and scheduling all tasks for all members of the project development team. The project manager must also communicate current project activities and status to management and end-user representatives. Further, the project manager acquires any resources or materials needed by the project or the team members.

The application architect is responsible for providing technical advice and guidance to the project manager. The application architect assists the project manager in identifying project tasks and the order in which they should be completed. The architect also helps the project manager identify needed materials and resources, including guiding the selection of other team members and validating their skill sets from a technical standpoint.

Business Analyst

The business analyst is responsible for working with end users to define the application requirements and the detail necessary to design and build the application. Because end users and developers often use different terminology, the business analyst is responsible for translating communications between end users and developers. Often the business analyst has experience on both the end-user side and the information technology side of the enterprise.

As a project progresses, the business analyst's role diminishes but does not disappear. Developers typically have additional business questions that come to light during coding and testing activities, and the business analyst works with the business side to get these questions answered.

The application architect is responsible for ensuring that the application requirements determined by the business analyst are adequate. It's unreasonable to expect 100 percent of the analysis to be complete and correct. After all, analysis is to some extent subjective. However, the analysis needs to be complete enough to warrant proceeding with design.

Solution Architect

The solution architect ensures that the application adheres to any technical standards enforced across the enterprise. For example, many organizations standardize the databases and application server software used. Should the application team encounter technical problems that have been solved elsewhere in the enterprise, the solution architect will guide the application architect toward re-using what has already been developed in the enterprise. Sometimes solution architects are organized by business area and are able to assist business representatives in deciding which application development efforts to fund. It is common for the application architect to fill this role, especially for smaller organizations.

Graphic Designer

Many applications, especially those that are publicly available, need professional graphics or layout designers. Most developers, left to their own devices, can produce functional web pages, but those pages are typically ugly and hard to use. Graphics design is more art than science. The graphic designer will focus on user interface design, graphics, and overall usability of the application. Usually, the graphic designer works primarily with the business analyst and other representatives of the business side to work out the design. But the graphic designer may also work with the presentation-tier developer to create a prototype.

Some larger organizations distinguish between a "graphic" designer and a "transaction designer." The transaction designer will design the page flow and controls to fit the business process, as opposed to being concerned with aesthetics. Most organizations don't distinguish between the two roles and combine them into one role.

The application architect is responsible for ensuring that the layout is technically feasible. I've seen many web page designs that use text effects that are available in word processors but are not supported by HTML—for example, a design using text rotated 90 degrees. The architect is in a position to catch and correct these kinds of problems early in the development process.

Presentation-Tier Developer

The presentation-tier developer is responsible for coding all HTML, Javascript, template markup, JSPs, and/or servlets for an application. In general, anything directly involved in producing the user interface is in the purview of the presentation-tier developer. Typically in collaboration with the layout designer, the presentation-tier developer builds the prototype and develops the working version. And with the application architect, the presentation-tier developer and graphic designer determine the structure and design of front-end navigation.

The application architect is responsible for ensuring that design patterns can be maintained and extended. Navigation issues are often complex and can easily degrade into hard-to-maintain code. The application architect is in a good position to identify and correct maintenance issues as well as other technical problems that arise.

Business Logic Developer

The business logic developer is responsible for coding all invisible parts of the application, including enterprise beans, web services, batch jobs, business objects, and data access objects. Some people refer to these invisible parts as the server-side components of the application. The business logic developer is often a Java specialist who works closely with the application architect and assists in performance tuning as needed.

The application architect provides guidance for the business logic developer. It's important for business logic to be readily usable by the presentation-tier developer. It's common for technical issues and problems to arise in server-side components, which are usually the most complex pieces of an application. Thus, the application architect often acts as a mentor to the business logic developer.

Data Modeler

The data modeler uses information from the business analyst to identify, define, and catalog all data the application stores in a database. Data modeling typically involves documenting application data in entity-relationship (ER) diagrams. The database administrator then uses the ER diagrams to produce a physical database design. Thus, it is common for the roles of data modeler and database administrator to be combined.

The application architect is responsible for ensuring that the data model is adequate. As with business analysis, it's unreasonable to expect the data model to be 100 percent complete. If the data model is largely complete and in third normal form, future changes in the model (and thus the database) are likely to be minor.

Database Administrator

The database administrator is responsible for formulating a database design based on the business requirements for the application, and for creating and maintaining database environments for the application. Typically, the database administrator assists with performance tuning and helps the business logic developer diagnose application development issues regarding data access. Sometimes, the database administrator doubles as a business logic developer or data migration specialist.

The application architect works with the database administrator to resolve any issues or problems involving database storage. However, the database administrator primarily interacts with the data modeler and the business logic developer.

Data Migration Specialist

Some applications, such as those for data warehousing, depend heavily on data migrated from other sources or from a legacy database. The data migration specialist writes and manages all scripts and programs needed to populate the application databases on an ongoing basis. When an application has few migration requirements, this role may not be necessary or may merge with the database administrator's role.

The application architect ensures that data migration requirements are provided for the migration specialist. Working with the data migration specialist to solve any technical issues or problems that might arise is another aspect of the application architect's role.

Infrastructure Specialist

The infrastructure specialist is responsible for providing all development, testing, and production environments as well as the deployment methods. A formal infrastructure for development and deployment saves lots of time and effort. The idiosyncrasies involved in administrating containers, writing deployment scripts, and assisting other developers in diagnosing problems with their test environments represent a unique and challenging problem set.

Usually, the infrastructure specialist works with the organization's system administrators and database administrators to provide these environments. Most organizations provide resource provisioning services through centrally managed groups. For example, in most organizations, the infrastructure specialist wouldn't physically install or define a build server; he or she would specify requirements for that build server and a system administrator would actually define it. The same can be said for the physical creation of databases. The point is that the infrastructure specialist is responsible for seeing that the environments get created and properly configured.

An infrastructure specialist is often essential when you are working with or designing a continuous integration environment, are providing build automation, or are dealing with complex hardware infrastructures that involve clustering and other nontrivial environment setup.

The application architect defines infrastructure requirements for the infrastructure specialist. The architect works with the specialist to determine the number and nature of the environments needed and what level of support is required for each environment. Many projects need at least one development, testing, and production environment. Some organizations combine the role of infrastructure specialist with that of application architect.

Testing Specialist

A testing specialist is typically a detail-oriented person who makes sure that the application produced matches the specifications and is reasonably free of bugs. Typically, a testing specialist has at least a basic knowledge of the business area.

The application architect works with testing staff to identify any infrastructure requirements and support needed. The project manager and the business analyst usually work with the testing specialist to establish the content of test plans and the testing methodology. Therefore, the architect's role in testing is usually support. For larger development efforts, the testing specialist role could be staffed by entire testing teams and a testing manager.

Testing Automation Specialist

A testing automation specialist is usually necessary for larger projects where it is anticipated that multiple application iterations and versions of the application will be delivered. The test automation specialist can script integration tests that can be performed as part of an application regression, and that can be executed on a per release basis or as part of a continuous integration environment where tests are executed on every successful build.

PROJECT LIFE CYCLE APPROACHES

There are differing schools of thought as to what the Java EE project life cycle should be. This section describes these schools of thought and presents my personal views on the topic. The guidelines presented in this book are intended to be compatible with any methodology.

Waterfall Approach

The waterfall approach entails performing all analysis and design for a project before coding and testing. This approach was commonly used when most development was mainframe-based and is still the one most companies prefer.

Projects developed under the waterfall approach tend to be large and have long delivery times. Hence, they entail more risk. These projects usually don't require business participants to learn as much technical terminology, and the business-side interface is tightly controlled.

Compared with other approaches, the waterfall approach to project development does not provide feedback as early in the process, but it delivers a more complete solution. Waterfall projects tend to fit neatly into the budget planning cycle, which may be one reason for the popularity of this approach.

Because of the length of time waterfall projects typically require, the business requirements often change during the project. Project managers then face a dilemma: if the project doesn't change with the business, the resulting application won't provide as much benefit; and if the project changes course to follow business requirement changes, the time and resources needed for the project will be negatively affected.

Agile Approaches

Agile approaches strive to separate a project into small component pieces that typically need few resources. Thus, agile approaches are the antithesis of the waterfall approach. Agile approaches can be viewed as a "family" of approaches with many varying implementations. The most popular implementation of agile methods at the time of this writing appears to be Scrum. Other examples of agile implementations are Extreme Programming (XP), Lean, and Crystal. For the context of this discussion, I use Scrum as the primary example of agile methodologies as it appears to be the most well known.

The central objective of agile methodologies is to reduce the technical risks and project costs that plague the waterfall approach. Agile methodologies use the following assumptions:

- Catching mistakes earlier is cheaper in the long run.
- Reducing complexity also reduces technical risk and is cheaper in the long run.
- Short iterations lead to improved return on investment (ROI) and the ability to more quickly adapt to changing business requirements.
- Focus on test automation results in more efficient use of development resources.

Agile approaches dictate that you break the problem up into many small problems (called stories) that take three weeks or less to implement. Each story is co-developed by two programmers using one machine. The programmatic test to determine if the new story functionality works is developed and added to the regression test suite when the story is developed. These programmers ignore every aspect of the application except the story they are working on. A business participant is dedicated to the project and is immediately available to answer any business questions that arise.

Using pairs of programmers to code everything theoretically reduces the probability that an error survives to deployment. Using pairs also tends to make code simpler because it takes time to explain the concept to another person. The more complicated the algorithm, the harder it is to explain. The emphasis on reducing complexity makes it less likely that mistakes will occur.

The emphasis on testing, creating, and frequently running a regression test suite catches mistakes early and reduces the probability that any change will inadvertently introduce new bugs or have other unintended consequences.

Scrum and other agile methodologies reduce risk by providing feedback early. A development team proceeding down the wrong track will be alerted and corrected earlier, when it's much cheaper to make changes.

Rational Unified Process

The Rational Unified Process (RUP) is a formalized development methodology. Most RUP literature describes it as an iterative approach, but that's only half the story. RUP emphasizes starting with requirements gathering, analysis, and design activities for the entire project—including object and data modeling—before proceeding to construction. In this sense, RUP takes a waterfall approach to analysis and design but an iterative approach to construction and delivery. By encouraging early requirements gathering and analysis, RUP seeks to keep the project aligned with user expectations.

RUP mitigates risk by encouraging the team to develop the riskiest portions of the project first, allowing more time to recognize and respond to issues and problems. It also reduces rework when the design requires alteration.

Which Approach Is Most Popular?

I'm not prepared to declare any of these approaches "best." They all have advantages and disadvantages. The waterfall approach appears to be the most commonly used in corporate environments where budgeting is paramount. Many companies use (and are more comfortable with) a waterfall approach to initial development and major enhancements. While enhancements are more iterative with the waterfall approach, the iteration size is usually much larger than with agile approaches.

Agile methodologies are rarely used in pure form. This isn't a judgment; it's merely an observation. Given that, measuring the adoption rate for agile methodologies is problematic. Two recent attempts to measure adoption rates are the following: http://visual.ly/agile-2012-state-union and http://www.klocwork.com/blog/agile-development/agile-adoption-an-update/. From these surveys, some observations can be made.

Scrum appears to be the most popular of the agile methodologies. This is substantiated by keyword statistics from Google Trends (figure 1.1). However, it also appears that organizations using agile methodologies use agile for some, but not all, of their development. It could be that different managers within larger organizations have different preferences. It could also be that some projects lend themselves to agile methodologies better than others.

Figure 1.1: Search Engine Keyword Trend Statistics for Different Agile Methodologies

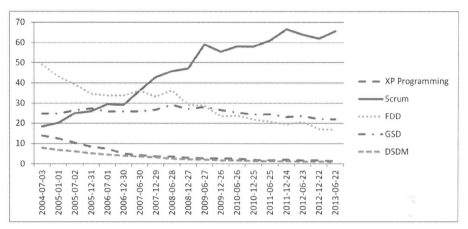

Source: Google Trends taken on November 25, 2013.

What I Think

This book is largely compatible with either approach. Scrum users and other agile enthusiasts would merely choose much smaller iteration sizes than my illustrations. Because one approach rarely has a monopoly on common sense and is rarely devoid of disadvantages, I prefer a hybrid approach.

Agile's emphasis on testing has great value. I've adopted the practice of coding test sequences for everything I write and combining them into a full regression test. I've even seen a team go so far as to put a full regression test in the build and force the deployment to fail if all the tests don't pass. I find that the mistakes avoided by this practice more than pay for the extra time and effort required to develop and maintain test scenarios. Having said that, I've also seen organizations invest in unit tests, only to discard them when maintaining them becomes too resource-intensive.

Agile's tendency to reduce project size has great value. Project risk appears to be proportional to the size of the unit of work. Hence, reducing the size of the unit of work reduces the business risk of undertaking the project. I don't have empirical evidence to prove this statement, but I've observed it in the field on several occasions.

Agile's war on complexity has value. Simpler is better. Ignoring all stories but the one you're working on does produce simpler code in the short term. But it also introduces a higher probability of rework (or refactoring, in more modern parlance), for which many projects have no budget. If refactoring isn't done properly or the developers are under time pressure, the code can easily end up being unnecessarily complex anyway. Also, many developers use the "complexity" excuse to ignore business requirements.

RUP's emphasis on centralized analysis and design has great value. Some agile methodologies assume that developers can take a parochial view of the story they are working on and ignore anything else. This can cause some amount of rework. All developers should really have a larger focus. Because RUP concentrates analysis and design at the beginning of a project, it represents a sensible compromise between a purely iterative approach and the waterfall approach.

It is necessary to control communication with end users. Some agile methodologies assume that any member of the development team should be able to talk to an end-user representative. Developers and end users usually have very different perspectives and use different terminology. In practice, many developers have trouble adapting to nontechnical terminology; they simply can't translate business terminology into technical terminology, and vice versa. Some centralization of communication to the business side is necessary as a practical matter.

FURTHER READING

Beck, Kent. 2000. *Extreme Programming Explained*. Reading, MA: Addison-Wesley.

Brooks, Frederick P., Jr. 1995. *The Mythical Man-Month: Essays on Software Engineering, Anniversary Edition*, 2nd ed. Reading, MA: Addison-Wesley.

Cockburn, Alistair. 2007. *Agile Software Development*, 2nd ed. Reading, MA: Addison-Wesley.

Kroll, Per, and Philippe Krutchen. 2003. *The Rational Unified Process Made Easy: A Practitioner's Guide to the RUP*. Boston: Addison-Wesley.

Larman, Craig. 2004. *Agile and Iterative Development: A Manager's Guide*. Boston: Addison-Wesley.

Johnson, Hilary and Chris Sims. 2012. *Scrum: a Breathtakingly Brief and Agile Introduction*. Dymaxicon.

Stephens, Matt and Doug Rosenburg. *Extreme Programming Refactored: The Case Against XP*. Berkeley, CA: Apress.

CHAPTER 2

DEFINING THE PROJECT

The first step in developing any application is performing analysis to define its purpose, scope, and objectives. A Java EE application is no exception. Including analysis in the development process is basic common sense, but I'm continually amazed at how many projects muddle through without defining their target first.

The application architect is not directly involved in defining the project; that is the job of the project manager, business analyst, and end user. However, the architect is responsible for ensuring that the project is defined with enough consistency and detail that it can be physically designed and implemented. Because most other members of the Java EE development team don't know what information is required to design and implement an application, the application architect often facilitates project definition discussions.

The application architect must possess analysis skills. Without analysis skills, an architect will not be able to recognize the weak points and gaps in project definition at the onset of the project, which is when those weak points are cheaper to address. On the other hand, architects with analysis skills are more likely to anticipate future feature requests because they are able to understand the business processes involved. While no effort will be put into constructing those expected features before they are requested, design choices can be made that will make it possible to add those features later. As an example, if I expect that at some point in the future the customers may be able to have multiple accounts, although they can't today, I'll make design choices that allow for that possibility.

I can hear the groans of developers as I write. Technical people want to hear more about coding techniques than project definition and analysis-gathering strategies. I completely understand. There's nothing I like more than producing good code that does something useful. However, to get good code, you need good analysis and good project definition. My experience is that the probability of getting useful code without doing decent analysis first is slim to none.

Use-cases are an important tool in analysis. The Unified Modeling Language (UML) specification was created to describe and document analysis and designs for systems that use object-oriented languages like Java. The main construct UML has for describing what an application will accomplish is the *use case*. This chapter defines the term *use case*, guides you through writing use cases for a project, lists some common mistakes made in creating use cases and how to avoid them, and presents and discusses an example of use cases written for one project.

This chapter does not contain a comprehensive synopsis of use cases with respect to the UML specification. I present the subset of the specification that is commonly used and is practical. For a thorough treatment of the UML specification, see Booch, Rumbaugh, and Jacobson (1999).

Although some developers distinguish between use cases and requirements, I see no difference. Requirements are the specific features, written in business terms, that an application must provide. Therefore, requirements typically are use cases written in summary form.

If you're using agile methodologies, such as Scrum, you create *user stories* rather than use cases. Both constructs fulfill the same purpose: communicating user requirements. User stories are a brief statement of what a user does or needs to do with an application. For example, "The application needs to remember my last product search and pre-fill the filters I specified last time; I do the same search most of the time." User stories do not contain enough detail to allow for implementation; verbal communication with the user representative is required to flush out the details. Use cases, in contrast, have enough of detail to allow for implementation. Whether the user writes use cases or arrives at the requirements using user stories and verbal communication is simply a difference in form and tactics.

Additionally, I like to prototype the user interfaces. A prototype is an excellent vehicle for enabling the business side and developers to understand the target of a development project. I usually have no trouble getting the business side interested in the prototyping process because it concretely represents what they're going to get. Prototyping also helps refine the use cases.

Once you've defined a project's use cases (or stories), you can create a fairly detailed definition of the project, written in business terms, that both developers and businesspeople can understand. This allows the business side and any management stakeholders to provide feedback early. Getting a formal sign-off for the use cases in a particular project enables the project manager to contain project scope.

IDENTIFYING PROJECT SCOPE

A high-level project definition and preliminary idea about scope is needed before use-case analysis and prototyping exercises can be effective. Most developers are detail oriented and will consider this high-level definition too vague to be useful. Keep in mind that the purpose of this high-level project definition is only to determine scope for the use-case analysis (not for coding).

Here is an example of a high-level project definition statement:

- Build a system that assists project managers in planning tasks, tracking the activities of every team member, and estimating completion dates. The project-tracking application should allow the user to do the following:
  - Define a project and its tasks.
  - Record people assigned to project tasks and estimate the time needed to complete each task.
  - Record the order in which tasks will be completed.
  - Record project progress and mark tasks as completed.
  - Automatically schedule the project.
  - Create reports of project progress.

As vague and simplistic as the statement is, it provides a starting point for identifying actors and constructing use cases.

IDENTIFYING THE ACTORS

The first step in use-case analysis is to identify the actors. An *actor* is the user type or external system serviced or affected by the use case. Although the word *actor* has connotations of being an actual person, a UML actor can be an external system or an organization type or role.

The following is a list of actors for a report generation application I architected:

- Trust customer user
- Trust customer organization
- Banking support user
- Report template developer
- Document delivery application interface
- Report template definition interface

- Data warehouse application interface
- Report request application interface
- Application administrator

And here's a list of actors for a cash-tracking application I architected:

- Cash manager user
- Transaction approver user
- Senior transaction approver user
- Banking support user
- Fund accounting application interface
- Application administrator

You may have noticed that in each example I listed individual user groups as separate items. I did this primarily because every user group has different capabilities. While some use cases apply to all types of end users, others are user-group specific. In each example, we had far fewer different types of end users when we started use-case analysis than we had when we finished. During the course of writing the use cases, we began to realize that there were different user roles that required different capabilities.

It is possible for a user to represent multiple actors. For example, a user who provides banking support may also assume the role of a cash manager or transaction approver.

Consider the application administrator as an actor for any large application. This forces some attention to support—which increases availability and in turn makes other actors (who happen to be people) happy.

Make sure that all actors are direct. Sometimes people are confused by the external system interfaces and want to list as actors the end users serviced by an external interface. For example, if a security-trading system is one of the external interfaces, you may be tempted to list traders as actors because they are serviced indirectly by your application. However, the security-trading system is the actor, and the traders are indirect end users.

Facilitate identifying actors by beginning with a small group. Application architects and business analysts can facilitate the discussion by making assumptions about who the actors are and reviewing them with other members of the team and the business side. In my experience, people are much better and quicker at critiquing something in place than they are at adding to a blank sheet of paper. You will probably discover additional actors as use-case analysis proceeds.

WRITING USER STORIES

A *user story* is a short description that contains an actor, that actor's want or need, and the expected benefit the actor will experience when that need is met. Usually, user stories are one sentence. User stories do not contain enough information for developers to implement the feature. The intention is that the details needed to implement the feature are obtained in conversation with the business representative.

A common form for user stories is as follows:

- As an <actor>, I want <want or need> [so that <expected benefit>].

Some consider the "expected benefit" part of the user story to be optional, whereas the actor and short description of the want or need is required. Examples of user stories from some of my recent projects are:

- As a registrar, I want to produce transcripts that can be distributed electronically because that's what students want.
- As a security administrator, I want a report that tells me which users have which role.
- As an executive, I want to be able to attach comments to budgeted items to communicate with other executives and accounting.
- As an academic administrator, I want to be able to publish class syllabi stored in our course application for prospective students.
- As an application administrator, I would like to be notified by text when an out-of-memory condition is reached.

Additional requirements obtained in conversations should be documented. Unless the project is very small and your organization is devoid of corporate politics, you need a written record of the implementation details. The documentation doesn't have to be elaborate or lengthy. Ensure that you share it with the business representative(s) you conversed with to obtain the information; if there is a misunderstanding about the requirements, it's best to flush it out early.

WRITING USE CASES

A *use case* is a description of something a system does at the request of, or in response to, an action by one of its actors. You should write use cases in business terms, not technical ones. Anyone on the business side should be able to read the text without a translator or technical glossary. Use cases containing technical terms often indicate that technical design assumptions are being made at this stage, and they shouldn't be. Use cases can also serve as a casual "contract" between the business and development sides of the organization as to what will be delivered in what increments.

There is no specific format for a use case. However, use cases usually contain a title, description, actor list, precondition list, trigger, main process flow, and alternative process flows.

Use-case description text should begin with: "The system (or application) will . . ." If you identify a use case that cannot be written in this form, it's likely not a valid use case but rather part of another one. Note that use cases often service multiple actors. I recommend explicitly listing all affected actors in the use case.

The following are examples of use case descriptions from a reporting system I implemented:

- The system will provide an interface that will allow users to run reports from data defined in an existing MVS/CICS application.

- The system will allow application administrators to control the reports that members of a trust customer organization can run.

- The system will allow application administrators to define new reports and publish them to users.

An actor list describes the users who directly participate in the use case (see section "Identifying the Actors" in this chapter). Some also list a brief reason for the actors' involvement in this use case. An example might be:

- Trust customer user, who wants to obtain information about his or her investments.

- Application administrator, who wants to define additional reports and publish them to customers.

A precondition list is a list of business conditions that must take place for this use case to occur. Examples include:

- A trust customer has been obtained and is logged in.
- A new report has been requested.

A trigger is an event that starts processing for the use case. Examples include:

- A trust customer desires to run a report.
- An application administrator starts work on defining a new report.

The main process flow of a use case is a step-by-step description of use case processing with no errors. An example for a customer running a report might be:

1   User displays a list of available reports.

2   User selects a report to run.

3   User inputs any parameters needed to run the report.

4   User inputs a format for the report (e.g., HTML, PDF, Excel, etc.).

5   User views the report.

Alternative process flows describe abnormal events that can happen during execution of the use case.

- If the user doesn't input all required parameters, the system will display an error message listing the parameters that are still required.

- If the report execution errors out, the system will display a generic error page and notify an application administrator with details of the error.

Use cases can be written with a more formal organization and content. See Cockburn (2001) for more details.

Use cases should be one to three pages in length. The length recommendation is provided by Cockburn (2007). Use cases that are longer than three pages tend to have material that isn't appropriate for the use case; for example, wire frame graphics are not generally appropriate material for a use case. Lengthy use cases tend to contain a term glossary or wire frame graphics. For each use case, I find it helpful to start with and include a summary that is no longer than two sentences. This simplifies organizing the use cases as the list grows. As analysis proceeds, you will attach additional detail to most use cases.

Avoid use-case diagrams. The UML specification does define a graphical representation scheme for use cases. However, graphical schemes are rarely used, and I purposely do not discuss them in this book. My experience has shown that use-case diagrams confuse both the business side and developers, and that the costs of creating, explaining, and maintaining these graphical constructs far outweigh any benefits they provide.

Writing use cases requires in-depth participation from the business side. From the technical side, some business analysts may be able to help construct an initial draft, but the process should not end without direct business side participation and review. Although enlisting the involvement of business users is sometimes easier said than done, their input is valuable. In my experience, insufficient business support for analysis efforts like use-case review can cause a project to fail.

Facilitate use-case analysis by starting with a small group. Application architects can speed this process along by working with one business side user or a business analyst to draft a set of use cases that can initiate discussion. These draft use cases will be incomplete, and some will be incorrect, but you'll get feedback easier and quicker than you would if you started with a blank sheet of paper. You can use objections to your assumptions to refine and improve the draft use cases.

Enlist someone to act as "scribe" for the use-case discussions. When you're facilitating a discussion, you won't have time to take good notes. Having someone other than the facilitator write the discussion notes helps ensure that they will be complete and understandable.

Write use cases so they can be amended as more information becomes available. Use cases are always evolving. If you discover additional information in the modeling phases or in later portions of the project, add this material to the use cases.

Use-case analysis is finished when team members feel they can estimate a time to implement each use case. Estimates may be in terms of number of weeks rather than hours. Some developers don't feel comfortable providing estimates until they've essentially coded the application. You may need to gently remind these developers that some difference between the estimate and the actual amount of time a task takes is expected. Note that it is common for developers to only include an optimistic development time in their estimates; I habitually double estimates provided by many developers I work with.

Do not slow down if the group has trouble articulating requirements. Make assumptions and proceed. If your use cases are not right, the objectors have the responsibility to tell you what's wrong so you can correct the problem. You can use that information to refine and improve the use cases.

COMMON MISTAKES

This section contains examples of use cases that have various defects.

Imposing a technical design assumption under the guise of a requirement. This is the mistake I see most frequently. Consider the following use case paraphrased from the reporting system example used earlier in the chapter:

- ▪ The system will allow application administrators to limit system load by setting rules that prohibit report execution for groups of users or redirect their execution to a batch stream.

This use case made several unwarranted assumptions and had us solving the wrong problems. It assumed that the hardware/software architecture used by the application could not be scaled to handle the load and that some alternative processing route was necessary. It assumed that the application could not be made as efficient as the "batch stream" mentioned. And it assumed that the batch stream environment in fact had surplus capacity to handle load that the application should have been handling.

Even if some of the assumptions made in this use case turned out to be true, we should have started by planning an architecture that more than supported our load. In fact, most of the assumptions turned out to be false: the architecture could handle the load efficiently; the batch stream was a frequent performance bottleneck and, in fact, did not have surplus capacity; and the efficiency of the application more than satisfied users.

A better way to write this use case would have been:

- The system will support up to 200 concurrently running reports with a maximum daily volume of 500,000 reports.

Including physical design assumptions in use cases. For example, one of the developers submitted the following use case for the reporting system:

- The system will insert a row into the report request table after the request is completed.

This use case made the physical design assumption that we were recording request runs in a table. But at that point we had not decided whether we would or wouldn't do so, and nor should we have. After some discussion, I learned that application administrators needed a way to know what reports a user ran so they could reproduce problems a trust customer reported to the help desk. Given these requirements, a better way to word the use case would have been:

- The system will record report request history for at least thirty-six hours for the benefit of application administrators and report template developers investigating reported problems.

Not keeping analysis sessions productive. Analysis efforts can stall for many reasons, including ineffective facilitation or leadership, an extremely low level of detail in the discussion, and lack of information. It's also possible for requirements obtained from analysis sessions to be incomplete or otherwise ineffective. Application architects can steer the development team away from all these problems. Rather than see a session stall, I'll create a "parking lot" for items or issues to be addressed later, after additional information can be obtained. Parking lot items are documented and tracked and then discussed at a later time.

Failing to document use cases, even when the project is small. Most developers assume that documenting use cases is unnecessary when the project has only one developer. The use cases should be documented anyway. However, with small projects, the use case set could be an informal one with a simple bullet list.

Documented use cases target the development effort and make tangents less likely. Further, documented use cases communicate the objectives of the development to management and the business side and assist in project transition if additional developers join the team or the project is assigned to another developer.

Repeatedly defining terms in every use case. Even for complicated applications, it's unnecessary to define terms repeatedly in every use case in which they appear. Instead, you can define them once and then maintain them in a separate list of business terms. For example, *cash transaction* (a term used in an earlier use-case example) refers to money transferred from one account to another. The characteristics of a transaction are that it has an identifier, a date, a cash amount, at most one account from which the money is taken, and at most one account to which the money is transferred.

If you think writing use cases seems easy, you're right. The corollary to this is that if you think you're missing something and that writing use cases should be harder than this chapter makes it appear, you're making the task harder than it needs to be. If writing use cases required more than common sense, the practice could not be successful, because you would never get a roomful of people to agree on the outcome.

PROTOTYPING

At this stage, the development team usually has enough information to choose a user interface technology (which typically involves HTML because most applications are web-compliant these days). A user interface enables the prototype to become a part of the real application and guards against accidentally promising delivery of something that isn't technically possible.

Consider involving the layout designer in producing the prototype. In fact, the layout designer should facilitate this particular exercise instead of the application architect. I find that technicians usually don't make the most aesthetically pleasing user interface screens. I know I don't.

Remember that prototypes are not functional by definition. None of the prototype screens should have dynamic data. If you are responsible for developing the prototype and are using HTML, I highly recommend Castro (2006).

SWIM-LANE DIAGRAMS

It's not a part of any official methodology that I'm aware of, but I've had great success supplementing use cases and prototypes with swim-lane diagrams that describe major business processes. For those who aren't familiar with swim-lane diagrams, they describe business processes supported by the software being designed. Each individual swim lane in the diagram contains an actor or application. Different components and decisions made during the business process by that actor or application are denoted by process squares or decision triangles within the swim lane. Swim lanes labeled with an actor are manual processes. Swim lanes labeled with an application are processes performed automatically. The swim lanes are read left-to-right in chronological order. Figure 2.1 is an example.

Figure 2.1: Sample Swim-lane Diagram

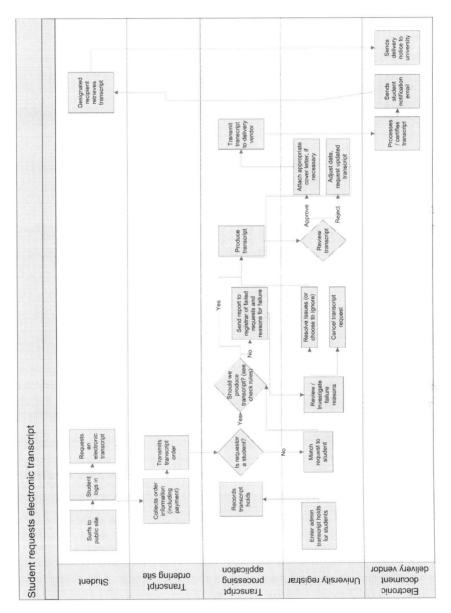

I find that end-users readily understand swim-lane diagrams without difficulty. They can effectively be used to describe which parts of a business process are manual and which are supported by software applications. End users are comfortable with this approach as it allows them to easily see if they've forgotten anything about the process that might be relevant to your project. Programmers also benefit from this approach as they can easily see the context in which their software product will be used.

NONFUNCTIONAL REQUIREMENTS

All project requirements discussed so far are functional requirements. *Functional requirements* define *what* the application is expected to accomplish. *Nonfunctional requirements* specify constraints on *how* the application will accomplish functional requirements. For example, a functional requirement might be that the application will allow a user to run a predefined report; whereas a nonfunctional requirement might be that all predefined reports should run within sixty seconds. Another example: a functional requirement might be that the application will allow a user to save a change to a customer account; whereas a nonfunctional requirement might be that backup needs to be taken for the application and that any saved transaction needs to be recoverable in the event of a hardware failure.

Typically, there will not be use cases or user stories for nonfunctional requirements. However, nonfunctional requirements occasionally impact functional requirements. For example, I received a functional requirement enhancement request to allow customer representatives to view users' passwords so they could communicate a user's password if the user had forgotten it. I informed them that there was a management directive that passwords were never to be stored in an unencrypted format. Furthermore, it was not possible to decrypt passwords with the encryption method used. The directive to encrypt passwords in such a way that they cannot be decrypted is an example of a nonfunctional requirement. In this case, a nonfunctional requirement definitely impacted a functional requirement.

IMPROVING YOUR ANALYSIS SKILLS

Sometimes developers and junior architects have trouble acquiring the business analysis skills needed to write good user stories and use cases. Business analysis requires good communication skills, both written and verbal, which not all developers have acquired. It requires that you be able to express a problem in business terms, leaving all technical terms (e.g., file, field, etc.) behind. It's an area that is not nearly as objective and precise as coding. Nonetheless, the ability to write effective use cases and user stories is a skill all architects need to develop. If you think it necessary, here are some things you can do to improve your analysis skills.

Get a mentor. Choose somebody, preferably working at the same organization, whose business analysis skills you respect. Have your mentor privately review your use cases, user stories, or whatever document style your organization uses to communicate functional requirements. Often, someone who is not directly involved is more objective and can provide you with valuable feedback.

Do a post-project review for your projects or assignments. This need not be done formally or publicized unless your manager requests that you do one. You can gather this information informally by discussing the project with the developers and end-user representatives involved. What user requirements were missed? What could you have asked that might have identified those missing requirements sooner? This is feedback you can use and attempt to correct with in future assignments.

Imagine that you had to do the user's task described by the use case or user story. What would you need to do to accomplish the users' goals if you were in their place? Doing this exercise can allow you to see aspects of the requirements you might be missing. Also, it gives you information about what the user does that might assist you with future assignments.

FURTHER READING

Booch, Grady, James Rumbaugh, and Ivar Jacobson. 2005. *The Unified Modeling Language User Guide*, 2nd ed. Reading, MA: Addison-Wesley.

Castro, Elizabeth. 2006. *HTML for the World Wide Web with XHTML and CSS: Visual QuickStart Guide*, 6th ed. Berkeley, CA: Peachpit Press.

Cockburn, Alistair. 2001. *Writing Effective Use Cases*. Boston: Addison-Wesley.

Cockburn, Alistair. 2007. *Agile Software Development*, 2nd ed. Boston: Addison-Wesley.

Fowler, Martin, and Kendall Scott. 2003. *UML Distilled: Applying the Standard Object Modeling Language*, 3rd ed. Reading, MA: Addison-Wesley.

CHAPTER 3

SCOPE DEFINITION AND ESTIMATION

In most organizations, the project manager works with the business side and management to establish project scope and to estimate time and resource requirements. And frequently the project manager relies on the application architect for assistance in these tasks. The scenario is no different for Java EE applications. This chapter is written for architects responsible for helping to define and estimate delivery for management. Readers not involved in these tasks can safely skip the chapter.

DEFINING SCOPE

Objectively define project scope in terms of user stories or use cases, and obtain the agreement of the business side. Changing scope during a project wreaks havoc with project timelines and lowers the morale of the development team. When the business side makes additional requests after development is under way, acknowledge them, record them in a use case, and schedule them for a future release. Often, making rough estimates for each use case provides information that the business side will find useful in deciding scope.

Get agreement on the use cases from the project sponsor. As use cases are written in business terms, they can be used as a "contract" with the business side and management as to what will be delivered when. Work with the business side to choose which use cases will be implemented in the current project. Anything else will be deferred. Even if scope is agreed on verbally, put it in writing and e-mail it to everyone remotely connected to the project. Make sure to keep a copy.

Diligently enforce project scope once it's determined. The most important thing the project manager can do once the scope of a project is determined is to enforce it. The application architect has the responsibility of alerting the project manager to scope changes. It's much harder to hit a moving target. Although I generally prefer to schedule all enhancements for future releases, the architect usually doesn't get to decide scheduling issues. I estimate the request in use-case form and provide a preliminary estimate. Usually, the project manager can use this information to steer the business side toward scheduling the request for a future release.

Document any assumptions made in determining project scope. There are usually unknowns about project requirements at this stage. Often it is not possible to pause the project while the unknowns are investigated. In these situations, I make my best guess as to what the requirements are and document those guesses as assumptions. It is imperative that management and the product manager or other business representatives be provided a copy of those assumptions. Should the assumptions be incorrect, you'll be notified and changes to the scope and resulting estimate can be made.

In the context of agile methodologies, such as XP or Scrum, the "project" is more likely to be referred to as an "iteration" and tends to be of smaller size. Note that most agile methodologies advocate fixing scope for the iteration that's currently in development. Agile methodologies accommodate change by providing flexibility (allowing changes in scope) to iterations currently not in development.

BASICS OF ESTIMATING

Many technical people consider estimating difficult; and indeed, at this stage, it is definitely as much art as it is science. This chapter presents a method of determining a gross estimate based on information you should have from the use-case analysis and the prototypes. I make no claims that my way of estimating is the *only* way. If you have an approach you're comfortable with, stay with it. It should be said that estimating the same project multiple ways can validate your confidence in the estimate, particularly if the different methods come up with similar answers.

Estimates formed at the beginning of a project should be revisited periodically and refined after more detailed planning and designing are done. After defining the external interfaces and completing object and data modeling, you will be in a better position to make more accurate estimates. Estimates you make now should be detailed enough that you can use them in estimating any combination of use cases. Ideally, the business side looks at cost/benefit comparisons when deciding on scope.

Estimate in terms of the slowest resource on the team. We all know that some people take less time on development tasks than do others. I would rather deliver a project early than have to explain why it's going to be late.

Estimates should be proportionally balanced. I have found that a typical development team spends about one-third of its resource budget planning and designing, one-third coding and unit testing, and one-third supporting system- and user-testing activities. Keep in mind that some portion of the planning and design budget was spent performing the use-case analysis described in the previous chapter (I usually assume that planning and design is 50 percent complete at this point). These ratios apply to the entire life of the project.

Estimates should be expressed in terms of the number of work hours. That is, estimate in terms of the number of work hours needed to complete a task. Most project management software will compute a date based on your project plan. If resources are diverted to other projects, you'll be able to more accurately advise management as to the resulting project impact of that decision.

Consider the time needed to set up the development, testing, and production environments. Most companies provide established environments at the enterprise level. For example, many companies have a central administration team to establish environments for development, testing, and production of new applications. If your company has such a team, time allocated to environment setup will be low and not usually material for preliminary estimates. If this isn't the case at your company, you should add an estimate for setting up environments.

Developers are more successful at estimating coding and unit-testing tasks than anything else. If you can get a reasonable coding and unit-testing estimate, you can extrapolate the rest using the ratios mentioned previously and get a ballpark estimate. Note that to extrapolate a total estimate based on those ratios, you just multiply the coding and unit-testing estimate by 2.5, assuming that planning and design is 50 percent complete at the time you estimate.

Validate your estimates by comparing them to historical data. I track the number of hours it takes to actually complete the tasks that were estimated. That allows me to identify estimating mistakes and correct them on future projects. Consequently, I have a library of tasks from previous projects with the time they actually took to complete. I look for comparable tasks (similar amount of work with similar difficulty) from this library. The estimates I'm evaluating for the current project should be roughly congruent with what was experienced with those comparable tasks. This is the same way real estate is valuated. Real estate professionals estimate a property's worth by looking at sale prices for similar properties nearby. The same methodology works for software estimation for most tasks.

An Algorithm for Estimating

It should be noted that application architects are responsible for estimating hours only. Project managers should be equipped to account for absences due to responsibilities to other projects and vacations.

Step 1: Quantify the application; determine a rough number of web pages, batch jobs, reports, database tables, and external application interfaces. From previous history, you should have timesheet data for comparable projects. From that historical data, derive an average number of hours to complete one web page (assuming that data access logic and business logic will need to be developed to support it). For example, with one of my current clients, my working average is forty to eighty hours per dynamic web page, depending on complexity. I have similar estimate ranges for batch jobs, reports, database tables, and external application interfaces. Database tables are in the list as there are data modeling and database design steps to be performed as well as physically creating the tables themselves. To derive a coding and unit-testing estimate, gather estimates of the following for the group of use cases being considered for the project:

- Screens/pages in the user interface (40–80 hours each)
- External application interfaces (80–120 hours each)
- Database tables (4–8 hours each)
- Conversion batch jobs (24–40 hours each)

If this is your first time estimating a project, you might not have historical data from comparable projects to draw upon; in which case, ask one of your colleagues who might. Ask your manager or one of the people you work with for sample project plans and estimates from previous projects.

Not all these items will exist for each use case. The basic estimates noted in parentheses in the preceding list are applicable if the development team hasn't been formed. If there is an existing team, more accurate estimates for each item may be possible. Estimates at this point will not be exact. Estimating based on the number of objects is more accurate, but that number is not available before object modeling exercises are done.

Step 2: Estimate coding and unit-testing time for each use case. Based on the information gathered in step 1, it is simple mathematics to get a base estimate for a combination of use cases. The *base estimate* is the length of time it takes for one developer to complete coding and unit-testing tasks. It may seem a bit strange to estimate coding and unit-testing time before design is complete, but few developers seem to be bothered by this ambiguity.

Many developers confuse unit testing with system testing. Unit testing is strictly at a Java class level. How well a class functions when called from other classes within the application is integration testing, not unit testing.

For example, for a set of use cases that involves four screens, two external interfaces, five database tables, no data conversions, and two environment setups, the base estimate is:

$$(4 \times 80 \text{ hrs}) + (2 \times 120 \text{ hrs}) + (5 \times 8 \text{ hrs}) + (0 \times 40 \text{ hrs}) + (2 \times 8) =$$
$$616 \text{ hours}$$

Step 3: **Multiply the base estimate from step 2 by 2.5 to account for analysis and testing activities for each user story or use case.** If coding and unit testing are about one-third of the overall cost of each use case, the total cost should be about three times the base estimate. Because the analysis is about 50 percent complete at this stage, estimate the total cost to be about 2.5 times the base estimate. Continuing the previous example, the total hours left for the project would be $600 \times 2.5 = 1,500$.

Step 4: **Inflate the estimate by 20 percent for each additional developer on the project.** The base estimate assumes that the project has just one developer. Each developer added to a project adds communication and coordination time (Brooks, 1995). Although necessary, time spent communicating and coordinating is time not spent developing. Therefore, inflate the base estimate by 20 percent (i.e., multiply by 1.20) for each developer added. For example, with a base estimate of 2,600 hours and five developers expected, estimate spending $600 \times (1.20)4 = 1,244$ hours to code and unit test. Incidentally, it's a good idea to round that number to 3,500 to avoid creating the mistaken impression that this is an exact estimate.

Assuming the project's five developers are dedicated full time (thirty-two hours per week, allowing for bureaucratic distractions, etc.), the development team could work a total of 160 hours per week. This means that project delivery would be approximately two to three months out. Specifically state the estimate in months or quarters at this point to avoid creating the impression that this is an exact estimate.

Step 5: **Review your estimates with the development team.** If developers don't have input, they won't feel bound by the estimates. It's important to remind developers that these estimates will be reassessed after design is complete.

More manpower rarely saves a late project's timeline. The communication/coordination penalty, as previously described, is the primary reason that adding people to a late project only makes it later. Architects are often asked for ballpark estimates before all the analysis is done. Even if it won't be literally correct, you can ballpark an estimate by filling it out with assumptions and documenting them with the estimate.

The time you spend estimating has diminishing returns. No matter what, the actual number of hours you work to complete the project will differ from your estimate. Applying more time to the estimation process will not make your estimate more accurate in most cases. This is an uncomfortable thought to many developers new to estimating, but it's one of those truisms that developers just have to learn to live with.

Those following agile methodologies with shorter development iterations will have lower estimates. However, the same concepts apply. If the story is to add a feature to an existing application, use estimates from past stories where you have historical data.

TRACKING THE ESTIMATE

If, in addition to your application architect role, you are filling the role of project manager as well, you should track your progress against the estimate on a periodic basis. Tracking your progress means gathering the number of hours developers are actually spending on assigned tasks and comparing those hours to what was estimated.

Estimate tracking documents the extent to which the project is on-time and on-budget. Most projects don't become two months late in one day—it's a symptom that appears over time. Most executives can accommodate a timeline issue if they see the problem far enough in advance.

Estimate tracking documents the effect of re-allocating resources to other projects. By tracking only those hours that are devoted to your project, you can alert management if not enough time is being given to your project to fulfill the timeline. I've often been able to defend projects that were delivered later than planned by pointing out that they weren't late at all in terms of the work performed. The project was late because resources were allocated to other projects—not because the team was mismanaged.

Tracking estimates enables you to improve them on future projects. For example, if I consistently underestimate the work involved in adding new screens/pages to an existing application, I may increase my estimates for similar tasks in future projects.

I tend to track progress weekly and include a progress summary (whether my team is ahead or behind) in my status report. Tracking progress weekly is often enough to be useful to management, but not so often that it consumes a large amount of time. Publishing your progress in your status report ensures that management isn't "surprised" by a late delivery. It also documents the effect should some of your resources be diverted to other projects.

NONFUNCTIONAL REQUIREMENT CONSIDERATIONS

As explained in the last chapter, nonfunctional requirements place constraints on how application requirements are met. As such, nonfunctional requirements often impact project estimates. For example, testing estimates will be higher if the application needs to support seamless fail-over in the event of a hardware fail-over. If there is a nonfunctional requirement that the application must be able to support 50 hits per second, then performance testing estimates need to reflect that. If there is an enterprise mandate that unit tests for an application must have at least 90 percent code coverage, then development estimates need to reflect that.

FURTHER READING

Brooks, Frederick P., Jr. 1995. *The Mythical Man-Month: Essays on Software Engineering, Anniversary Edition*, 2nd ed. Reading, MA: Addison-Wesley.

DeMarco, Tom, and Timothy Lister. 1999. *Peopleware: Productive Projects and Teams*, 2nd ed. New York: Dorset House.

CHAPTER 4

DESIGNING EXTERNAL APPLICATION INTERFACES

It is common for a Java EE application to interface with external applications we don't control. For example, a purchasing application may notify an accounting application of all purchases, or an inventory management application may notify an accounting application of all inventory receipts and customer shipments. The application architect is responsible for the design of application interfaces as well as the application itself. Application architects typically have a central role in designing application interfaces with external applications, especially when the external application is also a custom development (e.g., not a vended product with established interface capabilities). This chapter describes how to define external application interface requirements so that both application teams will have the information needed to perform design and implementation tasks.

Sometimes external applications are vended, and supported interface methods are established and readily consumable. Sometimes external applications are supported by another team or business area and don't yet exist. Common reasons for creating external application interfaces are as follows:

- To read external application data for reference or processing
- To leverage external applications to perform some body of work
- To publish functionality to external applications

Reporting applications are a common example of a need to read external application data. Rarely do reporting applications maintain the information needed for report content. It is more common for reporting applications to read data as required. It is also common that users want to reference data from an external application when using a feature of an application you're building.

Leveraging external application functionality or publishing functionality for other applications are examples of the Don't Repeat Yourself (DRY) principle. In fact, they only differ in perspective; every "external" application is an application that somebody supports and they look at your application as "external." Often it is not cost effective or desirable to replicate functionality in that external application for a specific use in your application. For example, let's say your application needs to initiate the recording of a customer charge. Nobody writes custom accounting applications these days. It's more likely that your application needs to leverage a vended accounting application to initiate that charge.

External interfaces create stability risk. Outages in external applications can cause partial outages for the application you're supporting. Furthermore, changes in external applications (e.g., product upgrades or product enhancements) can also force changes in the applications you support. Consequently, implementing interfaces in a way that mitigates or contains stability risk is usually a requirement. There are ways to mitigate these risks, and they will be discussed in this chapter.

External interfaces complicate development and support activities. Development and support are impacted as problems require personnel outside the team to resolve. Furthermore, it is not always easy to determine which application owns a particular defect. You may investigate a reported defect only to discover that it's really a defect in the external application and all you can do is report the issue to the team or vendor that supports that application. There are ways to reduce the complications external interfaces cause, and they will be discussed in this chapter.

Application architects are typically responsible for ensuring that external interfaces are formally defined and documented so that developers from both applications have a basis for object-modeling activities (described in chapter 6). The application architects for both applications need a basis for their modeling and implementation activities. Further, the project manager needs a contract between your development group and the external system developers that describes everyone's responsibilities.

The following aspects of external interfaces should be discussed with the external teams and agreed on among the teams:

- Interface method selection (e.g., web services, messaging)
- Published services or functions
- Data content structure

- Triggering events for content exchange
- Error-handling procedures and responsibilities

The application architect should facilitate interface design discussions. Part of the role of facilitator is keeping the discussions limited to the topics just listed. The internal design of either application is largely irrelevant to this discussion. The platform used by the external application is relevant because it could affect the ability of the Java EE application to use some interface methods. For example, if the external application is not written in Java, the Java EE application cannot use any form of communication that uses RMI, such as EJBs.

This chapter will describe commonly used interface methods and their advantages and disadvantages to help guide you in making design decisions about external interfaces.

STRATEGIES FOR CONSUMING EXTERNAL APPLICATION DATA

The most common type of external interface is needed to read data maintained by another application. Commonly used strategies include utilizing the external application database directly or utilizing an Enterprise Java Bean (EJB), Messaging technologies, REST service, or web service to obtain the information needed. Each of these strategies has advantages and disadvantages.

Reading External Application Databases Directly

The advantages of the strategy of reading external application data directly are the following:

- Is the simplest and cheapest to implement
- Requires little or no involvement from the external application vendor or application team
- Provides data that is always up-to-date

This strategy is used a lot because *initial* development is usually simple and cheap. It often doesn't take much interaction with external application personnel. Furthermore, database access is well known and easily understood by most developers.

The disadvantages of this strategy are the following:

- Increased risk of adverse impact from external application change
- Increased risk of unintended consequences on external application users (i.e., performance)

Reading external application databases directly makes use of application internals that were never intended to be published in many cases. If external applications are vended, it is common for product upgrades to contain database schema changes. If the external application belongs to a separate team or department, changes might occur in the external application database without notice. Consequently, it's often desirable to reduce exposure to these types of changes.

With the exception of Oracle, most databases issue locks on reads by default. This means that reading data isn't necessarily harmless. It is possible that this strategy adversely impacts performance (because of read locking) on the users of those external applications.

The risks of reading external application databases directly can be mitigated by using an operational data store. Essentially, your application reads a copy of the external application data instead of the external application database directly. This mitigates the risk of adverse impact from application changes by localizing that risk purely to the data extracts; most of your application code would be unaffected. If the operational data store is in a vendor neutral format (i.e., not just a replicated copy of the external application database), then the source of this data can even be changed to other products with minimal impact. For example, let's say the external application is an accounting package. Using this strategy, should your current accounting package be replaced with a competing product from another vendor, the impact of that change would be only to the extracts, not to the lion's share of your application code.

This strategy, illustrated in figure 4.1, also mitigates the risk of unintended negative impact on external application users since that access is scheduled and controlled. This strategy does mean that external application data will only be as current as the latest extract.

It's important to note that there are several Extract, Transform and Load (ETL) products on the market that provide support for these types of extracts. Some of these products are open source and freely available. Many ETL product suites are very dependency heavy and require a significant learning curve. My experience is that your extract and transformation needs have to be extensive before leveraging this type of toolset is cost effective.

Figure 4.1: Operational Data Store Strategy

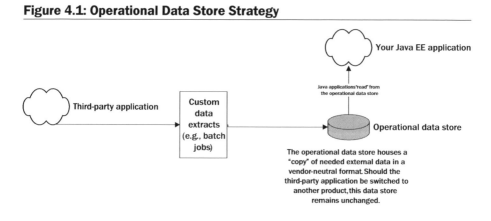

Writing to external application databases directly has considerable risk. This should be done only if there are absolutely no other options. It considerably increases the risk of unintended impact to users of the external application; if your code has a bug, the external application might not work properly. Furthermore, if the external application is a vended product, doing this may void your support contract.

Utilizing Web Services

Many vended products that support custom interfaces will provide web service libraries for this purpose. Like any interface choice, web services have several advantages and disadvantages.

Advantages of utilizing web services for applications interfaces are the following:

- Web service definitions are self-documented using WSDL.
- Web services have extensive product support.
- Web services provide a change insulation layer.
- Web services are platform neutral.
- Web services can be published securely over the Internet.

Web service interfaces are popular precisely because they are platform neutral. Given the choice, most organizations like preserving the flexibility of choosing alternate platforms should that become necessary. In addition, tool support for publishing and consuming web services has advanced considerably. For instance, the Java EE specification (JAX-WS portion) has added web service annotations that make it easier to publish web services. Additionally, there are numerous web service frameworks available for Java/Java EE as well as other development platforms.

Readers wanting code-level information on how to program web services using the JAX-WS specification can see the following tutorial: http://docs.oracle.com/cd/E17802_01/webservices/webservices/docs/2.0/tutorial/doc/JAXWS.html. From an architectural perspective, it is usually advisable to segregate code consuming or publishing web services from the rest of your application. This is an application of the "single responsibility principle" and provides an insulation layer that limits adverse effects of change on both sides. It also makes constructing unit tests easier. As an example, suppose your application needs to consume web services offered by a document management system (DMS) product. I typically would segregate code consuming the interface from the rest of the application, as illustrated in figure 4.2a.

Figure 4.2a: Example Web Service Client Design

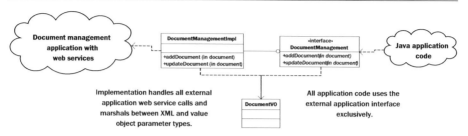

This design provides several benefits. Changes in the DMS product, such as product upgrades or even complete product or vendor replacements, only affect the web service client implementation; the rest of your application is unaffected. The DocumentManagement interface can be mocked; unit tests for your application do not need access to the DMS to run.

We can leverage this concept for web services we publish as well. Suppose that we support a reporting application and need to expose the ability to run reports to external applications. I typically would segregate the published web service from the rest of the application, as illustrated in figure 4.2b.

Figure 4.2b: Example Web Service Design

This design has several benefits. You are free to refactor and redesign the reporting application as desired. As long as the ReportService and associated arguments and WSDL specification are the same, applications that use your web service will not be impacted.

Additionally, providing a web service layer provides a natural insulation layer for external application change. Should you elect to publish a web service to expose functionality to external applications; as long as that web service interface remains consistent, your application can change with less risk of adversely impacting applications consuming your web services.

Disadvantages of utilizing web services are the following:

- Web services are often more expensive to develop and maintain compared to other interface methods.

- Web services are not optimized for retrieving large amounts of data.

■ Web services may be unavailable when needed; consumers need an outage strategy.

Despite increased tool support, publishing and consuming web services are not cheap compared to utilizing an external application database directly. Furthermore, web services often do not have good performance when used to retrieve large amounts of data. For this reason, I've seen many interfaces that *read* data using either the database strategy mentioned above or a REST service, but *write* data using web service interfaces.

If your Java EE application programmatically initiates processing in external applications, you should identify those applications as actors in the use-case analysis, as discussed in chapter 2. All specifics about the information transferred between the Java EE application and the external applications should be the subject of one or more use cases. For example, the fact that a purchasing system notifies the accounting system about all orders placed should be the subject of a use case.

Utilizing RESTful Web Services

RESTful web services work by using structured URLs to communicate specifics of an information request. For example, a RESTful web service URL like /customer/account/55555 might be a request for information for a specific customer account 55555. The return from the REST service call (which is HTTP) would be structured XML (or JSON) formatted data.

To further illustrate, consider the following example of a purchasing application using HTTP to request information from an inventory management system:

1 The purchasing application issues an HTTP request (using `java.net.URL`) to the inventory application requesting current inventory levels for an item (e.g., laundry detergent). With REST, the URL describes the content of the request. For example, the format of a REST-style request might be <server>/sku/<item sku number> (e.g., /inventory/sku/14678).

2 A servlet in the inventory management system receives the request, interprets request specifics from the URL, and initiates processing.

3 The inventory management system examines its database and determines the quantity of the requested item available at all warehouses.

4 The inventory management system constructs an XML document containing the item information.

5 The servlet in the inventory management system returns the XML document to the caller in the same way it would return HTML to a browser.

The purchasing application receives the XML document, parses it, and continues processing, using the inventory information received.

Advantages of utilizing RESTful web services for applications interfaces are the following:

- RESTful web services provide a change insulation layer.
- RESTful web services are platform neutral.
- RESTful web services are often easier to consume than web services.

Disadvantages of utilizing RESTful web services are the following:

- May be unavailable when needed; consumers need an outage strategy.
- Don't have a built-in documentation strategy.

Utilizing Messaging Services

Messaging services are an asynchronous communication method. That is, a request is sent, but a response may not be immediate. The Java EE provides formal support for messaging by a construct known as Message Driven Beans. Essentially, the container will act as a JMS message receiver and route all messages to a given destination to a class that implements the `MessageListener` (http://docs.oracle.com/javaee/1.3/api/javax/jms/MessageListener.html) interface.

The main advantage of Message services is that they can provide guaranteed delivery due to the fact that JMS messages are asynchronous. That is, the receiving application may be down when the message is sent, but when that application becomes available, the message will be received and processed. Consequently, applications consuming a messaging interface do not need to have an outage strategy. Note that messages that are never picked up and processed will eventually be noticed by end users.

Messaging can be platform neutral, but that depends on the messaging vendor. The JMS specification utilized by Java EE messaging is by definition Java-specific. However, some vendors that implement the JMS interface for Java applications also provide for clients using alternative development platforms.

Messaging is very useful in situations where one application needs to notify another application of a particular event. Using one of the other interface methods, external applications can "pull" information about that event on a scheduled basis, but that usually isn't as timely. Advantages of utilizing messaging services for application interfaces are the following:

- Messaging services provide guaranteed delivery.
- Messaging services are platform neutral.

▓ Messaging services have Java EE container support.

Disadvantages of utilizing messaging services are the following:

▓ Messaging services don't have a built-in documentation strategy.

Utilizing Enterprise Java Beans

Enterprise Java Beans (EJBs) are a pure Java method that could be used to call one application from another. Advantages of utilizing EJBs for application interfaces are the following:

▓ EJB definitions are self-documented using the published Java interface.

▓ EJBs have extensive product support.

▓ EJBs provide a change insulation layer.

Disadvantages of utilizing EJBs for application interfaces are the following:

▓ EJBs are restricted to Java-based clients.

▓ EJBs are not easily secured.

▓ EJBs may be unavailable when needed; consumers need an outage strategy.

While the Java EE specification has belatedly made Enterprise Java Beans (EJBs) easy to publish, and tooling support is readily available to consume them, web services are more popular. Web services provide the same functional features that EJBs do without limiting consumers to Java-based applications.

COMMON MISTAKES

Using databases and file systems as "message brokers." This error-prone strategy consists of writing a row in a database table (or a file in a file system) with the contents of a message. The second part to the strategy is writing an agent that "polls" the database (or file system) for new messages to arrive, reads and processes the message content, and then deletes the row or file.

In essence, this strategy is akin to writing your own messaging system. It is typically a frequent source of bugs. Why reinvent the wheel? Choose one of the existing forms of communication and concentrate on business logic, not low-level communication programming.

Using an asynchronous communication method, such as messaging, when a response is required. With this strategy, your application sends an asynchronous message to another application and waits for a return message from that application.

Using asynchronous communication when responses are required puts you in the position of programming an algorithm to wait for a response. How long do you wait? If you wait too long, you could be holding up a user. If you don't wait long enough, you could mistakenly report an error. This is akin to two people trying to find each other in the dark in an extremely loud room. If a response is required, use a synchronous communication method.

If the application initiating the message doesn't require a response, using asynchronous communication methods are less vulnerable to unplanned outages as the sender won't experience an error if the receiving application isn't currently available. The receiving application will merely consume the message when it comes back online. As asynchronous messaging requires messaging software, using asynchronous communication adds components and complexity to the application. Lest I leave you with the impression that using asynchronous messaging is dangerous, messaging technologies are mature, robust, and stable.

Not considering production environment requirements. For organizations that don't standardize load balancing options, communication protocols, and security methods, you will need to investigate what external application plans to use and accommodate those plans in the interface design. For organizations that standardize security concerns and hardware platforms across the enterprise, this information might already be known. One way to mitigate this risk is to do a small test implementation of the planned communication method upfront. That way you'll have more time to react if you need to modify your design.

DETERMINING A DATA STRUCTURE

Document all data passed to an external application. The communication structure or format, along with the conditions that dictate transmission, are part of your contract with the external system developers. The data structure should be documented in writing.

Use simple structured formats for interfaces to legacy platforms such as XML or CSV. XML can be a headache for developers using legacy platforms if your company won't buy an XML parser. Open source parsers and other tools are not available for COBOL or PL/I at the time of this writing. This would be a valuable open source project. When the external application is a legacy system and the client doesn't buy XML tools to assist, custom formats are common out of practical necessity. Custom formats can have a keyword-type organization (like XML) or some type of positional organization. COBOL lends itself to fixed-length strings using a positional format.

You need to develop a DTD or schema, or otherwise document the XML document formats and tags with allowed values. Leaving this communication verbal is a recipe for disappointment and countless project delays. Chapter 7 includes material to help you design XML documents.

CSV formats appear widely supported by many purchased software products. However, although writing a specification for the CSV format has been attempted, there isn't formal agreement on what delimiters are permitted and what escape characters are supported for strings. For these reasons, I trend toward using XML if it's an option.

It is not necessary to validate XML documents for external interfaces. Developing a DTD to describe a document format does not mean that you have to "validate" the document when it's parsed. Validation works well for documents that were directly written by people and thus more likely to contain errors. Application interfaces are mechanical. Aside from initial development, the probability of receiving a malformed XML document that was programmatically generated from another application is very low. Given this, the benefits of validation don't usually outweigh its performance costs.

Avoid sending serialized Java objects as message content. This effectively negates the benefits of loose coupling by making both applications dependent on the same classes. If a change is made to one of the objects referenced by the serialized class, the change would have to be deployed to both applications simultaneously. Further, serialization problems can occur if one of the applications upgrades its Java Virtual Machine (JVM). Serialized objects cannot be visually inspected to determine content; they must be programmatically processed. They also limit communication to Java applications.

ERROR-HANDLING REQUIREMENTS

Error-handling requirements need to be discussed, documented, and agreed to just as thoroughly as data formats do. Bad error handling will lead to high maintenance costs.

Error Notification Procedures

All external application interfaces should have error notification procedures. Some organizations provide centralized operations personnel responsible for notifying application support personnel of errors. This is often achieved through some type of console message. It's not uncommon for the console to be monitored 24x7x365. It's normal for organizations with this capability to provide some way to programmatically generate a console message that someone takes action on.

Use mechanical error notification. In companies that haven't established enterprise-wide error notification procedures, I typically include some type of e-mail notification for severe system errors. Merely writing errors to a log assumes that someone will look at them. Messages written to the log often go unnoticed. As most alphanumeric pagers accept message via e-mail, it's easy to include pager notification for severe errors. This should be used with caution for obvious reasons.

Don't be afraid to be verbose when logging for errors. My philosophy is that the error log should contain as much information as possible. While some of it might not be useful for a particular problem, it's better to have too much rather than too little when it comes to information. If logging is successful, a large percentage of errors should be diagnosable just from the error message without further need to reproduce the problem.

At some companies, commercial tool support is available to help with logging. BMC Patrol, EcoTools, and Tivoli are commercial network management toolsets that are often used to monitor the enterprise. OpenNMS (http://www.opennms.org) and Nagios (http://www.nagios.org/) are open source alternatives for network management.

Retry Procedures

Once initial development is complete, most errors with interfaces have environmental causes. Examples include someone recycling the database or messaging software, someone tripping over a network cord, and a server with a full file system. In most cases, the error is eventually fixed and the application interface resumes proper function.

However, with most applications, some type of recovery or retransmission procedure must be performed for the transmissions that failed. For example, messages recording customer purchases from the ordering application must be resent to keep accounting records accurate.

Make retry procedures mechanical. For transmissions that a user isn't physically waiting for, I often put a scheme for automatic retry logic in place. Environmental problems occur often enough in most companies to warrant including selective retry logic to recover from outages more quickly and with less effort. The objective of the retry mechanism is to automatically recover from a temporary outage without manual intervention by an application administrator.

The potential for complexity lies in discriminating between temporary outages and errors that won't magically go away over time. It's possible to take a shotgun approach and assume that all errors occur as a result of a temporary outage, and therefore always initiate retry logic. The danger is that the retry logic introduces an infinite loop for any situation other than a temporary outage. Consequently, you should use this approach with care.

All mechanical retry logic should have limits. It's important not to retry forever, essentially creating an infinite loop. Choose a sensible retry interval and number of retry attempts. It's also wise to make these limits configurable so they can be easily adjusted. Retry attempts should also be logged or possibly follow your mechanical notification procedure. Upon receiving notification of the retries, an application administrator might realize that corrective action should be taken.

EXTERNAL INTERFACE GUIDELINES

Many Java EE applications communicate with external systems, some of which may not be Java applications. As an application architect, you'll probably have an opportunity to facilitate design and implementation of external interfaces. Over the years, I've adopted several techniques for creating successful external interfaces.

Record every request or transmission from or to an external application. This should be the first task in any external interface. Be sure to log this information so that you know the time (and node if you're in a clustered environment). If there's a problem with work you initiated in an external application, you'll want to be able to tell those developers exactly what calls they made and when. If there's a problem processing a call from an external application, you'll want enough information to replicate it and fix any problems quickly.

This documentation practice helps prevent you or any member of the development team from being blamed for the mistakes of others. Without facts, anyone can make accusations, and in too many corporations you're guilty until proven innocent. Having a transmission log will make it easier to determine which application has a problem.

Create a way for an application administrator to resubmit a work request from an external application. When your application experiences an environmental problem and you're able to fix it, the application administrator should be able to resubmit the work that failed. This limits the impact on end users and limits the number of people (and thus the time) needed to fix a problem. Sometimes, resubmission isn't possible or applicable. But it can save you time for activities that are more fun than maintenance.

As an example, one of the applications I supported provided scheduled reporting capabilities. An application administrator could resubmit any report that wasn't being delivered to a browser by an administrative web-based utility.

Collect the identity of the transmitter. Part of every transmission should be information that indicates the identity of the caller. This is meant as a way to reduce your maintenance time, not as a security mechanism. In the case of an inappropriate call, you want to be able to quickly notify the application making it. If you don't know where it's coming from, finding it and getting it fixed takes longer.

Develop a mechanical way to "push" errors to the transmitter. If there is a problem processing a request made by an external application, administrators from that application need to be notified. If the interface has a tight coupling (e.g., session bean, RMI service), all you have to do is throw an exception. Whatever mechanism the external application uses for error processing will be able to handle the error.

If the interface has a loose coupling (e.g., uses messaging technologies), you need to construct a way to mechanically notify administrators from the external application of the error. Most often, I've seen e-mail used as an effective error notification channel for these cases. As most alphanumeric pages accept e-mails, paging is a possibility. However, I would thoroughly test your error processing before hooking it up to a pager.

Ensure that you adequately test error-handling logic. Often developers will neglect the testing of error handling. Errors in error-handling logic can easily mask the underlying problem, making production support much more difficult.

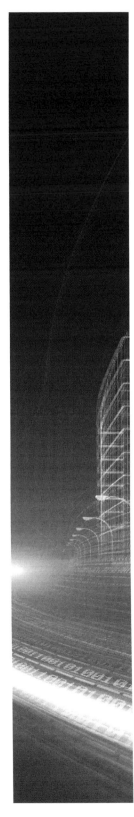

SECTION II

DESIGNING JAVA EE APPLICATIONS

The application architect typically leads and facilitates all application design activities. In this section, you will learn how to:

- Document application designs with object models so other development staff can easily understand the design.

- Understand software layering concepts and how to use them to organize J2EE applications into smaller and more manageable sections.

- Apply common design patterns at each software layer.

- Document application storage requirements using data-modeling techniques.

- Design XML document formats.

- Refine project estimates after the design phase.

CHAPTER 5

A LAYERED APPROACH TO JAVA EE DESIGN

Application architects, by definition, must supply application developers with an overall design. It is important that developers understand the overall design so they can make lower level coding decisions; architects can't expect developers to follow a design they don't understand. Furthermore, if developers have disagreements with the intended design, it's best to resolve those disagreements before too much code is written.

Although extensive documentation is frowned upon these days as many trend toward agile methodologies, some amount of design documentation is needed. The larger the effort (and the number of developers), the more extensive this documentation needs to be. Having some amount of documentation allows you to more quickly and easily involve additional developers in the effort, should that be needed.

This chapter presents and explains a general approach to designing Java EE applications. This discussion is necessary background to the next chapter, which offers tips and techniques for transforming the use-case analysis described in previous chapters into a concrete design. It is a general approach that can be applied to all business applications.

The fact that my approach to all Java EE business applications is consistent allows me to minimize the design documentation needed for each application built. Since developers who have worked with me on previous projects are already familiar with the concept, there's less time spent getting developers up to speed on my designs or transferring developers between development efforts. It also minimizes the number of support developers needed for each application.

Object models are the most popular mechanism for documenting Java EE application designs. The application architect is typically responsible for facilitating creation of object models for the most complex portions of the application to be developed. For those using agile methodologies with very short iterations (e.g., two weeks per iteration), this is a short exercise at the start of the iteration.

In addition to object models for the most complex portions of the development effort, I often have illustrations that describe major business process flows. I generally use swim-lane diagrams for this purpose. This chapter will provide a more in-depth description of these and a sample.

Java EE application design is a vast topic. Entire books have been written about design techniques, design patterns, and object modeling with UML. And like most large and complicated methodologies, UML is only partially applied in business applications. Thus, although I don't want to discourage learning, I do take a streamlined approach to the topic in this chapter. For instance, of the hundreds of design patterns that have been identified and cataloged, this chapter focuses on the handful of patterns most commonly used in business applications today.

OVERVIEW OF THE LAYERING CONCEPT

A common framework for Java EE applications is *software layering*, in which each layer provides functionality for one section of the system. The layers are organized to provide support and base functionality for other layers. For example, the data access layer provides a set of services to read and write application data. An inventory management application needs services that can read information about specific items and warehouses.

Layering is not a new concept; operating systems and network protocols have been using it for years. For instance, anyone who's worked with networks is familiar with telnet, FTP, and Internet browsers. All these services depend on a TCP/IP networking layer. As long as the interface to TCP/IP services stays constant, you can make network software advances within the TCP framework without affecting telnet, FTP, or your web-browsing capability. Typically, the TCP/IP layer requires the services of a device layer, which understands how to communicate with an Ethernet card.

Business applications can make strategic use of the same concept. For example, it's common to make data access a separate portion of an application in order to make it easier to consolidate data access logic used in multiple portions of an application. For instance, a customer lookup by ID might be used in several portions of an application. With data access separated and consolidated in one layer, existing code is easy to recognize and reuse. In addition, should your data access method change in some way (e.g., you switch your underlying database from MySql to Oracle), the way the application physically reads and writes data may change without affecting application processing or business logic.

To continue the inventory management example, suppose the data access layer had a method to look up the information for an inventory item given a UPC code. Suppose that other parts of the application use this method when information about items is needed (e.g., a customer viewing that item on a web page or an inventory analyst ordering stock for that item). As long as the methods for accessing item information remain the same, you should be able to reorganize how you can store information about items and warehouses without affecting the rest of the application.

In essence, a layered approach mitigates the risk of technical evolution. If you use this concept to separate your deployment mechanics (e.g., Java Server Faces or Struts), you can add new deployments without changing your business logic or data access layer—for example, if you decide to expose application functionality via web services. If your application effectively separates your business logic and data access logic from the rest of your application, you can freely add a web services deployment without having to change the entire application. Table 5.1 lists common software layers used in Java EE applications.

Table 5.1: Typical Software Layers in Java EE Applications

LAYER	ROLE
Data access object layer	Manage reading, writing, updating, and deleting stored data. Commonly contains JDBC code, but could also be used for XML document and file storage manipulation.
Business logic layer	Manages business processing rules and logic.
Entity objects layer	Lightweight structures that are mapped directly to relational database tables.
Value objects layer	Lightweight structures that facilitate display of summarized business information.
Deployment layer	Publishes business object capabilities.
Presentation layer	Controls display to the end user.
Architectural component layer	Generic application utilities. Often, these objects are good candidates for enterprise-wide use.

Software layering implements an architectural concept called the *separation of concerns*. The separation of concerns principle states that software components should have a single focus and be concerned with only what they need to accomplish and nothing more. Furthermore, the focus of one software component should not overlap with that of another component. The basic idea of this principle is to simplify software development by breaking large complex problems into multiple smaller and therefore simpler problems. This principle also incents reuse. More information on the separation of concerns principle can be found here: http://aspiringcraftsman.com/2008/01/03/art-of-separation-of-concerns/. Cases where this principle is violated are commonly referred to as a *leakage of concerns.*

Typically, calling patterns between software layers are tightly controlled. Any class in a software layer can call any other class in the same layer. For example, classes in the data access layer can leverage any other data access class. However, data access layer classes do not call business logic layer or presentation layer classes as those classes aren't directly involved with reading or writing stored data. Business logic layer classes can call other business logic layer classes as well as data access classes when they need to initiate reads or writes for stored data. Business logic layer classes do not issue SQL or initiate any reading or writing of stored data themselves; that activity is delegated to the data access layer. Figure 5.1 illustrates typical software layering calling patterns for Java EE applications.

Figure 5.1: Software Layering Calling For Java EE Applications

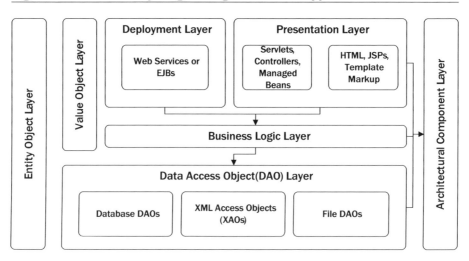

Note that entity and value object classes are used by all layers as they are used to pass information between other software layers.

When this boils down to code, I usually implement the layers as separate packages. Here's an example package structure:

`com.jmu.app.dao`	Data access object layer
`com.jmu.app`	Business logic layer
`com.jmu.app.entity`	Entity objects

`com.jmu.app.vo`	Value objects
`com.jmu.app.ui`	Presentation layer
`com.jmu.app.util`	Architectural component layer
`com.jmu.app.services`	Deployment layer/web services

I use the abbreviation jmu for "just made up." Also, you'll want to replace the app abbreviation with a meaningful application name.

It's important to note that the only layer that directly utilizes the data access layer is the business object layer. One question I commonly hear is, why not call the data access object layer directly from the presentation layer? Although calling the data access object layer directly can save some code by eliminating a couple of layers, it means placing any business logic either in the data access object layer or the presentation layer, which makes those layers more complex. Software layering works on the premise that it's easier to solve multiple small problems than fewer large ones. Experience has taught me two lessons:

- Should the data layer be modified, fewer touch points will be affected as they are all consolidated in the business logic layer.

- There is tremendous value in consistency.

There is value in consistency for maintenance purposes. For instance, if some JSPs call data access objects directly while others work through business objects and others use deployment wrappers, to make a change to code you're unfamiliar with, you have to do an audit of the whole action sequence. This defeats the purpose of separation of concerns and software layering.

I've had the privilege of utilizing a consistent architecture across an enterprise for one of my clients. At that particular client site, we typically are able to support a dozen applications with 2.5 support developer resources. At all other client sites I'm aware of, it takes multiple developers to support most applications. The consistency of the architecture is one of the largest reasons my client gets such good developer efficiency.

DATA ACCESS OBJECT LAYER

Data access objects (DAOs) manage access to persistent storage of some type. Usually, the storage used is a relational database, but DAOs can manage access to NoSQL databases, files, XML documents, and other types of persistent storage as well.

NoSQL (short for Not Only SQL) databases are gaining popularity. NoSQL is a term that describes databases that don't use SQL as a primary syntax for interacting with them. There are many products within the "NoSQL" umbrella. In fact, there are several categories of NoSQL databases, such as document stores, key value stores, graph databases, etc. NoSQL databases vary widely and have drastically different strengths and weaknesses. Because of that, describing the various advantages and disadvantages of the various products with a "NoSQL" designation would require a book in itself.

There have been attempts, however, to generalize the more popular NoSQL database products and provide a general overview of their strengths and weaknesses. The best synopsis that I have found can be viewed here: http://kkovacs.eu/cassandra-vs-mongodb-vs-couchdb-vs-redis. As a very broad generalization, a NoSQL database is a possible candidate for any data store that doesn't easily fit the relational database model and for which the queries you plan to execute against the data store are known and well-defined. Logging seems to be a popular use for NoSQL databases. NoSQL also appears to be commonly used for Content Management Systems (CMS) applications. However, at the time of this writing, relational database access still predominates. As such, relational database access will have a much larger focus in this book.

The primary reason to separate data access from the rest of the application is that it's easier to switch data sources and it's easier to share DAOs between applications. Furthermore, in cases where there are multiple applications using the same database, it may be possible to consolidate data access layer code and leverage the same access code across multiple Java EE applications.

A couple of patterns for data access objects are the most common. The simplest pattern has each persistent object represented as a DAO. I call this the *simplified data access pattern*. The more complex, but more flexible, pattern in common use is a factory-based pattern. In fact, it's called the *data access object pattern*. I'll define each pattern later in the section.

For convenience, I separate DAO objects in the package hierarchy (e.g., `com.acme.appname.data` or `com.acme.appname.dao`). I only mention this because some modeling tools (e.g., Rational Rose) encourage you to decide your package structure at modeling time. Some developers also add a DAO suffix to data access object names; for example, a customer DAO might be named `CustomerDAO`.

Choosing a Database Persistence Method

The question of which persistence method is best is the subject of considerable disagreement and debate. Although the Java EE specification provides for entity beans, other popular forms of database persistence exist. The degree to which developers take sides in the debate is akin to a discussion of religion or politics; the debate is not entirely rational. I'll take you through my thoughts on the different options, what I see in the marketplace, and what I prefer to use. However, the modeling concepts in this chapter are applicable to all persistence methods.

When beginning object-modeling activities, you can identify a DAO without choosing the persistence method you'll use at implementation.

For instance, the DAO could be a custom-coded JDBC class, a class using the Java Persistence API (JPA) (e.g., Hibernate), or an object utilizing an object-relational (O/R) mapping tool such as Ibatis. Java EE applications are compatible with all these persistence methods.

In making a decision, I first consider what needs to happen at the data access objects layer. I then grade each persistence method according to how well it achieves the goals, using the following rating system:

- High (best rating): Gets high marks toward achieving the stated goal.

- Medium (middle rating): Moderately achieves the stated goal.

- Low (lowest rating): Doesn't achieve the stated goal very well.

Table 5.2 lists the goals and ratings of several data persistence methods. Following the table are explanations of my reasoning in determining the ratings. I consider the first four goals listed in the table to be the most important to the majority of my clients.

Table 5.2: Ratings of Data Persistence Methods

Goal	JDBC	JPA	O/R Tool
Minimize learning curve	High	Medium	Medium
Minimize code and configuration files written and maintained	Low	Medium	Medium
Maximize ability to tune	High	Low	Low
Minimize deployment effort	High	Medium	Medium
Maximize code portability	Medium	High	High
Minimize vendor reliance	High	High	Low

Minimize the learning curve. Because JDBC was the first persistence API for databases, it is the most familiar to most, if not all, Java developers and thus has the lowest learning curve. To use the JPA or an ORM toolset, developers need to understand JDBC in addition to the technology they are directly using. The reason for this is: when errors come up, it is necessary to understand what your JPA or ORM implementation is doing to diagnose the error.

Minimize code and configuration files written and maintained. People have a tendency to consider the number of lines of code only when evaluating ease of development. I view any configuration file (e.g., an annotation or XML configuration file) as code with a different syntax. JPA implementations and most O/R toolsets I'm familiar with save some percentage of code in most situations.

Maximize the ability to tune. Because it's the lowest level API and closest to the database, JDBC provides unfettered ability to tune database SQL. Every other choice relies on a product to generate the SQL used. For instance, most JPA implementations and object-relational mapping tools generate the SQL executed; it's usually harder to tune without direct control of the SQL used.

Minimize the deployment effort. Deployment hassles negatively impact development and maintenance time. In this case, all product choices appear to be roughly equivalent in terms of effort needed to redeploy changes.

Maximize code portability. Being able to port data access code from one database to another is a consideration for some applications. In this sense, JPA implementations can offer the best opportunity for writing truly portable code that can run using any of the popular relational databases. For many business applications, needing to switch the underlying database vendor is a rare event. In which case, this criterion should receive less weight.

Minimize vendor reliance. You need to reduce your dependence on vendors that provide Java EE container services, JDBC drivers, JPA implementations, and O/R toolsets. This is desirable from a business standpoint should a vendor fail or change its cost structure. You can change vendors for JDBC drivers easily; I've done it many times with multiple database vendors. Switching JDBC vendors is usually just a jar file change along with a container configuration change. Most applications do not use JDBC vendor-specific classes and will not require change should you switch vendors.

Changing container vendors is moderately easy. You do have the possibility of performance-tuning issues, particularly with JPA vendors. With O/R toolsets, application code directly uses vendor (or vendor-generated) classes. Switching O/R toolsets requires significant development in most cases.

I think about the use of software toolsets in the same way an economist thinks about market efficiency. Financial analysts and economists have a theory that financial markets are efficient. That is, when a new piece of information becomes public, the stock prices of all companies related to that information change accordingly over time. For example, when the Enron and United Airlines bankruptcies became publicly known, the news had profound effects on their stock prices.

When new software paradigms are introduced, if they provide benefits that exceed their costs, over time developers will switch to them. The time frame in which this happens for programming paradigms is much slower than that for financial markets, but the general concept is much the same. When I wrote the first edition of this book, the "market" consensus regarding database persistence appeared to be favoring native JDBC. However, search engine keyword interest in Hibernate (a JPA implementer) has interest in JDBC. The inference is that developers are trending toward JPA implementations such as Hibernate. It's also possible to use job posting data as a proxy for market consensus; job posting data show that employer interest in Hibernate has surpassed that of JDBC. The search engine keyword data I refer to comes from Google Trends and is presented in figure 5.2. Job posting data I refer to can't be included because of licensing restrictions.

Figure 5.2: Search Engine Keyword Statistics with Persistence Technology Terms

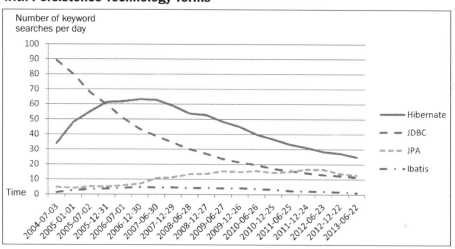

Source: Google Trends taken on November 17, 2013.

Simplified Data Access Pattern

Of the two patterns for data access objects that are most common, this is the simplest. In this pattern, there is a one-to-one correspondence between the physical storage construct (e.g., relational database table, XML document, or file) and the DAO that manages it. For example, you might have CUSTOMER_DAO manage access to a CUSTOMER table in a relational database. Although you haven't identified methods yet, you can imagine that this class will have methods to search and return information on one or more customers using search criteria as arguments. It might have methods to insert, update, and delete customers as well.

The advantage of this pattern is that it's simple. Its chief disadvantage is that it's often specific to one data source type. The code involved in manipulating an XML document is quite different from the JDBC and SQL required to use database tables. Switching the data source type would be a major overhaul to most methods in the class.

This pattern is usable no matter what database persistence mechanism you choose. Your data persistence method choice merely dictates how DAO classes are constructed internally. Figure 5.3 illustrates an object model for this pattern.

Figure 5.3: A Simplified Data Access Pattern

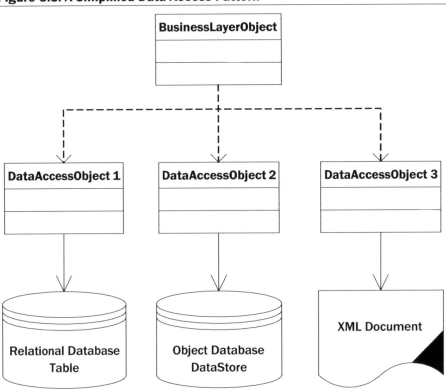

Supporting Multiple Databases

For an application that supports multiple types of databases, the data access object pattern, which is factory based, is quite common. This pattern implements the DAO as an interface. A factory is required to produce objects that implement this interface. In addition, you will have an implementation of this interface for each type of data source. The factory is smart enough to know how to instantiate all implementations. Figure 5.3 illustrates an object model for this pattern.

Figure 5.4: Data Access Object Pattern

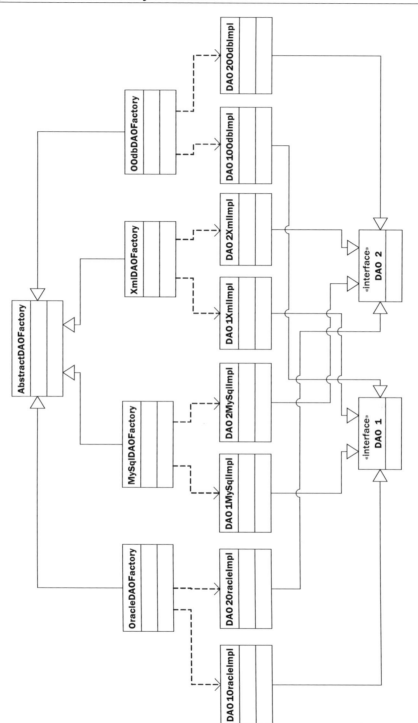

For example, consider a customer DAO implementation. It would have a CustomerDAO interface that would specify a variety of search methods as well as an update, delete, and insert method. It would also have a customer DAO factory (`CustomerDAOFactory`) responsible for providing a DAO for the application to use. It might also have an implementation for all relational databases it supports (e.g., `CustomerDAOOracleImpl`, `CustomerDAOSybaseImpl`, `CustomerDAOMySQLImpl`, etc.). The business object code would use the `CustomerDAO` interface exclusively so it could use any one of the implementations.

Another reason you might need this level of configuration in the data access layer is for unit testing purposes. When unit testing the business logic layer (which is the chief consumer of the data access layer), it is often useful to stub out the data access layer for business layer unit tests. This eliminates the dependency on a specific database.

Consider using an Inversion of Control (IOC) product in place of manually coding the object factories. Current popular IOC implementations are Spring, Google Guice, and Pico. These products eliminate the need to code factory classes, but introduce some level of configuration and complexity.

The data access object pattern is overkill if you don't foresee a need to support multiple database vendors and do not plan to maintain unit tests for the business layer. Few business applications need to be able to support multiple databases. While most developers employ some level of unit testing, many do not practice test driven development rigorously as it is more code to maintain. If your organization is diligent about writing and running automated unit tests, then you likely need to use the data access object pattern. If your organization doesn't support this level of testing, then you get no benefit for the additional complexity this pattern requires. Software vendors are more likely to need this pattern than business application developers. I discuss it at length because it has an unqualified recommendation in many texts.

ENTITY OBJECT LAYER

Most applications use relational databases for storage. Entity classes have a one-to-one mapping to one of the application's relational database tables. For example, if you have a `Customer` table, there will also be a `CustomerEntity` class that represents that table in Java. That class will have fields that correspond to columns on that table. For all practical purposes, an instance of `CustomerEntity` represents a row in the `Customer` table. For all practical purposes, the entity object layer represents a "Java" version of the application's relational database.

Data access classes in one sense are factories for entity classes. They use relational database data as "input" and produce one or more instances of entity classes as output. They also translate data in entity classes and persist it to the applications database.

Typically, entity classes are separated into a different package structure (e.g., `com.acme.appname.entity`). In addition, it's often helpful to use a naming convention for entity classes so that the fact that a class is an entity class can be easily identified. Often, I use an "Entity" suffix for entity classes (e.g., `AccountEntity`). If the database design adheres to 3rd normal form (which will be described in a separate chapter), entity classes derived from that design will closely match what would have been identified from an object modeling perspective. For example, the "customer" and "account" tables discussed earlier are logical candidates for Java classes in an object modeling exercise. Every application has data items that logically belong and typically are used together.

Typically, entity classes have accessor and mutator methods, but usually little else. They are typically referenced in all other application layers.

VALUE OBJECT LAYER

In addition to entity classes, which represent data that will be saved and later retrieved, every application has transient data items that logically belong, and typically are used, together. Transient data is data that exists only to facilitate a specific body of work, but isn't directly saved. Value object (VO) classes represent this data. For example, value objects might be used to represent aggregate sales information for user display (e.g., `SalesDisplayVO`). Aggregate sales information isn't often stored directly, but summarized from detailed sales data when needed for display or reporting.

There is some labeling confusion surrounding the topic of value objects. My definition of "value object" is very close to a Data Transfer Object (DTO). A definition of a DTO can be found here: http://martinfowler.com/eaaCatalog/dataTransferObject.html. For years, the Java EE community promoted use of DTOs as the preferred way to transmit data between session beans (EJBs) and their clients (hence the word transfer in its title). As use of the term DTO implied use of enterprise session beans, many began using the term "value object" to avoid that implication. It should be said that the term value object has a different meaning in C++ circles. In those circles, value objects describe one value in a meaningful way (e.g., money, date, etc.).

In the early days of Java EE, enterprise beans (EJB) were much more widely used than they are today. With enterprise beans, value objects were used to optimize network transmissions between the beans themselves and their callers. As EJB use has declined, most applications don't need that level of distribution, so using value object classes for this purpose is less relevant.

It's programmatically convenient to treat this logical group of data items as a separate object. This type of object is commonly known as a value object (VO), although some texts refer to it as a data transfer object. If Java had a "structure" construct, as C/C++ and many other languages do, a VO would be a structure.

For example, you could combine various pieces of information for a report template into a VO. Methods needing a report template argument could then accept the `ReportTemplateVO` instead of individual arguments for all components of the structure.

Typically, a VO has accessors and mutators but little else. And usually a VO implements `java.io.Serializable` so it can be transmitted to remote application clients or serialized in session. Java EE containers and RMI services serialize the content of Java classes before transmitting them to a remote machine. A common convention is to give value object names a VO suffix, as in `CustomerVO`.

Common Patterns

The value object originates from a formally defined pattern. In some texts, this pattern is called the value object pattern (Alur, Crupi, and Malks, 2001). The VO pattern enhances EJB performance but is useful in communication among all layers of the application.

You can combine the VO pattern with the composite pattern, which is used when something contains other things. For instance, a report template often contains multiple parameters. Using the composite pattern, the `ReportTemplateVO` contains an array of `ReportTemplateParameterVO` objects, as illustrated in figure 5.5.

Figure 5.5: Composite Pattern with Value Object Context

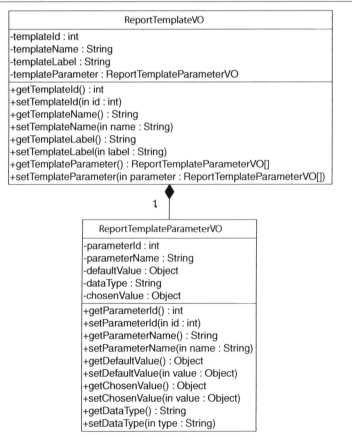

BUSINESS LOGIC LAYER

Objects in the business logic layer combine data with business rules, constraints, and activities. Business objects should be separated from DAOs, entity objects, VOs, and the service layer, such as web services, to maximize the possibility of reuse. Business objects often use and coordinate the activities of multiple data access objects.

Business objects should be deployment independent and self-contained. Business objects should be easily usable in batch jobs as well as web applications or thick-client applications. Business logic objects utilize data access classes and reference entity and value objects, but don't reference anything in the presentation layer. We will find out that the presentation layer uses the business logic layer, not the other way around.

Business logic contains transaction scripts for any work performed by the application. For example, if credit checks are automatically initiated for new customers, the business logic class managing saving new customers' information might also initiate the credit check for that customer. This action might be initiated by a business user via a web application or initiated by a batch job processing a purchased customer base. The business logic class makes no assumptions as to the context of its execution.

Common Patterns

One of the most frequently used patterns in the business logic layer is the *Transaction Script pattern*. This pattern basically looks at an application as a series of discrete transactions. For example, in banking, common transactions are defining a new customer and opening new bank accounts for that customer. You can imagine transactions to find an account balance as part of validating a financial transaction, as illustrated in figure 5.6. A more detailed definition can be found here: http://martinfowler.com/eaaCatalog/transactionScript.html.

The Transaction Script pattern is often criticized as not being object oriented. That is true. It is so popular because it adheres to the practice of keeping software as simple as it can possibly be.

Figure 5.6: Transaction Script Example

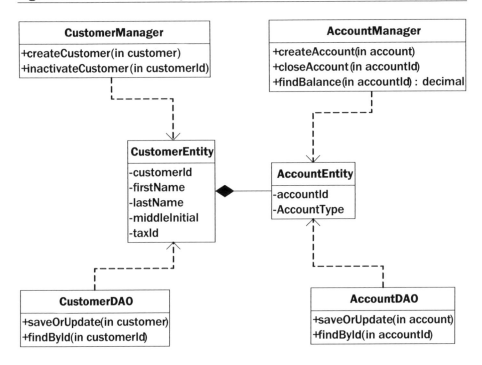

Layered initialization is a pattern you will commonly use when you have different varieties of the same object. For example, most applications have different types of users. As shown in figure 5.7, you might have trust customer users, corporate customer users, banking support users, application administrator users, and so on. All these users share commonality but also have aspects that are unique.

Figure 5.7: Layered Initialization Pattern Example

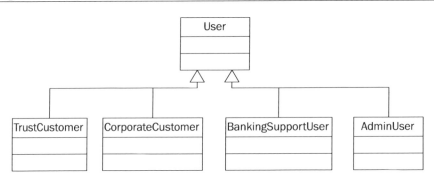

When the same business object might have to produce different outputs or use different inputs, you will most likely use the *adapter pattern*. Consider the example shown in figure 5.8, a reporting business object that has several different delivery mechanisms—e-mail, ftp—but all other processing is the same. Furthermore, there are existing utilities to perform the e-mail and ftp deliveries, but they don't implement the interface currently needed for the application. The adapter has the responsibility of implementing the interface and utilizing any third-party product needed to actually accomplish the report delivery.

Figure 5.8: Adapter Pattern Example

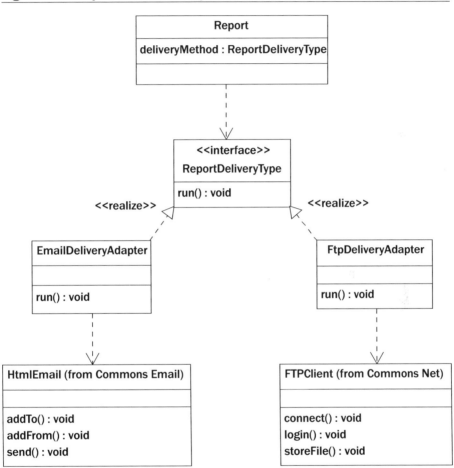

Like the adapter pattern, the *strategy pattern* is used when the activities of a business object are likely to vary according to the context. However, the adapter pattern leaves the activities of a class constant while dynamically varying its inputs and outputs, and the strategy pattern makes the activities of a class dynamic while using constant inputs and outputs. It's largely a difference in the perception of "who's the client." Figure 5.9 illustrates the strategy pattern.

Figure 5.9: Strategy Pattern Example

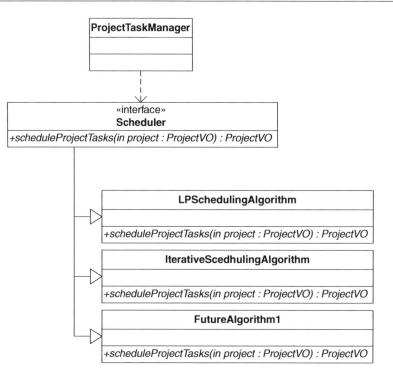

DEPLOYMENT LAYER

Deployment wrappers publish business object functionality to Java classes that could be on separate machines (including anything in the presentation tier). Examples of deployment wrappers include enterprise beans (e.g., session beans, message-driven beans) and web services.

Promoting reuse is the motivation for deploying business functionality so that it can be called by other applications. That is, it's better to reuse existing functionality than to reinvent it. Sometimes the functionality to be reused is changing frequently or has onerous resource requirements that make it difficult to merely include that functionality in your application as common code.

Deployment layer classes publish business logic. Service layer classes utilize business logic classes and reference entity classes and value objects. They do not reference data access classes directly.

Do not implement business logic directly within deployment layer classes. Some developers consider enterprise beans to represent business logic. Although it is technically possible to consolidate what I call business objects and enterprise beans into the same class, I don't recommend it. Keeping the business logic separate gives you complete deployment flexibility. You can deploy the same business object as an enterprise bean, a message-driven bean, a web service, or even a client application with no changes to the underlying business object. Separating the business logic into deployment-independent classes does create additional classes, but the classes are less complex.

Trend toward publishing that is an independent unit of work. If a remote call succeeds, any changes made by that remote call will be committed and will not participate in a rollback. If you need the ability to rollback the work performed by a remote call, it would be better to include the business logic code in your application where you can control the transaction strategy.

Trend away from publishing remote functionality with expected high transaction volume. Remote calls have network overhead that local calls don't. This is true regardless of the deployment wrapper chosen.

Choosing Deployment Wrappers

You can have multiple deployment wrappers for the same business object. For example, it is not uncommon to create a message-driven bean and a web service deployment for a customer object.

Each type of deployment wrapper has its advantages and disadvantages. Choosing which type of deployment wrapper to use is difficult if you haven't substantially completed use-case analysis and prototyping (chapter 3) or defining application interfaces (chapter 4). Table 5.3 summarizes the differences between the types of deployment wrappers.

Table 5.3: Features of Deployment Wrapper Types

Feature	EJB	Web Services	Messaging/ JMS	RMI	HTTP
Caller platform requirements	Java-compliant only	Any	Any	Java-compliant only	Any
Communication method supported	Synch. only	Both	Both	Synch. only	Synch. only
Coupling	Tight	Loose	Loose	Tight	Loose
Supports clustering for scalability and availability?	Yes	Yes	Yes	No	Yes

Faced with deciding which deployment wrappers to use and which business objects to publish, ask yourself the following questions; your answers will help you navigate through the decision-making process.

Is your business object called from applications that aren't Java?

This functionality is commonly published as a web service. Web services completely eliminate any language-to-language restrictions by encoding all communication in XML using a SOAP format. Because web services don't represent a programmatic coupling, they need very little deployment coordination. Web services are widely used and often the preferred deployment wrapping technology.

If your messaging vendor supports JMS and also has a native API for the foreign application platform, you should be able to deploy this functionality as a message-driven enterprise bean.

Does your business object receive and process messages via JMS?

Functionality supporting JMS message receipt and processing is commonly implemented via a message-driven enterprise bean. That bean utilizes business logic classes to perform whatever work is required to process the message. Although the JMS standard was created and refined in the last few years, messaging technology has existed for more than a decade. Most messaging technology vendors have implemented the JMS interface. Messaging is good for transmitting information. This technology is designed more to guarantee delivery than to issue a sub-second response time.

Does your business object require two-phase commit functionality?

If it does, deploy the business object as a session bean. Two-phase commit functionality requires JTA and is provided by Java EE containers. Web services or servlets running from within a Java EE container will have access to JTA, but these deployments may be used in environments that don't support JTA.

Common Patterns

The pattern commonly used for deployment wrappers is a combination of the session façade pattern and the proxy pattern. This combination (or slight variations thereof) works for all the deployment wrappers that I can think of. The session façade pattern has been especially popular with EJB deployments, but the concept is valid for most types of distributed objects.

Two common design goals for deployment wrappers such as enterprise beans or web services are to minimize network traffic and to minimize changes. Façades minimize network traffic by allowing the published functionality to be coarse-grained. That is, using façades, remote calls to the remote service can initiate processing of business logic over a larger amount of data or combine lower level business logic features in a single call. It is often more important to minimize the number of calls to remote services, even if some of the data in those calls or returns from those calls are larger as a result.

Façades allow you to minimize changes in features published to remote callers. That is, it preserves the ability to refactor and change the business logic layer or other layers of the application and keep the façade publishing that functionality to remote applications unchanged. This is customer friendly in the sense that the service's remote applications are calling change less frequently. It also preserves your ability to refactor and change the application publishing the service without accidentally impacting customers.

Some developers like to publish the business logic layer objects directly as web services or enterprise beans. This is usually an attempt at simplification and reducing complexity. But the trouble with that approach is that changes to the business logic layer then potentially change how those services are called and used. This means that an innocent refactoring in the business logic layer might have unintended consequences for applications calling those services. Figure 5.10 graphically illustrates how you can effectively combine the session façade and proxy patterns.

Figure 5.10: Session Façade Pattern with Proxy Pattern

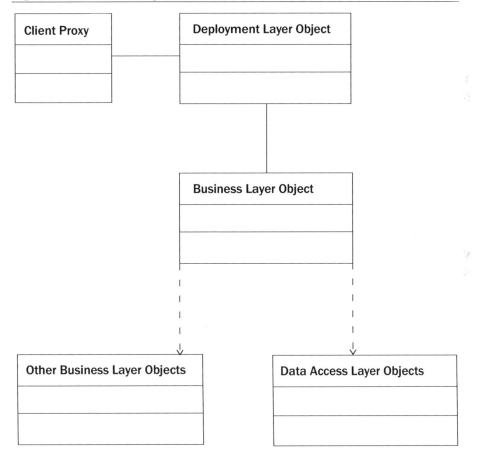

FURTHER READING

Gamma, Erich, Richard Helm, Ralph Johnson, and John Vlissides. 1995. *Design Patterns*. Reading, MA: Addison-Wesley.

CHAPTER 6

CREATING OBJECT MODELS

Application architects are responsible for leading the application design process. In this role, the architect is as much a facilitator as an application designer. This chapter shows you ways to utilize use-case analysis along with the layered approach described in the previous chapter to construct effective designs for Java EE applications and document them in an object model. Along the way, I'll share some techniques for leading a group design process.

Finished use cases are essential for effective application design. Without them, the object-modeling sessions will produce more questions than answers. If you do find vague points or unaddressed issues in the use-case documentation, apply the technique of making assumptions to fill the gaps. Document the assumptions you make so you can confirm them with the business side later. Your use-case analysis is more likely to be incomplete when you're working on a large project.

Object-modeling exercises are applicable for the Java portions of a Java EE application that are custom written (e.g., not provided by a software vendor). Modeling of third-party software components should be limited to those classes directly called by your application.

It is not necessary to model 100 percent of the application. This is particularly true when layered architectures are utilized. Object models will most likely be needed for the value object and business logic layers. For instance, the object model of the entire entity layer will be obvious once you've completed the data modeling portion of the design (covered in the next chapter) as each class will have a one-to-one relationship with a table. Furthermore, many JPA implementations will generate classes mapped to a database. Similarly, the data access layer classes usually have a one-to-one relationship with entity classes (e.g., a customer entity class will likely have a customer data access class to handle I/O). Concentrate modeling activities on the most complex portions of the application (typically in the business logic layer).

The application architect is responsible for facilitating design discussions, which should involve the business logic and presentation-tier developers in the design process. Because of its subjective nature, the object-modeling process can be a large source of frustration and a project bottleneck. I've seen some projects where the architect produces the object model privately and then attempts to coerce other developers to follow. Although a lone modeler may be able to produce an object model more quickly than a team, the model is more likely to contain errors and omissions, and only the architect understands it and is loyal to it.

When the model is produced privately, it doesn't get substantive developer support. After all, if developers can't understand or agree with a plan, they certainly won't want to follow it. Many developers react to architect-produced models by ceasing to contribute anything meaningful to the project from that point. The architect may want to "draft" a model as a way to move the design process along, but developers should clearly understand that this draft is presented solely to prompt discussion and is entirely subject to change.

As a practical matter, when I need to get meaningful support from multiple developers, I go through the longer exercise of forming the plan collectively. Developers who have had input to a model and repeated opportunities to suggest enhancements to it are going to be more enthusiastic about implementing it.

Appoint a scribe for all modeling sessions. It's difficult to facilitate design sessions and take accurate and complete notes of the items discussed at the same time. As the architect is usually leading the session, one of the developers should act as scribe, perhaps on a rotating basis. After the design session, the scribe is responsible for updating the object model to reflect changes discussed in the session.

The remainder of this chapter presents a framework you can use to guide development staff through the object-modeling process. The first step in the process is to identify the major objects in your application using the use cases as a guide. Next, you refine these objects into classes, determine how they interact, and identify attributes and methods. Throughout the chapter, I show you how to streamline the process and avoid those annoying bottlenecks.

IDENTIFYING OBJECTS

Identify the most important constructs. Nouns in use cases are generally good candidates for classes. Thus a good way to start identifying objects is by reading the use cases and extracting a list of all the nouns. (You can ignore system in the beginning phrase "The system will" because it's merely part of the use-case format.)

At this point, you should interpret my use of the word *object* loosely. In the early stages of development, it's impossible to know enough about these objects to understand exactly which classes you will derive from them. Note that my use of the term *object* differs from some texts that use the term to refer to an instance of a class.

Don't bother with attribution or relationships at this stage. Attribution and relationships are important, but identifying them too early will bog you down in too much detail and will throw the team into frequent tangents. For now, try not to be concerned about process; focus instead on data organization.

As objects are identified, record persistence requirements. Some classes will represent data that your application has to store, usually in a database, and are said to be persistent. In fact, persistent objects frequently appear as entities in the data model. I often record objects with persistent data as entities in the data model when they're identified in the object model. I discuss data modeling in detail in chapter 7.

Objects identified at this stage are high level. You will further refine and expand them later in the process, using objects to determine specific classes.

OBJECT IDENTIFICATION EXAMPLE

Let's use an example paraphrased from a reporting system I recently implemented. The team defined the following use cases:

- The system will provide an interface that will accept report template definitions from an existing MVS/CICS application. A report template consists of an ID, a name, a list of parameters required to run the template, and a list of data items produced by the template.

- The system will allow application administrators to control the report templates that users belonging to a trust customer organization can run.

- The system will run reports at least as fast as its predecessor system did on average.

- The system will restrict reported data for all trust customer users to that of the trust customer organization to which they belong.

- The system will allow banking support users to execute all report templates using data from any trust customer organization.

Looking at the nouns in the use cases in order (ignoring *system*, as mentioned earlier) gave us the list that appears in the first column of table 6.1.

Table 6.1: Object Identification Example

Noun (from use case)	Object
Interface	`ReportTemplateInterface`
Report template	`ReportTemplate`
List of parameters	`ReportTemplateParameter`
Data item	`ReportDataItem`
Application administrator	`ApplicationAdministrator`
Trust customer organization	`TrustCustomerOrganization`
Trust customer user	`TrustCustomerMember`
Reported data	`Report`
Banking support user	`BankingSupportUser`

Next we rephrased the nouns to make them self-contained object names, as shown in table 6.1. By self-contained, I mean that object names shouldn't depend on context to provide meaning. For instance, *interface* from the first use case became `ReportTemplateInterface` and *list of parameters* became `ReportTemplateParameter`. The fact that our use case referred to a "list" of parameters was documented as a relationship. The more descriptive the object name, the better. All the objects were persistent except `ReportTemplateInterface`. (Note that the word *interface* in this use case refers to an application interface and may not imply use of a Java interface construct.)

Three types of users appear in the list: application administrator, trust customer member, and banking support user. When we got to attribution, we recognized that there was another object, User, with different subtypes. Inheritance relationships like this are easier to recognize when it comes time for attribution, so let's leave the object list as it is for now.

An alternative to merely identifying nouns is to do the data-modeling exercise first. All identified entities are good object candidates. Many of the objects we identified in this example would make good entity candidates as well. See chapter 7 for details.

Some of these objects were implemented as classes in multiple software layers in the application. This process is the focus of the next section. Defining and illustrating these layers was described in chapter 5.

TURNING OBJECTS INTO CLASSES

Once you have identified major objects in the application, you need to refine those objects into classes and organize them in a framework.

After identifying objects, you need to identify which layers they pertain to. It is common for objects to have multiple roles. Any object you have identified as playing multiple roles (e.g., manage data access, implement business rules, etc.) must get counterparts in multiple layers. For example, `ReportTemplate`, `ReportTemplateParameter`, and `ReportDataItem` from table 6.1 had persistence requirements as well as requirements as business objects. Therefore, they appeared as classes in at least the data access layer, the business object layer, and the entity layer.

Define separate classes for each object in each layer. If you define the same class for each of these roles, the classes get too large to effectively maintain and you lose all the benefits from software layering.

From the object identification example, consider `object ReportTemplate`. Class `ReportTemplateDAO,` residing in the data access layer, was responsible for reading and writing template information using a relational database. `ReportTemplateEntity` in the entity layer described all characteristics of a report template (e.g., its name, data type, display length, etc.). `ReportTemplateManager` in the business logic layer coordinated and enforced all rules for creating a new report template. And `ReportTemplateManager` coordinated report template information, template parameter information, and any other information necessary for running or editing a report.

DETERMINING RELATIONSHIPS

A *relationship* describes how different classes interact. You can determine relationships after you've identified individual classes. The UML literature documents several categories of object relationships. Most applications only need the four types described in the following paragraphs.

Dependency (uses) relationship documents that one class uses another class. At a code level, *using* another class means referencing the class in some way (e.g., declaring, instantiating, etc.). Because this relationship type is strikingly similar to the association relationship type, I usually ignore the difference between the two types as unnecessary complexity. The relationship in figure 6.1 is read as "`Customer uses Account.`"

Figure 6.1: Dependency Relationship Illustration

Generalizes (extends) relationship documents that one class extends, or inherits the characteristics of, another class. Most medium to large applications have a handful of this type of relationship.

An extends relationship is denoted by a solid line with a hollow arrow. The relationship emanating from `TrustCustomer` in figure 6.2 is read as "`TrustCustomer extends Customer.`" The attributes of Customer will be available and usable in all children.

Figure 6.2: Extends Relationship Illustration

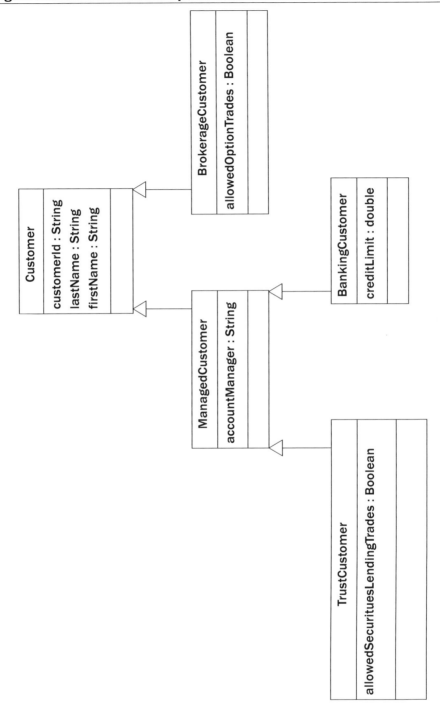

Realization (implements) relationship documents that a class implements an interface. An implements relationship is denoted by a dotted line with a hollow arrow. The relationship in figure 6.3 is read as "E-mailDeliveryType implements ReportDeliveryType."

Figure 6.3: Implements Relationship Illustration

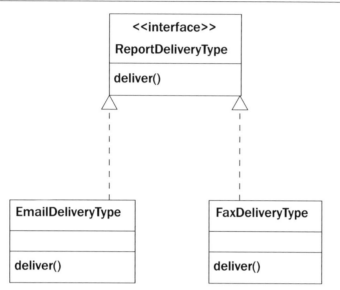

Aggregation (collects) relationship documents that a class collects multiple occurrences of a class. A collects relationship is denoted by a solid line with a diamond next to the class doing the collecting. The relationship in figure 6.4 reads "Customer collects Account."

Figure 6.4: Collects Relationship Illustration

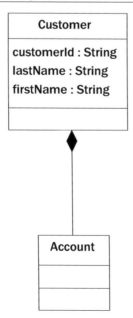

Don't document formal relationships to value objects or entity objects. VOs and entities have so many relationships that if they are documented, the model becomes unreadable and unusable. After all, the purpose of creating the class diagram is to make the application easier for the team to understand and implement. In any case, VO relationships are easy for developers to figure out from the method signatures.

IDENTIFYING ATTRIBUTES

Attributes are fields that a class contains. At a code level, attributes are instance-level variable declarations. Most attribution occurs with VOs, with other object types receiving little attribution.

Ideally, attributes should be base, not derived. A *base attribute* is atomic—that is, its value is not derived from the value of other elements or the result of a calculation. Conversely, a *derived attribute* is made up of the values of other elements. For example, consider a `CustomerVO` class that has `firstName`, `lastName`, and `fullName` attributes. The attribute `fullName` is derived because it is made up of the first and last names.

Avoid declaring derived attributes. Derived attributes, like fullName mentioned in the previous paragraph, only give you more to maintain. If a customer changes his or her last name, the values of two attributes need to change. Instead of making fullName an attribute, it would be better to create a convenience method, such as getFullName(), that does the concatenation.

IDENTIFYING METHODS

Methods are where the action is. Methods are invoked primarily when a user does something, when something that was scheduled occurs, and when something is received from an external interface. A common way to identify methods is to analyze each event and document the methods needed along the way. During the course of identifying the methods you'll need, you'll usually identify new classes.

Starting with user actions, I use screens from the prototype to drive method identification. Consider an application login as an example. Most applications customize the main screen based on a user's identity and preferences. For the moment, assume that authorization and authentication is provided by the enterprise architecture and not at an application level. Further assume that you need to invoke something that will get user specifics from the security package, invoke something to retrieve that user's options settings, and display the main application page.

If you use Struts, you'll need some kind of action class that can get user specifics from the security package, using the package to look up customer preferences (which will be used to generate the main page). If you haven't yet identified an action class to do this, add it to the model. Ignoring the security package itself, since it's out of scope, you then need a method somewhere that allows the user preference lookup.

Remember from our discussion of software layering in chapter 5 that classes in the presentation tier use business logic layer classes rather than using DAOs directly. Most applications identify a user object (or something similar) that manifests into a DAO class, an entity class, and a business object. It would be logical to add a `findById(String userId)` method to our user business logic layer class. It would also be logical for that method to return a `UserEntity,` which includes information about preferences, as a result of the call.

Pass and return VOs or entities instead of individual data items. Doing so decreases the number of arguments passed between method calls and makes for more readable code.

The physical lookup of the user preferences is usually delegated to at least one DAO. It would be logical to have a `UserDAO that has a findById()` method on it that would do the lookup.

By now, you're probably wondering why you don't just have the `Action` class invoke the DAO directly. It would appear to be simpler because it would cut out several layers of classes that, in this example, appear to be adding very little to the functionality of the product. Technically, you could have had the `Action` class invoke the DAO directly, but doing so would have greatly added to the complexity of the `Action` class, which isn't easy to debug, and would have eliminated the insulating benefits of software layering, as discussed in the last chapter.

Figure 6.5 illustrates an object model for the example just discussed.

Figure 6.5: Object Model Example

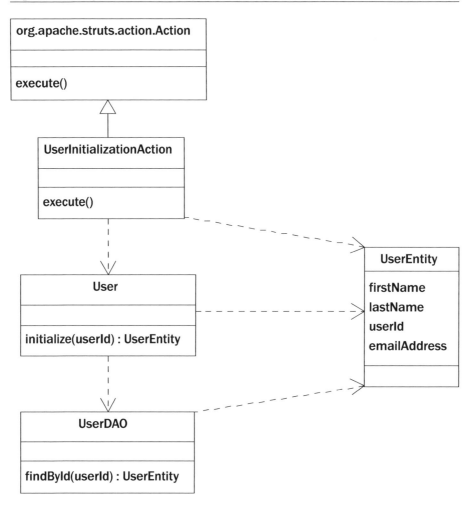

SHORTCUTS

Over the years, I've adopted several shortcuts that decrease the time and effort required in the object-modeling phase.

Assume that all documented attributes will have accessors (get methods) and mutators (set methods). This simplifies the model and eliminates a lot of boring busywork. It also makes the model easier to read and thus more useful. For example, if you document that a CustomerVO class has a lastName attribute, you should be able to assume the existence of getFirstName() and setFirstName() methods without explicitly documenting them in the model.

Omit relationships to objects in the JDK. Including these relationships adds very little value but a lot of complexity, making the model hard to read. For example, many attributes in the JDK are strings. Technically, any class containing a string attribute should have a relationship to the java.lang.String class.

In a typical application, documenting these types of relationships would add hundreds or thousands of relationships to your model and provide no benefit.

Forget about generating code from UML. My experience is that it's usually a net time loss. The minute level of detail you have to type in the model usually exceeds the time it would take to code it using any integrated development environment (IDE). On the other hand, generating UML from existing code can be extremely valuable and easy to do if your IDE supports it.

Don't attempt to micromanage the coding when determining methods. Leave some work to the developer. If the development team starts documenting private methods, it's going too far.

EXAMPLE: ADMIN4J

Admin4J (www.admin4j.net) is an open source product that provides basic Java EE application administration and support features for support developers. One of its features is to track and summarize exceptions generated by applications so that ongoing application issues can be easily identified and prioritized. In the interest of full disclosure, I'm a committer for the Admin4J project.

A detailed description of this feature taken from the Admin4J project website is as follows: Admin4J tracks all logged exceptions and combines and summarizes all "like" exceptions. Currently, exceptions logged with Log4J and JDK Logging are tracked. Additional loggers will be added as user demand dictates.

- Display Features
  - Exceptions are sorted from the most frequent occurring to the least.
  - Exceptions are persisted and survive a container recycle.
  - Administrators can delete exceptions that they deem dated and no longer occurring.
- The length of time covered by exception statistics is configurable (defaults to thirty days).

In addition to these explicit requirements, there are a couple of implicit requirements to keep in mind. This feature needs to be easily installable. An install process that is difficult to understand or has a large number of steps is not likely to be used; most developers are very busy people. Secondly, the performance impact of this feature needs to be minimal. Ideally applications will throw exceptions rarely, but that isn't always the case. Should this feature accidentally cause a material performance impact to end users, it would be promptly uninstalled.

Although this feature set is not really written as use cases, it conveys much of the information that would be in those use cases and can be used in a similar way. In examining this feature set within the context of a software layering framework as discussed in the last chapter, we can start associating these features with appropriate software layers.

I often start by identifying entity classes that are passed among the data access, business logic, and presentation layers of an application. As entity classes are stored and are typically nouns, the entity most easily identified with this feature set is `Exception`. As the entity name "Exception" is already taken by the JDK, and the information that needs to be stored is really information and statistics regarding that exception, the entity was named `ExceptionInfo`. If we look at the screen shot in figure 6.6, specific information retained about an exception is the following:

- Class name
- Message from last occurrence
- The total number of exceptions tracked
- First and last occurrence dates
- Associated stack trace

It foreshadows the next chapter, but performing a data modeling exercise is appropriate at this point. As explained in the next chapter, a data model will make identifying the entity classes very easy.

The stack trace associated with the exception needs additional thought in that it isn't a base attribute. It's actually a collection of execution points expressed as a class, method name, and line number combination. The order of the execution points within the collection indicates the call hierarchy. As it turns out, the JDK already has a representation for these execution points in a class called `java.lang.StackTraceElement`.

An object model for the entity layer portion can be found in figure 6.6. Note that I've *assumed* the existence of accessors and mutators and not directly modeled them. Also, I normally don't directly model classes in the JDK and relationships to them, but this particular relationship is important and is needed by developers to understand the design. Furthermore, `StackTraceElement` is really a value object and is not nearly as innocuous as the use of most other classes in the `java.lang` package.

Figure 6.6: Admin4J Exception Feature Entity Layer Diagram

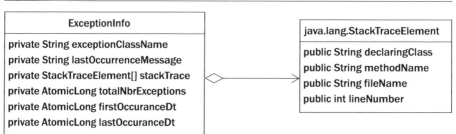

Having identified the relevant entity classes, we can start modeling the data access layer. The feature requirements for persistence don't specifically specify a storage mechanism. In fact, the only requirement is that the product remembers exception statistics between container recycles. While we might want to provide additional reporting features down the road, display requirements don't suggest any type of flexible search requirements regarding exception statistics. It appears that all we really need to do is a mass read and write of exception statistics.

Depending on how large the exception statistics information turns out to be, reading and writing en masse on a frequent basis *might* be material for some users. Given this, a decision was made to separate reading and writing activity from the activity trapping logging of exceptions. That is, we made the decision to conduct the reading and writing activity in a thread separate from the threads running user work. We didn't want to slow down user activity with the storage of exception statistics that would be used for later analysis.

In addition, we wanted to keep resource consumption by Admin4J to a minimum. Rewriting exception statistics after every update would ensure that up-to-date statistics are current, but the resource consumption would have been large in situations where large numbers of exceptions were being thrown. As a compromise, a decision was made to persist exception statistics on a configurable interval. That would allow users to effectively balance resource consumption with the need to persist current statistics. As a consequence of this decision, the data access layer only needs to read and write exception statistics en masse; there was no need for single read and write operations.

With a software package such as this, minimizing the dependency list is always a consideration. With that in mind, we decided to use XML as a storage mechanism for the first release and keep our options open for other storage mechanisms in the future. While this choice doesn't offer the same flexibility as a relational database of some sort, it reduces dependencies for third-party database software. It also reduces the install effort required. Given that the decision has been made to support multiple storage mechanisms, a full data access object pattern is appropriate.

Generally, a data access class is a factory for entity classes, and generally, there will be a one-to-one correspondence between entity classes and data access object interfaces. An object model for the data access layer for this feature can be found in figure 6.7.

Figure 6.7: Admin4J Exception Feature Data Access Layer Class Diagram

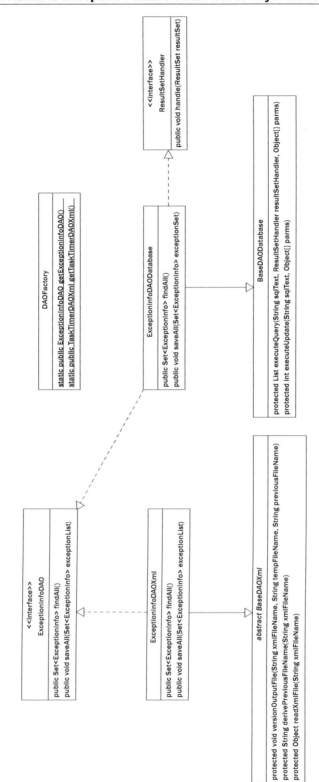

At this point from the model of the entity classes, we have a plan for organizing exception statistics and a list of what specific statistical attributes we're tracking. From the model of the data access layer, we understand how input/output for this section of the application is going to work. We have not modeled the section of Admin4J that actually examines exceptions that are logged, analyzes them to see which exceptions are identical to those that have been logged previously, and updates the relevant statistics. We've also made mention of the decision to store exception statistics at a configurable interval to keep resource utilization low. This activity occurs in the business logic layer. For a product such as this, the nature of the logic layer is more technical in nature than you find in most Java EE applications. A class diagram for the Admin4J business logic layer can be found in figure 6.8.

Let's start by identifying a preliminary list of classes that will be needed in the logic layer. Something needs to be responsible for analyzing generated exceptions, determining whether or not an exception like it has been previously observed, and updating the statistics associated with that exception. For the lack of a better term, let's call the class that does this an `ExceptionTracker`.

From the planned feature set, `ExceptionTracker` needs methods to initiate the "tracking" of an exception and retrieving exception statistics. Furthermore, to support the feature that "Administrators can delete exceptions that they deem dated and no longer occurring," a method to delete the reference to an existing exception is also needed. As exception statistics are persisted, it follows that the `ExceptionTracker` will rely on the data access layer.

At this level, we also needed to formulate a plan for observing logged exceptions. How this is accomplished is dictated more by the logging products than anything else. Regarding Log4J, the easiest way to observe logged exceptions is to implement a Log4J `Appender`. This is accomplished by extending a Log4J class called the `AppenderSkeleton`. Class `Log4JExceptionAppender` from figure 6.8 accomplishes this. It stands to reason that this class will rely on the `ExceptionTracker` to analyze the exception and update exception statistics.

Regarding the logging framework that's incorporated in the JDK, exceptions can be observed by extending a `Handler` class (`java.util.logging`). Class `JdkLoggingExceptionHandler` from figure 6.8 accomplishes this. It stands to reason that this class will rely on the `ExceptionTracker` to analyze the exception and update exception statistics.

We also need a plan to support work that will happen in a separate thread (e.g., the periodic storing of exception statistics at a configurable interval and purging aged exception statistics); we need a daemon thread for that type of work. In the class diagram, we've named this class `ExceptionTrackerCleanupTask`. This class leverages a generic daemon class used by other portions of Admin4J. That information is really out of scope for the portion we're modeling here and hasn't been included. What's important is that we've identified a class to perform this work and the fact that it operates in a daemon thread.

The decision to persist statistics on a configurable time interval makes it possible to lose track of exceptions generated between the time statistics were last persisted and shutdown of the JVM (e.g., application is shut down for maintenance or software updates). To minimize information loss, we've implemented a shutdown hook that will be executed with a graceful shutdown. This hook will persist statistics and terminate. We will still lose information if the JVM process is killed or suffers some other type of nongraceful shutdown.

Figure 6.8: Admin4J Exception Feature Business Logic Layer Class Diagram

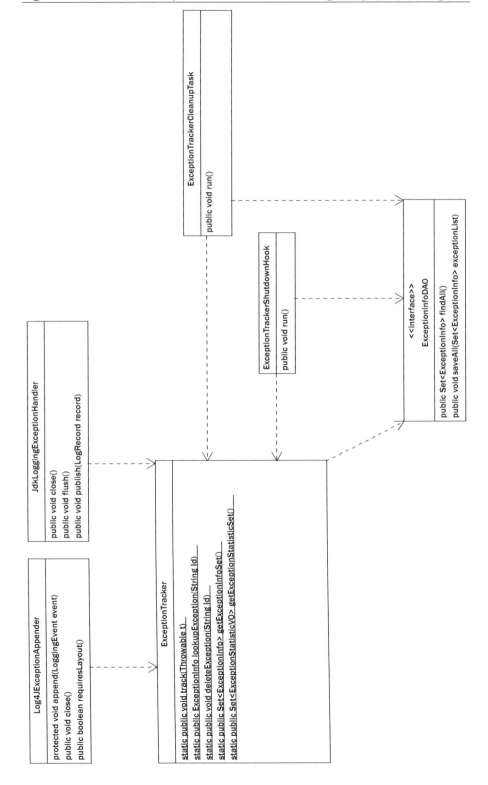

At this point, all that remains from a modeling perspective is the presentation layer. As Admin4J is a generic tool, we can't assume the existence of any presentation framework, such as Struts, Java Server Faces, Wicket, or anything else. Nor do we want to impose a large configuration effort on users. At the same time, writing and maintaining user display logic entirely within servlet code is tedious and time consuming.

To minimize our dependency and configuration footprint, yet provide some basic presentation capabilities, we adopted Freemarker (http://freemarker.sourceforge.net/) as a display mechanism. We configured our use of it so that all templates we use are sourced from the Admin4J jar. We didn't want users to have to copy templates or individual JSPs into their application web root.

This presentation method requires users to register a servlet in the applications web.xml file. As all of Admin4J's display pages follow a similar architecture, we became concerned that the servlet registration requirement would become oppressive. To solve that issue, we created a home page servlet that contains links for all Admin4J pages, including the exception statistics display page we're discussing in this example. Users need only register the home page servlet once, and all other pages are handled automatically. Of course, users can still install pages separately if they don't want to install all Admin4J features, but that's the user's decision.

The `ExceptionDisplayServlet` handles display for the exception statistics display page. The `ExceptionDisplayServlet` extends the `AdminDisplayServlet`, which provides basic plumbing code to generate output from Freemarker templates and writes that generated content to a user's browser. Both of these servlets rely on functionality contained in the `Admin4JServlet` class, which handles basic configuration tasks for all Admin4J functionality.

A class diagram for the presentation layer for this portion of Admin4J can be found in figure 6.9.

Figure 6.9: Admin4J Exception Feature Presentation Layer Class Diagram

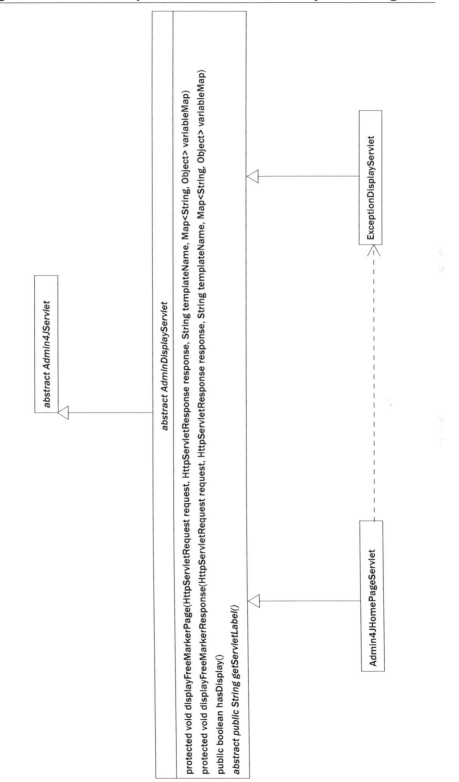

After the reader has reviewed this example, I expect several follow-up questions.

Do I need to model every portion of all applications in this much detail? In all probability, models such as these usually aren't updated over time. Consequently, they have the most value for the initial development effort. The amount of modeling performed should be just enough to support the initial development effort.

Furthermore, let's distinguish between "modeling" and the act of documenting that model in a modeling tool or graphics design package. For those with much modeling experience, the latter usually takes more time than the former. I mentally construct models for most of my projects regardless of whether or not I write those models down as a communication mechanism with other team members. It leads to cleaner code and more maintainable applications. Furthermore, it helps me work in an organized fashion.

The amount and quality of model documentation needed depends on project complexity, the size of the project, and how many developers on the project don't have experience working with you on previous projects. For a project with one or two developers, much less documentation is needed than for a project with a team of twenty developers. In fact, for a project with only one developer, a formally documented object model might not be needed.

Also, if you're working with developers unfamiliar with your methods, they will need more guidance than those who've worked with you before. With one team I've worked with for several projects, I can model the entity layer and the most complicated portions of the business logic layer, and not formally document other portions of the model.

The entity layer largely dictates the organization of the data access layer. Consequently, once the entity layer model documentation is produced, you might not have to document the data access layer completely. Once you communicate the data access pattern to be used, it can be applied to any entity. For example, the data access layer persisting performance statistics for Admin4J is very similar in concept to what was presented regarding exception statistics.

If you encounter a portion of your development project that is difficult for you to model, that's an indicator that the model for that portion of the application should be documented and discussed with the development team. If it's difficult for you, it will likely be difficult for others, and all developers for the project should be on the same page and understand the design being constructed. Furthermore, the perspectives and opinions of others might help you clarify issues and concerns.

What modeling tools do you use? I use what my clients use. For those without modeling tools, I recommend ArgoUML (http://argouml.tigris.org/). It's a very active open source project that I find moderately easy to use. In fact, object models for Admin4J in this example were produced using ArgoUML.

How can you validate that your object models are correct? Good question. We don't have compilers or other tools that will validate object models. One way to test is peer review by developers. Hold a review session with others familiar with the requirements and provide them with a review and explanation of your models. Often, others will have insight and may point out defects or issues before construction. Furthermore, defects in the model will become more apparent during construction.

Compare your model to the code actually developed. There will always be subtle adjustments made to the design (e.g., attributes added, methods added). But if fundamental classes and relationships between software classes as constructed differ substantially from your model, it could indicate defects in the model. For this reason, I usually participate in the construction phase so that I can learn from my mistakes.

FURTHER READING

Gamma, Erich, Richard Helm, Ralph Johnson, and John Vlissides. 1995. *Design Patterns.* Reading, MA: Addison-Wesley.

CHAPTER 7

CREATING
THE DATA MODEL

Most books about Java EE skip the data-modeling and relational database design phases of development. But I have found that both steps are critical to the success of a Java EE application. As part of the development team, an application architect should have a basic knowledge of data modeling. Further, in some companies, the architect is responsible for designing the application database. Just as object-modeling exercises help produce good code, data-modeling exercises help produce good database designs. (I have to admit, however, that the many years I spent as a database designer and administrator may have prejudiced my views as to the importance of data modeling.)

Even if your organization delegates relational database design and data modeling tasks to a separate team, application architects should understand data modeling concepts. In an organization with separate data modeling teams, the application architect usually communicates requirements and coordinates with that team to get the database designed and implemented. Understanding data modeling concepts will allow the architect to streamline this process.

I also rely on these concepts when modeling the entity layer, as most object mapping technologies rely on a one-to-one correspondence between entity classes and database tables. For example, a banking application with a database table called `Account` might be mapped to a Java class in the entity layer call `AccountEntity`. In fact, creating a database model for an application can make modeling of the entity layer in the application much easier. It is not unusual for data modeling and object modeling activities to occur concurrently.

As the data model (and resulting database design) greatly impacts the design of the entity layer of your application, a poor database design will create coding problems and difficulties. I've seen poor database designs inflate the amount and complexity of application code produced. With that increased complexity often comes an increased frequency of bug reports and a larger resource requirement to diagnose and fix those bugs. Ensuring that developers are working with a high quality data model (and resulting database design) should be a high priority for application architects.

In addition, I find data-modeling concepts very useful in designing XML document formats, such as DTDs and schemas. Applying data-modeling concepts to XML document design is a bit unconventional. The thought process behind deciding if a data item is an element or an attribute is very similar to deciding between entities and attributes in data modeling. In addition, one-to-many relationships in data modeling translate directly to the child element concept in XML documents. I'll provide some details and examples in this section to show how you can implement data models as XML document formats.

Although the popularity of NoSQL databases has grown in recent years, I don't see any signs that relational database technologies will be replaced any time soon. NoSQL databases are targeted at extremely large data stores that don't have the same transaction guarantees that relational databases do. In other words, NoSQL databases are used in cases where approximate answers are acceptable. Furthermore, as NoSQL products vary widely and have drastically different strengths and weaknesses, any advice on how to design NoSQL databases tends to be product specific. The best attempt I've seen to document generalized data modeling techniques for NoSQL databases has been this article: http://highlyscalable.wordpress.com/2012/03/01/nosql-data-modeling-techniques/. For now, because relational databases are part of most Java EE applications, most application architects need to have at least a basic understanding of relational data-modeling concepts. The rest of this chapter will focus on relational databases.

If you're more comfortable with data modeling than with object modeling, feel free to take the easier path by doing data-modeling activities before object modeling. All the *entities* (defined in the next section) in the data model are potential identifications of classes in the entity layer. Although the two modeling disciplines use different terms, they are quite similar conceptually.

KEY TERMS AND CONCEPTS

An *entity* is something you want to keep information about and thus represents information that persists (i.e., is written to media). Usually, an entity is a noun. Although most entities are implemented as database tables, the terms *entity* and *table* are not synonymous. An entity is purely a conceptual construct, with its closest counterpart in object modeling being a class. Good examples of entities are customer, account, user, customer order, and product.

In a relational database, an entity is implemented as a table. When you implement your data model as an XML DTD or schema, each entity becomes an element.

An *entity occurrence* (sometimes shortened to occurrence) is an instance of an entity. If you're more comfortable with object modeling, you can think of an entity occurrence as similar to instantiating a class. If you can't resist the urge to equate entities and tables, consider an entity occurrence as a row in a table. And for XML users, an entity occurrence is like an individual element in an XML document.

An *attribute* is a characteristic of an entity. Although attributes can be nouns, they usually don't make sense outside the context of an entity. For example, attributes of a CUSTOMER entity could be CUSTOMER_ID, FIRST_NAME, LAST_NAME, STREET_ADDRESS, CITY, STATE, and ZIP_CODE. Attributes should be atomic—that is, they should be self-contained and not derived from the values of other attributes.

A *primary key* is the one attribute, or combination of attributes, of an entity that uniquely identifies an entity occurrence. For example, CUSTOMER_ID would be a good primary key for the CUSTOMER entity, and ACCOUNT_NUMBER and ORDER_NUMBER taken together would be a good primary key for an entity called CUSTOMER_ORDER.

Every entry must have a primary key. If, by chance, no combination of attributes uniquely identifies an entity occurrence, make up an attribute to serve as a key. For example, most manufacturers assign unique identifiers (UPC codes) to their products; but when they don't, you might have to make up product identifiers to serve as the primary key.

A *relationship* is an association between two entities. Out of the many types of relationships that exist, three are commonly used: one-to-many, many-to-many, and super-type/sub-type. In a *one-to-many* relationship, one occurrence of an entity is associated with possibly multiple occurrences of another entity. For example, a single customer could have multiple accounts or place multiple orders. Often, the entity with a single occurrence is called the *parent*, and the entity with multiple occurrences is called the *child*. Figure 7.1 illustrates a one-to-many relationship.

Figure 7.1: One-to-Many Relationship ER Diagram

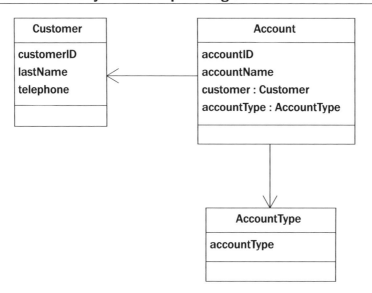

Notice in the figure that the ACCOUNT entity contains the primary key (PK) columns of the ACCOUNT_TYPE and CUSTOMER entities. Each additional column in ACCOUNT is a foreign key (FK). Foreign keys are the primary keys of related entities that an entity uses for lookup purposes. The existence of a foreign key is an implicit result of creating a one-to-many relationship. For example, given an occurrence of ACCOUNT, related CUSTOMER and ACCOUNT_TYPE information is easy to determine.

Some data-modeling tools provide for many-to-many relationships between entities. In a *many-to-many* relationship, each entity has a one-to-many relationship with the other. For example, customer orders can contain many products, and each product can be purchased by multiple customers. It is common to rewrite a many-to-many relationship as two separate one-to-many relationships with a new entity defined as a cross-reference. Figure 7.2 is an example of a many-to-many relationship.

Figure 7.2: Many-to-Many Relationship

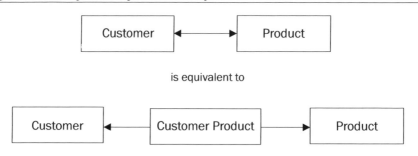

In a *super-type/sub-type* relationship, an entity refines the definition of another entity much the same way as inheritance does in the Java world. For example, in banking, a customer entity might be too generic for a bank that has trust customers, private banking customers, corporate customers, broker-age customers, and so on. In a Java world, this very well might be modeled as an *inheritance* relationship where banking customers are represented by a class that extends `Customer` (as in figure 7.3a).

Figure 7.3a: Inheritance Relationship

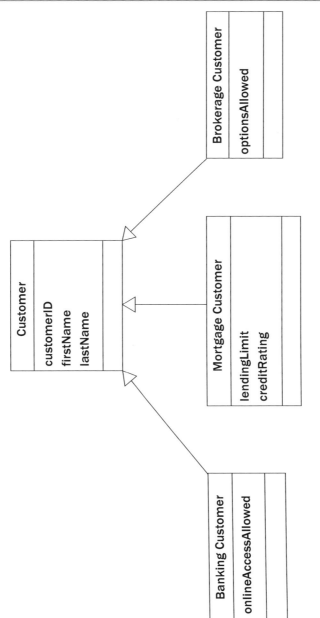

Using data modeling terminology, we would identify a `Customer` entity that is the super-type. We would also identify the `Banking Customer`, `Mortgage Customer`, and `Brokerage Customer` as sub-types. The `Customer` entity contains all attributes common to all three sub-types. Each occurrence of `Customer` has a corresponding occurrence in one and only one of the sub-type entities. The terminology differs, but the concept is very similar to an inheritance relationship on the Java side.

Super-type/sub-type relationships can be physically implemented in two ways. They can be expressed as separate entities or combined into one entity. Figure 7.3b illustrates a relationship of this type. Notice that the relationships in this example are all one-to-one and are all optional. Notice that attributes common to all are assigned to the `Customer` entity while the sub-type entities contain attributes specific to their respective type.

Figure 7.3b: Inheritance Expressed as Separate Entities

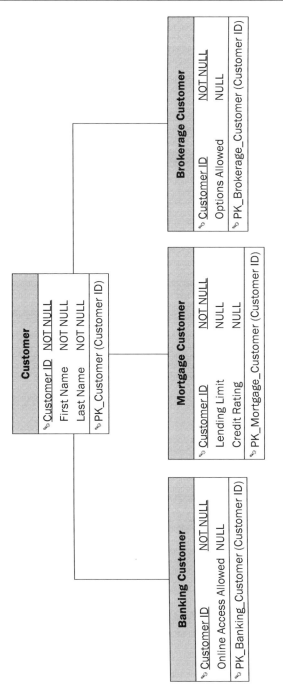

The second option for implementing super-type/sub-type relationships is to combine all entities into one. With this method, the `Customer` entity contains all attributes from all four entities, along with a "type" field (e.g., `Customer` type) that indicates what type of entity represents that particular row.

For example, if the `Customer` type is `Banking,` that occurrence is a banking customer and only attributes pertaining to banking customers (`ONLINE_AC-CESS_ALLOWED, CUSTOMER_ID, FIRST_NAME,` and `LAST_NAME`) have values. An illustration of this type of implementation can be found in figure 7.3c.

Figure 7.3c: Inheritance Expressed as Combined Entity

Customer	
Customer ID	NOT NULL
Customer Type	NOT NULL
First Name	NULL
Last Name	NULL
Online Access Allowed	NULL
Lending Limit	NULL
Credit Rating	NULL
Options Allowed	NULL

Many developers prefer to combine super-types and sub-types in this manner as it reduces the number of entities and relationships. However, using this pattern, which attributes apply to which sub-types is not documented in the model and may cause confusion in the implementation.

It is possible to have entities related to themselves. This is called a *recursive* relationship. For example, consider an `EMPLOYEE` entity with `EMPLOYEE_ID` as the primary key. A recursive one-to-many relationship could be used to indicate the manager of each employee. As a result of the relationship, a foreign key, say `MANAGER_ID`, would be used to cross-reference employees with their managers.

DESIGN PRACTICES AND NORMAL FORM

Normal form is a set of rules that guide you in identifying entities and relationships. In fact, there are many different degrees of normal form; but in practice, third normal form is the one most frequently used. For that reason, I limit the discussion here to third normal form. If you are interested in other normal forms, I recommend Date (2003).

To qualify for third normal form, entities must satisfy three conditions:

- All repeating attribute groups should be removed and placed in a separate entity.
- All non-key attributes should be dependent only on the primary key.
- All non-key attributes should be dependent on every attribute in the primary key.

Suppose the `CUSTOMER` entity has the attributes `ADDRESS_LINE_1`, `ADDRESS_LINE_2`, `ADDRESS_LINE_3`, and `ADDRESS_LINE_4`. Technically, such an entity isn't third normal form because it's a repeating group and violates condition 1. Figure 7.4a illustrates the example of this bad practice, and figure 7.4b illustrates a possible correction.

Figure 7.4a: Violation of the First Condition of Third Normal Form

Customer	
Customer ID	NULL
Customer Name	NULL
Address Line 1	NULL
Address Line 2	NOT NULL
Address Line 3	NOT NULL
Address Line 4	NOT NULL

Figure 7.4b: Violation Corrected

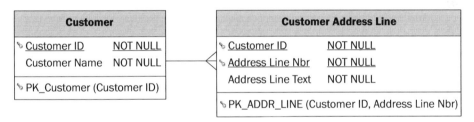

Suppose the ACCOUNT entity contains the attribute ACCOUNT_BALANCE. This isn't third normal form because it violates condition 2. ACCOUNT_BALANCE is fully dependent on outstanding orders, the line items on them, and the payments that have been made—items in other entities. Another problem with ACCOUNT_BALANCE is that it isn't atomic. ACCOUNT_BALANCE is computed based on previous orders and customer payments. Since ACCOUNT_BALANCE is completely derived, it shouldn't be physically stored and in the data model.

Suppose the CUSTOMER_ORDER entity (which has a primary key that combines ACCOUNT_NUMBER and ORDER_NUMBER), has the attributes ACCOUNT_NAME and ADDRESS_INFORMATION. This technically isn't third normal form because these attributes relate to the account but not the specific order, which violates condition 3. Figure 7.5a illustrates the order violating third normal form, and figure 7.5b illustrates a corrected version.

Figure 7.5a: Violation of the Third Condition of Third Normal Form

Customer Order	
Account Nbr	NOT NULL
Order Nbr	NOT NULL
Account Shipping Name	NOT NULL
Account Shipping Address	NOT NULL
Account Shipping City	NOT NULL
Account Shipping State	NOT NULL
Account Shipping Zip Code	NOT NULL
Shipping Charge	NOT NULL
Primary Key (Account Nbr, Order Nbr)	

Figure 7.5b: Violation Corrected

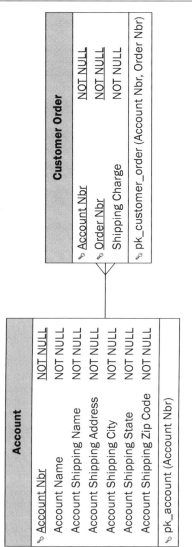

In the early days of relational databases, third normal form was considered inefficient, and "denormalization" in the name of performance was commonplace. Despite decades of technological advancement, there are a surprisingly high percentage of developers who still subscribe to this idea. The usual reason given is that joins (which occur more often in a normalized database) are inefficient.

The main side-effect of denormalization is the additional code and processing needed to keep all copied and derived data synchronized on update. In the example above, if you include account information on the customer order to "denormalize" and eliminate the need for queries to join between the two tables, then you've effectively copied the account information once per order. When that account information changes, it must be changed on the orders as well.

These days, joins are efficient, and denormalizations should be a rare event. If you want to make queries easier for support developers who write ad hoc queries to investigate defect reports, then create a series of views for that purpose.

CREATING DATABASE SCHEMA DEFINITIONS

Typically, database administrators use the data model to create relational database schemas for the rest of the team to use. And most database administrators use modeling tools to do the dirty work. Unfortunately, few open source tools for creating schemas are available. Although the process is a bit more involved than what I illustrate in this section; with the help of a qualified database administrator, you can create schemas using the following central algorithm:

1 Directly translate each entity into a table. All attributes of an entity become columns in the table. Explicitly define the primary key in each table.

2 Assign a foreign key in the child entity of each one-to-many relationship. Remember, a foreign key is the primary key of another entity that exists so that you can match data in one entity to another. For example, CUSTOMER_ID will appear as a foreign key in the ACCOUNT table so that you have a way to associate an account with a specific customer using an SQL join. It's a good idea to index all foreign keys to facilitate query joins.

3 Rewrite each many-to-many relationship by adding an associative table and two one-to-many relationships. An associative table has a primary key that is made up of two foreign keys. For example, look back at figure 7.2 to see the many-to-many relationship between CUSTOMER and PRODUCT. This will get implemented by creating a new table (called CUSTOMER_LINE_ITEM, for example) that relates customers to products.

COMMON DATABASE DESIGN MISTAKES

Denormalizing the database out of habit. Denormalizing a database means replicating information to avoid lookups and enhance performance. Consequently, denormalization can introduce maintenance problems if the copies get out of synch.

In the early days of relational databases, denormalization for performance was a must. However, the technology has advanced to the point where forced denormalizations are rare. Today, denormalizations are done more out of (bad) habit than for performance reasons.

Dropping database integrity constraints for programmatic convenience. Some developers like to shut off the foreign key relationships between tables. Not using database integrity constraints initially saves the programmer time because it permits invalid inserts, updates, and deletes. But I've found you lose much more time than you save because you end up having to fight bugs created by flawed inserts, updates, and deletes. The sooner you catch a bug, the cheaper and easier it is to fix.

Attempting to use relational data modeling concepts to design NoSQL databases. The data modeling concepts described in this chapter apply to relational databases only. Most NoSQL database products aren't designed to support the wide variety of queries and relationships within the data that relational databases are designed to handle.

IMPROVING YOUR DATA MODELING SKILLS

Get a mentor. Choose someone whose data modeling skills you respect to review your models for current assignments. Often, someone outside the project can provide a more objective viewpoint. This can be done privately unless your manager requests otherwise.

Audit relational databases for applications you support. What mistakes do you see? Are there any violations of third normal form? Is there any denormalization or data duplication present? Is there anything here that you would have modeled differently if you were given the chance? Take note of these items. You may not get the opportunity to fix the mistakes that you find, but you might be able to avoid making the same mistakes on future assignments.

CREATING XML DOCUMENT FORMATS

In addition to their use in database design, data-modeling techniques can easily be applied to designing XML documents. The same data models that database administrators use to create physical database designs also readily translate into XML document formats, such as DTDs or schemas. XML is most often used as a means of communication between applications.

The first step in creating any XML document is to identify the document root. XML documents usually contain lists of things identified in the data model. For instance, a `<customer-update>` document might contain a list of customer-related elements that contain information that has changed. A `<purchase-order>` document might contain a list of order-related elements describing one or more purchase order contents.

Entities in a data model translate to elements in an XML document. Only implement the elements that are needed for the documents you're creating. Chances are that you don't need all entities translated into elements. Entities that represent small lookup value domains (e.g., CUSTOMER_TYPE, AC-COUNT_TYPE, etc.) are usually implemented as attributes rather than elements in an XML document.

Attributes of an entity become attributes of the corresponding element. For example, the `<customer>` element from figure 7.1 would have the attributes `customer-id`, `last-name`, `first-name`, and `telephone`.

A one-to-many relationship implies that one element is the child of another in an XML document. Unlike relational databases, a foreign key to the parent element isn't needed because it's indicated by segment ancestry. Ancestry is indicated naturally within the XML syntax. For example, the `<customer>` element from figure 7.1 would have an optional `<account>` child element.

As a more complete illustration, listing 7.1 is a sample XML document for the data model in figure 7.1.

Listing 7.1: XML Document Example

```
<?xml version="1.0" encoding="UTF-8"?>
<customer-update>
   <customer customer-id="C123"
     first-name="Derek"
     last-name="Ashmore"
     telephone="999-990-9999">
     <account account-id="A1"
       account-name="Personal Checking"
       account-type="checking" />
   </customer>
</customer-update>
```

As we normally describe XML formats in terms of schemas these days, listing 7.2 contains an XML schema for the document we've been discussing.

Listing 7.2: XML Schema Example

```
<?xml version="1.0" encoding="UTF-8"?>
<schema xmlns="http://www.w3.org/2001/XMLSchema"
    xmlns:tns="http://www.example.org/foo/"
    targetNamespace="http://www.example.org/foo/">

  <complexType name="CustomerType">
    <sequence>
      <element name="account" type="tns:AccountType"></
        element>
    </sequence>
    <attribute name="customer-id" type="string"></attribute>
    <attribute name="first-name" type="string"></attribute>
    <attribute name="last-name" type="string"></attribute>
    <attribute name="telephone" type="string"></attribute>
  </complexType>

  <complexType name="AccountType">
    <attribute name="account-id" type="string"></attribute>
    <attribute name="account-name" type="string"></attribute>
    <attribute name="account-type" type="string"></attribute>
  </complexType>


  <complexType name="CustomerListType">
    <sequence>
      <element name="customer" type="tns:CustomerType"></
        element>
    </sequence>
  </complexType>

  <element name="customer-update"
        type="tns:CustomerListType"></element>
</schema>
```

Rewrite all many-to-many relationships by choosing one of the entities of each relationship to be a child element. For example, consider a many-to-many relationship between customer orders and products. This relationship would be rewritten as two one-to-many relationships using the entity OR-DER_LINE_ITEM as a cross-reference. An <order-line-item> element could be a child of the <order> or <product> element, or both. Chances are that both do not need to be implemented and that <order-line-item> would be considered a child of <order>.

COMMON XML DESIGN MISTAKES

Declaring attributes as elements. One of the most common XML design mistakes I see is making data elements that should be attributes. For example, in listing 7.1, some developers would have made "account-name" a separate element instead of an attribute of <account>. Misusing elements in this way is likely to cause lower parsing performance and slower XSLT transformations.

FURTHER READING

Date, C. J. 2003. *An Introduction to Database Systems*, 8th ed. Boston: Pearson/Addison-Wesley.

Fleming, Candace C., and Barbara von Halle. 1989. *Handbook of Relational Database Design*. Reading, MA: Addison-Wesley.

CHAPTER 8

PLANNING CONSTRUCTION

Okay, you've read the chapter title and you're thinking, "What's a chapter on project planning doing in an application architect's handbook?" But remember: part of the application architect's role is to give the project manager information on construction tasks, the order in which they should be completed, and what dependencies exist. And these days, application architects are often called on to assist or even fulfill the project management role.

This chapter is included for those in organizations using non-agile methodologies for which project planning is more relevant. Most agile methodologies rely on teams to be self-managing; hence, project planning at the level described in this chapter doesn't usually take place.

This chapter develops, and adds detail to, the high-level requirements described in chapter 3. After completing use-case analysis and object and data modeling, you should have enough information for a more detailed plan. My project plans typically include the following types of activities:

- Business requirements gathering
- Technical design
- Database design
- Environment setup
- Project setup
- Data migration/conversion activities
- Coding and unit testing
- System testing

- Performance/load testing
- User acceptance testing
- Deployment activities

Many of these categories can be divided into lower-level tasks. For example, you could break down "business requirements gathering" into prototyping and use-case analysis activities. Typically, I divide "coding and unit-testing" activities into smaller sections that can be assigned to individual developers.

Some of these categories are applicable only to the development of new applications, as opposed to enhancements of existing applications. For example, new applications likely need tasks for "environment setup" and "project setup," whereas in most cases, existing applications already have these and they are not needed for projects enhancing existing applications.

Figure 8.1 shows a template project plan I use for Java EE web applications. Tasks are listed roughly in completion order. I use the open source product OpenProj (http://sourceforge.net/projects/openproj/).

Figure 8.1: Java EE Web Application Project Plan Template

Task Name	Work
J2EE Application Development	
Business Requirements	
Prototypes	
Prototype 1	8 hours
Prototype 2	8 hours
Prototype 3	8 hours
Prototype Presentation 1	8 hours
Prototype Presentation 2	8 hours
Use Cases	
Use Case 1	8 hours
Use Case 2	8 hours
Technical Design	
Database Design/Data Modeling	16 hours
Third-party Product Research	16 hours
Object Modeling	16 hours
Process Flows	16 hours
Environment Setup	
Project Setup	
Source Control Repository Setup	4 hours
Development Build Script	4 hours

Continuous Integration Setup	4 hours
Deployment Setup	
Development Database	8 hours
System Test	8 hours
User Acceptance Test	8 hours
Production	8 hours
Coding and Unit Testing Tasks	
Entity Classes	8 hours
Data Access Object Classes	
DAO 1	16 hours
DAO 2	16 hours
Business Logic Layer Classes	
Logic 1	16 hours
Logic 2	16 hours
Presentation GUI	
Section 1	16 hours
Section 2	16 hours
Batch Jobs and Web Services	
Job 1	8 hours
Job 2	8 hours
System Testing Activities	8 hours
User Acceptance Test Support	8 hours

It's possible that some of the tasks presented in my template don't apply to some projects. For instance, if the project is an enhancement to an existing application, the project and environment setup tasks may not be needed, as they already exist.

TASK ORDER AND DEPENDENCIES

The most common planning question I get from project managers is how to effectively order construction and unit testing. I usually advise the following order:

- DAO (with testing classes) and entity classes
- Business objects (with testing classes)
- Presentation layer
- Batch jobs, web services, and application interfaces

Architectural components of a project need to be constructed before they are needed. There is no way to make more detailed recommendations for architectural components because they can be used in all layers of the project.

You will find that most business objects rely heavily on DAOs and entities. As such, you cannot complete most business objects until the classes they use are complete. If you're using project management software, you should ensure that these dependencies are properly reflected in the plan.

The presentation layer actions and JSPs would logically be completed after the deployment layer is coded. If the presentation layer coding and construction must start first for political reasons, then stub the business logic classes; these "stubs" are throwaway work.

The tasks at this point in the project should become granular enough that most developers will feel comfortable providing estimates. As a result, the project plan can be more accurate now than in the preliminary stages described in chapter 3.

If you're using a project management tool, and the work schedule it computes doesn't make sense, the most likely cause is that some dependencies are incorrect or missing. Many people circumvent the management tool and manually compute and enter start and end dates for all the tasks. I prefer to fix the dependencies rather than produce an unrealistic plan.

Another consideration is project risk. If there are portions of the application that present more risk, those tasks should be completed as soon as possible. For example, if you're using an unfamiliar technology, it's possible that you will encounter unexpected difficulties. Completing these tasks upfront gives you more time to react should problems arise, with less impact on the total project.

Critical Path

The *critical path* is a set of dependent tasks that must complete on time for the *project* to complete on time. In effect, the critical path determines the length of the project. A delay of one day to a task in the critical path will delay the project by one day. Conversely, one day saved in the critical path may allow the project to come in one day early. Let's use an example everybody can relate to: I'm doing laundry on the side as I write this. My laundry project isn't software-related, but all of the concepts are exactly the same. It takes me about ninety minutes to do one load of laundry: thirty minutes to wash, fifty minutes to dry, and ten minutes to fold. If I only need to do one load, all three tasks are on the critical path. Every minute I delay transferring clothes from the washer to the dryer is a minute I add to the entire project.

Sometimes, not all tasks in the project are on the critical path. Noncritical-path tasks can usually be delayed or rescheduled without impact to the project completion time. Suppose I need to do two loads of laundry (and I have one washer and one dryer) and wish to complete the project in 120 minutes. The first wash is on the critical path, but the second wash isn't. I could start the second wash immediately after transferring the first load from the washer to the dryer, but I don't have to. I can safely wait twenty minutes to start the second wash without affecting the project end time, as the dryer takes twenty minutes longer than the washer. In this example, the first wash load, both dry loads, and the folding of the second load are on the critical path.

If you're an application architect doubling as a project manager, pay more attention to the critical path than to anything else. Most project management software packages highlight the critical path if you have entered all the resource assignments and dependencies completely.

The corollary is that time saved on noncritical path tasks will *not* allow the project to finish earlier. The reason is that those tasks aren't currently determining the project timeline; critical path tasks are. Furthermore, a critical path can shift; that is, tasks on the critical path can change if your project plan changes. If you save enough time on a critical path task, it's possible that it isn't on the critical path anymore—something else is. If a long delay occurs for a task that is not on the critical path but is still essential, the task might become part of the critical path.

For example, financial analysis software I helped develop included a component responsible for generating analysis, using company financial information and financial models that users input. In the beginning, this component was not part of the critical path. But as the project proceeded, the critical path changed to incorporate the component because the developer leading the effort to write it didn't have enough knowledge and experience for the task.

The best books I've encountered on the importance of the critical path (and planning in general) are by Goldratt (1992, 1997). Although both books use factory assembly lines as examples, the concepts are applicable to Java EE projects (and with their novel-like format, the books are entertaining reads).

COMMON MISTAKES

Going straight to code. Many developers are impatient with design. They view object-modeling and data-modeling activities as boring compared with coding. I've seen many projects proceed to coding without doing enough modeling to first figure out what the target is. Although most of those projects eventually were finished, they typically used more resources than was necessary. Sometimes, targetless efforts can use two to four times the required resources.

A good analogy is residential construction. When contractors build houses, they create the blueprints first to avoid costly mistakes and rework. Object models and data models are effectively blueprints for Java EE applications.

Permitting a moving target. Once scope is decided for the project (e.g., it has been decided which use cases will be implemented, and the content of those use cases has enough detail from which to design), discourage or even outlaw scope increases. I know this is easier said than done. McConnell (1998) suggests installing a change control board, which is charged with reviewing and authorizing all change requests once a project has progressed passed analysis and high-level design. The existence of a change control board effectively discourages scope increases by creating bureaucratic red tape.

If you can't avoid adding something to a project late in the game, make sure the additional activities, time, and costs get added to the project plan. Also, make sure that the revised project plan reflects the fact that the time spent on analysis and design for the new features zapped time from what you were supposed to be doing (making it late too). If the new feature causes rework on tasks already completed, make sure that those costs are also documented for all to see.

Think of the residential construction analogy again. Changes in what the homebuyer wants cause rework and impact the delivery date.

Not correcting personnel assignment mistakes. Of course, it's best to avoid making mistakes in the first place. But when mistakes happen, your best course of action is to recognize and fix them rather than ignore them. The most damaging mistakes in large projects are in the areas of personnel task assignment. This type of mistake is so damaging because most managers are unable to gather the courage to correct the mistakes and therefore allow them to continue.

Although the project manager traditionally handles personnel assignments, the architect (with more knowledge of technical skill sets) should at least be in an advisory role. DeMarco and Lister (1999) make some interesting observations:

- Count on the best people outperforming the worst by about 10:1.
- Count on the best performer being about 2.5 times better than the median.

In addition, people generally are extremely good at some tasks but poor at others. Good project managers learn to recognize the differences and adjust assignments appropriately. For example, someone might be a whiz when it comes to coding the presentation tier but a complete dud at coding architectural components. Some people can perform testing with ease but are poor at coding.

Saving integration testing activities until the end of the project. Analysis and design mistakes and omissions often aren't visible until construction begins. Integration testing the application makes analysis and design mistakes visible, even if the application is only partially functional. Finding these mistakes earlier in the project gives you a chance to correct the error with fewer effects to the project timeline.

IMPROVING YOUR PROJECT PLANS AND ESTIMATES

Track your time. It is important to track your time in such a way that you can easily map that time to specific tasks you've been given. If you lead other developers, have them track their time as well. It is also important that you estimate the time it will take you to complete a task before you complete it and measure the time you spend doing it. The time you estimate will rarely equal the time that you spent. With this process, you'll be able to begin understanding how close your estimates are to reality. Over time, you will notice the difference between your estimates and the time that you spend get smaller.

Don't discard estimates and time tracking records from past assignments and projects. When you need estimates for future projects or assignments, it's helpful to look at comparable assignments or projects that you have done in the past. This is similar to how real estate agents decide if the price of a property is too high or low; they look for recently sold properties similar to it and check their selling prices.

Have a colleague review your estimates. Someone not involved with the project may easily see things that you have missed.

FURTHER READING

DeMarco, Tom, and Timothy Lister. 1999. *Peopleware: Productive Projects and Teams*, 2nd ed. New York: Dorset House.

Goldratt, Eliyahu. 1992. *The Goal: A Process of Ongoing Improvement*. Great Barrington, MA: North River Press.

———. 1997. *Critical Chain*. Great Barrington, MA: North River Press.

McConnell, Steve. 1998. *Software Project Survival Guide*. Redmond, WA: Microsoft Press.

SECTION III

BUILDING JAVA EE APPLICATIONS

Once the design is complete, the application architect is often asked to guide application construction. Activities that are the direct responsibility of the application architect during construction include setting coding standards; mentoring junior developers through more difficult programming tasks; and establishing conventions for logging, exception handling, and application configuration. In addition, the architect (or senior developer) is usually responsible for coding any custom architectural components the application requires because of the difficulty involved in the task.

This section guides you through the application construction process. In it, you will learn how to:

- Establish coding conventions for all software layers.

- Choose a database persistence method (e.g., JDBC, JPA, etc.).

- Set conventions and guidelines for transaction management.

- Understand how to make architectural components easy for developers to use.

- Set guidelines for logging, exception handling, threading, and configuration management.

The first edition of this book relied on an open source

123

product called CementJ (http://sourceforge.net/projects/cementj/), which was provided as a shortcut for implementing the layering concepts presented in this book. CementJ also provided numerous time-saving static utilities that turned common coding tasks into one-liners. CementJ is now obsolete.

Since that time, numerous open source projects have matured to provide this functionality in a more robust way. Consequently, CementJ has been replaced by several common open source projects from the Apache Commons (http://commons.apache.org/) family of projects including:

- Apache Commons Lang (http://commons.apache.org/lang/)
- Apache Commons Collections (http://commons.apache.org/collections/)
- Apache Commons BeanUtils (http://commons.apache.org/beanutils/)
- Apache Commons DbUtils (http://commons.apache.org/dbutils/)
- Apache Commons IO (http://commons.apache.org/io)
- Google Guava Core Libraries (https://code.google.com/p/guava-libraries/)

CHAPTER 9

CODING VALUE OBJECTS AND ENTITIES

Just as value objects (VO) and entities are similar in that they combine logical groups of data items into a single logical construct; the coding standards and guidance for them are similar in many ways. The largest difference between them is that entity classes have a map to a database table and are persisted, while VO classes are transient in nature. In the early days of Java EE, value objects were used to minimize network transmission between enterprise beans and their remote callers. As the use of enterprise beans has declined—since in many applications it is an unnecessary complexity—this purpose for value object classes has been reduced.

At first glance, my broader definition of a value object or entity class appears to contradict the principles of object-oriented design that tell us to combine data with the business logic. Object orientation principles would have us think of "employee" as an object that contains its data (e.g., last name, first name) and methods like `add()`, `terminate()`, and `oppress()` that represent business logic. For many practical considerations, such as reducing complexity, we need to have the option for referencing data outside the business logic context.

Chapter 11 will show you ways of constructing objects in the business logic layer that adhere to object-oriented design principles and also allow you to reference the data portion of these objects as a value object. For example, the `Employee` class could easily provide a `getEmployeeVO()` accessor that provides the data for an employee without its business logic.

Figure 9.1: Using Value Objects and Entities within a Layered Architecture

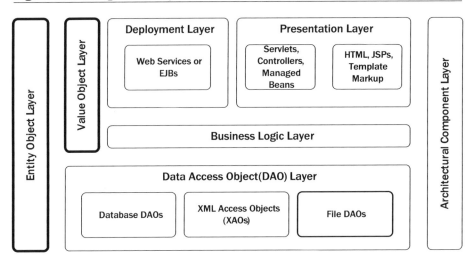

Because the application architect is responsible for establishing coding standards and guidelines and for mentoring development staff, this chapter provides several implementation tips and techniques for value objects and entities. Additionally, the chapter explains several concepts needed for effectively structuring value objects and entities. And to make implementing these recommendations easier and less time consuming, the chapter presents a base value object class, which I've included in the source bundle (`j2ee.architect.handbook.common.BaseVO`). As we will discuss, it's much more difficult and dangerous to provide such a base class for entities.

IMPLEMENTATION TIPS AND TECHNIQUES

Always implement `java.io.Serializable`. For a value object or entity to be usable as an argument to any type of distributed object, such as enterprise beans or RMI services, it needs to implement `Serializable`. There are no methods required by `Serializable`, so implementation is easy. You're better off not putting anything—such as a database connection— in a value object that isn't serializable. But if you must put a non-serializable object in a value object, declare it transient so it's bypassed during any serialization attempts. Listing 9.1 is an extract of value object code.

Listing 9.1: Sample Value Object Code

```
public class SalesSummaryVO implements Serializable,
        Comparable<SalesSummaryVO> {

    private static final long serialVersionUID =
        -4099990023592442788L;

    private String  salesRegion;
```

```
private Integer salesYear;
private Double  salesQuarter1;
private Double  salesQuarter2;
private Double  salesQuarter3;
private Double  salesQuarter4;

// Code suppressed for brevity

}
```

Source: /src/j2ee/architect/handbook/chap09/sample1/SalesSummaryVO.java

Always populate all fields of a value object or entity. Some programmers, for the sake of convenience, don't take the trouble to populate all fields of a value object or entity if they only need a subset of the fields in it. This is less likely with entities as they usually are populated by the JPA implementation. In my experience, this practice saves time during construction, but it inevitably causes bugs that show up as `NullPointerException` exceptions when something attempts to use a field that is not populated. Furthermore, partial population of a value object or entity creates an inconsistency that developers will find confusing. I recommend either populating all fields of a value object or creating a new value object with the new field set.

Always type fields accurately. I've often seen programmers implement dates and numbers as strings, usually to save time when initially coding a value object or entity. The motivation for this is facilitating display or the coding of a specific process. But as the application gets larger, this practice can cause confusion and inevitably results in additional conversion code where the field is used. It also leads to confusion for maintenance and causes bugs, because someone will format the strings inappropriately.

Check dependence on third-party classes in value objects. Value objects are used as arguments for distributed objects, such as enterprise beans and RMI services. If your value objects rely on third-party classes, your callers will have to include them in their class path to call you. This can be an inconvenience for your callers and make your distributed objects harder to use.

Always override method `toString()`. If you don't override `toString()`, the resulting text is not very meaningful. An example from the default implementation of `toString()` is `com.myapp.Test@3179c3`.

Since there are enough classes in the JDK that accept `Object` arguments and expect to be able to execute method `toString()`, you should provide an implementation. The implementation of `toString()` inherited from `Object` isn't all that useful.

Consider overriding methods `equals()` and `hashcode()`. If a value object is ever used as a key in a `HashMap`, `Hashtable`, or `HashSet`; `equals()` and `hashcode()` are used for key identification. The definition of these methods, inherited from

`Object`, dictates that for two value objects to be equal, they must literally be the same class instance. For example, consider a `CustomerVO` with `firstName` and `lastName` fields. You could have two instances of "John Doe" that will look unequal using the `equals()` inherited from `Object`. You will have to override both `equals()` and `hashcode()` for a value object if you want it usable in any type or `Map` implementation, such as `Hashtable`, `HashMap`, or `TreeMap`.

The behavior differences between a meaningful implementation of `equals()` and the implementation inherited from `Object` confuses many developers. The example in listing 9.2a should help alleviate any confusion.

Listing 9.2a: Sample `Object.equals()` Implementation

```
public void showObjectEqualImplementation()
{
  ObjectWithoutEqualsImpl fiveAsObject =
      new ObjectWithoutEqualsImpl("5");
  ObjectWithoutEqualsImpl anotherFiveAsObject =
      new ObjectWithoutEqualsImpl("5");
  ObjectWithoutEqualsImpl sevenAsObject =
      new ObjectWithoutEqualsImpl("7");

  System.out.println("Object equals() demo:");
  System.out.println(
    "\tfiveAsObject.equals(anotherFiveAsObject): "+
  fiveAsObject.equals(anotherFiveAsObject));
  System.out.println(
    "\tfiveAsObject.equals(sevenAsObject): " +
   fiveAsObject.equals(sevenAsObject));
}
```
Source: /src/j2ee/architect/handbook/chap09/sample1/EqualsDemonstration.java

Listing 9.2a uses a simple class that does not override method `equals()` and uses the implementation inherited from `Object`. The variable declared in line 3 with the value 5 should be "equal" to the object declared in line 5. However, if you were to run the sample, you would see that the variables are actually not considered equal. Output to the sample is provided in listing 9.2b.

Listing 9.2b: Output from Listing 9.2a

```
Object equals() demo:
    fiveAsObject.equals(anotherFiveAsObject): false
    fiveAsObject.equals(sevenAsObject): false
```

If you were to run a different sample using class `String` instead of `ObjectWithoutEqualsImpl`, the output would be more what you would expect because `String` *overrides method* `equals()`.

The method `hashcode()` returns an integer that is guaranteed to be equal for two instances of `Object` that are equal. The logic behind constructing an algorithm to do this can get intricate. Fortunately, a good implementation of `hashcode` logic has been implemented in the Apache Commons Lang product (http://commons.apache.org/lang/) in class `HashCodeBuilder`. Listing 9.3 illustrates an effective implementation of `hashcode()`.

Listing 9.3: Sample `hashcode()` Implementation

```
@Override
public int hashCode() {
return new HashCodeBuilder(17, 37).
   append(this.salesRegion).
   append(this.salesYear).
   append(this.salesQuarter1).
   append(this.salesQuarter2).
   append(this.salesQuarter3).
   append(this.salesQuarter4).
   toHashCode();
}
```

Source: /src/j2ee/architect/handbook/chap09/sample1/SalesSummaryVO.java

Implementing `equals()` is similar in that we once again utilize the Apache Commons Lang product. This is shown in listing 9.4.

Listing 9.4: Sample `equals()` Implementation

```
@Override
public boolean equals(Object obj) {
if (obj == null) { return false; }
if (obj == this) { return true; }
if (obj.getClass() != getClass()) {
 return false;
}
SalesSummaryVO rhs = (SalesSummaryVO) obj;
return new EqualsBuilder()
    .append(this.salesRegion, rhs.salesRegion)
    .append(this.salesYear, rhs.salesYear)
    .append(this.salesQuarter1, rhs.salesQuarter1)
    .append(this.salesQuarter2, rhs.salesQuarter2)
    .append(this.salesQuarter3, rhs.salesQuarter3)
    .append(this.salesQuarter4, rhs.salesQuarter4)
    .isEquals();
}
```

Source: /src/j2ee/architect/handbook/chap09/sample1/SalesSummaryVO.java

Consider implementing `java.lang.Comparable`. If you ever use a value object in a sorted collection (e.g., `TreeSet` or `TreeMap`), you must implement `Comparable` for sensible sort results. Implementing `Comparable` requires the implementation of a `compareTo()` method that returns 0 if the two objects are equal, a negative number if the `Object` is less than the argument passed, and a positive number if the `Object` is greater than the argument passed. Fortunately, Apache Commons Lang comes to our assistance with the `CompareToBuilder` class. Listing 9.5 illustrates this.

Listing 9.5: Sample `compareTo()` Implementation

```
public int compareTo(SalesSummaryVO o) {
   return new CompareToBuilder()
   .append(this.salesYear, o.salesYear)
   .append(this.salesRegion, o.salesRegion)
   .append(this.salesQuarter1, o.salesQuarter1)
   .append(this.salesQuarter2, o.salesQuarter2)
   .append(this.salesQuarter3, o.salesQuarter3)
   .append(this.salesQuarter4, o.salesQuarter4)
   .toComparison();
}
```

Source: /src/j2ee/architect/handbook/chap09/sample1/SalesSummaryVO.java

VALUE OBJECTS MADE EASY

My laundry list of recommendations makes implementing value objects extremely boring, tedious, and time consuming. As an application architect, you have the option of mentoring developers as they follow these recommendations and, you hope, implement them consistently. Another option is to provide architectural utilities that make coding value objects easier and quicker and bring some consistency to value object behavior.

These goals are achieved by `BaseVO` included in the source bundle, a tool I created to provide architectural support for value objects. If value objects extend `BaseVO`, they get meaningful `equals()`, `hashcode()`, and `toString()`, and they `clone()` implementations automatically.

`BaseVO` does use reflection to achieve its magic, so it's slower than custom-coded value objects. Table 9.1 presents a performance comparison for our sample `SalesSummaryVO`.

Table 9.1: Performance Comparison for `BaseVO` for 100,000 Operations (JDK 1.7)

Version	Milliseconds per 100,000 Operations			
	clone()	toString()	hashCode()	equals()
VO extension	2214 ms	3511 ms	829 ms	940 ms
Custom	27 ms	774 ms	52 ms	9 ms

For the table, I arbitrarily chose 100,000 iterations to make the time differences more apparent. Most applications will have fewer executions of these methods per transaction.

By using `BaseVO`, you trade some performance for development and maintenance time. Most value objects in an application use these operations in large enough volume for the speed of `BaseVO` to be an issue. I recommend you custom code only the small number of value objects that you've determined to need faster execution time based on your performance-tuning efforts.

In addition, since value objects that extend `BaseVO` contain only small amounts of logic, if any; no test cases are necessary. If you choose to provide your own implementations of `equals()`, `hashcode()`, and `toString()`, you need to construct test cases for these methods.

Warning: It is dangerous to have entities extend `BaseVO`. There are several reasons for this. Entities are often related to other entities. When you reference them, queries are issued under the covers to find related entity instances. For example, a customer may have many accounts. When `BaseVO` formulates a `toString()` value using reflection, it will access all accounts and initiate a query to find that information. This would make the generic implementations found in `BaseVO` extremely expensive for entities.

COMMON MISTAKES

Populating VOs inconsistently. I've seen some applications where fields of value objects were populated with different value sets depending on usage context. For example, consider a CustomerVO with name, address, contact, and several other fields. I've seen developers use a structure like this, but only populate name and address in a specific section of code as that was all that section of code needed. This can cause developer confusion and bugs, as other fields are present but can't be relied on in this section of code to have data. To eliminate confusion, it would have been better to create a separate value object with only the fields used in that section of code. Usually, this practice is a red flag indicating that the design is process oriented instead of object oriented.

Using a blank string to avoid a `NullPointerException`. Some developers initialize all fields to a blank string or something that means "null" but really isn't, as in the following:

```
private String _customerName = "";
```

Although this kind of declaration eliminates `NullPointerException` exceptions, it doesn't prevent some other type of derivative exception from appearing down the line. This practice is akin to "sweeping dirt under the rug" and is best avoided. Furthermore, this kind of sweeping isn't necessary if you adopt the practice of validating all arguments for protected and public methods upfront as the error message received will be explicit.

Embedding formatting assumptions into entities or VOs. For example, some developers will return strings that represent dates or numbers as that's what's displayed in the presentation layer. Unfortunately, it limits reusability for the entity or VO as the presentation format desired for different applications or even portions of an application will likely differ. This is really a violation of the separation of concerns principle in that the entity or VO is given display responsibilities as well as data retention responsibilities. Keep formatting concerns in the presentation layer.

It should be noted that representing date and time as anything other than a `java.util.Date` is also an example of embedding formatting assumptions. For example, some developers use `java.sql.Date` or `java.sql.Timestamp` in VOs or entities; these classes wrap `java.util.Date` for purposes closely tied to JDBC and database storage. Keep these formatting concerns in the data access layer, which by definition needs to concern itself with storage issues.

Maintaining parent-child relationships for VOs or entities in both directions. For example, the `CustomerEntity` would contain a collection of `AccountEntity` children, and each of the `AccountEntity` instances would contain a reference back to the parent. You run into the same problems with this practice as you do when you replicate data in relational databases. The result is double the maintenance when data is changed. Further, the practice is error prone and tends to be the root cause of bugs, including memory leaks.

EXAMPLE: ADMIN4J

Admin4J (www.admin4j.net) is an open source product that provides basic Java EE application administration and support features for support developers. Admin4J has several value objects that are used to facilitate user information display.

As suggested in this chapter, all value objects extend `BaseVO` and have meaningful `toString()`, `equals()`, `hashCode()`, and `clone()` implementations. An example value object extending `BaseVO` can be found in listing 9.5.

Listing 9.6: `PerformanceSummaryVO` **Value Object from Admin4J**

```java
public class PerformanceSummaryVO extends BaseVO {

    private static final long serialVersionUID =
        1280316263958819876L;
    private String label;
    private DataMeasurementSummaryVO summaryMeasurement;
    private DataMeasurementSummaryVO rollingTimeMeasurement;
    private DataMeasurementSummaryVO
        rollingNbrObservationsMeasurement;

    public String getLabel() {
        return label;
    }

    public void setLabel(String label) {
        this.label = label;
    }

    public DataMeasurementSummaryVO getSummaryMeasurement() {
        return summaryMeasurement;
```

```
    }

    public void setSummaryMeasurement(DataMeasurementSummaryVO
        summaryMeasurement) {
      this.summaryMeasurement = summaryMeasurement;
    }

    public DataMeasurementSummaryVO getRollingTimeMeasurement()
        {
      return rollingTimeMeasurement;
    }

    public void setRollingTimeMeasurement(
          DataMeasurementSummaryVO rollingTimeMeasurement) {
      this.rollingTimeMeasurement = rollingTimeMeasurement;
    }

    public DataMeasurementSummaryVO
        getRollingNbrObservationsMeasurement() {
      return rollingNbrObservationsMeasurement;
    }

    public void setRollingNbrObservationsMeasurement(
          DataMeasurementSummaryVO
        rollingNbrObservationsMeasurement) {
      this.rollingNbrObservationsMeasurement =
      rollingNbrObservationsMeasurement;
    }

}
```
Source: Admin4J source code distribution (www.admin4j.net)

As discussed, this value object relies on a base value object class providing meaningful implementations of `toString()`, `equals()`, `hashCode()`, and `clone()`. Source for this class can be found in listing 9.6.

Listing 9.7: BaseVO **Value Object from Admin4J**

```
public abstract class BaseVO implements Serializable, Cloneable
        {

    private static final long serialVersionUID =
        2618192279106780874L;

    /* (non-Javadoc)
     * @see java.lang.Object#hashCode()
     */
    @Override
    public int hashCode() {
        return HashCodeBuilder.reflectionHashCode(17, 37, this);
    }

    /* (non-Javadoc)
```

```
     * @see java.lang.Object#equals(java.lang.Object)
     */
    @Override
    public boolean equals(Object obj) {
        return EqualsBuilder.reflectionEquals(this, obj);
    }


    /* (non-Javadoc)
     * @see java.lang.Object#clone()
     */
    @Override
    public Object clone() throws CloneNotSupportedException {
        try {
            return BeanUtils.cloneBean(this);
        } catch (Exception e) {
            throw new ContextedRuntimeException("Error cloning
         value object", e)
                .addContextValue("class", this.getClass().
         getName());
        }
    }


    /* (non-Javadoc)
     * @see java.lang.Object#toString()
     */
    @Override
    public String toString() {
        return new ReflectionToStringBuilder(this).toString();
    }


}
```
Source: Admin4J source code distribution (www.admin4j.net)

Notice that the `BaseVO` class leverages various builder classes from Apache Commons Lang.

Some of Admin4J's value objects have custom overrides for `equals()` and `hashCode()` for performance. For example, a value object class `FileWrapperVO` has custom overrides for both `equals()` and `hashCode()`. Listing 9.7 contains source for both overrides.

Listing 9.8: `FileWrapperVO` **Value Object Overrides for** `equals()` **and** `hashCode()`

```
/* (non-Javadoc)
* @see java.lang.Object#equals(java.lang.Object)
*/
@Override
public boolean equals(Object obj) {
if (obj == null) {
    return false;
}
FileWrapper rhs = null;
```

```
if (obj instanceof FileWrapper) {
    rhs = (FileWrapper)obj;
    return this.file.equals(rhs.file);
}
return false;
}


/* (non-Javadoc)
 * @see java.lang.Object#hashCode()
 */
@Override
public int hashCode() {
return this.file.hashCode();
}
```

Source: Admin4J source code distribution (www.admin4j.net)

DIFFERENCES FROM THE FIRST EDITION

The first edition of this book introduced a technique for having value objects provide a textual description of themselves for error-logging purposes. This was achieved by having value objects implement an interface Describable. The objective was to standardize descriptions included with exceptions in a way that reduced the probability of erring out formatting the text of an exception.

Today, there is a much better and less invasive way of accomplishing the same goal. With version 3.0 of Apache Commons Lang, two exceptions were introduced: ContextedException and ContextedRuntimeException, which I contributed. These exceptions make it easy and safe to include additional information with thrown exceptions without fear of accidentally excepting in the formatting of an error message. As you might have guessed, ContextedException is checked; ContextedRuntimeException is not.

An example of how to use these exceptions can be found in listing 9.8.

Listing 9.9: Example of ContextedRuntimeException Usage

```
try {
   ...
} catch (Exception e) {
  throw new ContextedRuntimeException("Error posting account
        transaction", e)
      .addContextValue("Account Number", accountNumber)
      .addContextValue("Amount Posted", amountPosted)
      .addContextValue("Previous Balance", previousBalance)
}
```

This example will produce a message similar to that in listing 9.9.

Listing 9.10: Example of ContextedRuntimeException Output

```
org.apache.commons.lang3.exception.ContextedRuntimeException:
        java.lang.Exception: Error posting account transaction
Exception Context:
```

```
[1:Account Number=null]
[2:Amount Posted=100.00]
[3:Previous Balance=-2.17]


--------------------------------
at org.apache.commons.lang3.exception.
        ContextedRuntimeExceptionTest.testAddValue(ContextedExc
        eptionTest.java:88)
..... (rest of trace)
```

The contexted exceptions are null safe and will even trap errors produced by a faulty value having a `toString()` implementation that excepts.

CHAPTER 10

BUILDING DATA ACCESS OBJECTS

Data access objects read and write saved data and convert that format to entities usable by other layers in the application. You can think of them as "factory" classes for entities. For example, `CustomerDAO`, a DAO in a purchasing application, reads customer information from a database or some other form of saved storage and converts that information to entities (e.g., `CustomerEntity`) that the rest of the application can use. CustomerDAO also uses information in `CustomerEntity` to update or insert data in the database or file. The following are some methods `CustomerDAO` might have:

```
public CustomerEntity findById(Long customerId);
public void saveOrUpdate(CustomerEntity customer);
public void delete(Long customerId);
public List<CustomerEntity> findByPartialName(String name);
```

All logic that interprets and processes that data is in the business logic layer, not in the data access object layer. The DAO merely handles the I/O. It should be noted that while most classes in the DAO will target relational databases, any form of persistent storage should be managed at the data access layer. In other words, access to NoSQL databases should reside in the data access layer as well. There are several reasons for segregating data access.

First, it promotes reuse. For example, there might be several use cases in an application that need to read and process purchase order information. Segregating data access makes the example DAO usable for all of those processes.

Second, together with your package structure (which separates DAO classes into a separate package) it allows developers to quickly find data access that might need to be changed or enhanced.

Third, it facilitates changing your method of storage without affecting other parts of the application. For example, one of my clients migrated from using Sybase to Oracle. The migration was relatively easy in applications with segregated data access. Further, from a maintenance standpoint, it was easy to locate, modify, and enhance the data access object layer to handle minor changes, such as column additions.

Figure 10.1 Illustrates the Role of DAOs in the Software Layer Hierarchy

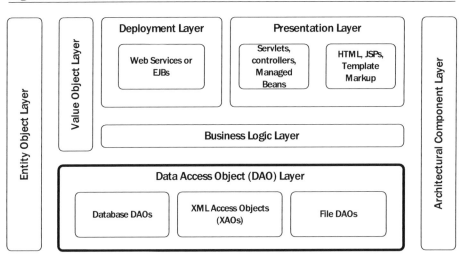

Most DAO classes in most applications are relational database DAOs; that is, they read and write data using relational databases such as Oracle or Microsoft SQL Server. If your application uses a JPA implementation like Hibernate, DAO classes is where you'll find Hibernate-dependent code. Ideally, other layers of the application (e.g., business logic layer) will never reference Hibernate classes. If your application uses JDBC, DAO classes is where you'll find any and all references to JDBC classes.

TRANSACTION MANAGEMENT STRATEGIES

All Java EE applications need a transaction management strategy. That is, a strategy that defines when commits and rollbacks are issued. There are three general strategies available: Servlet Filter strategy, Aspect-Oriented Programming (AOP) strategy, and Autocommit strategy.

The Servlet Filter strategy uses a Servlet filter, which is executed on all web transactions to issue all commits for successful transactions and rollbacks for all transactions that except. Listing 10.1 contains a short example of this strategy. Note that in this example, class `TransactionContext` retains the current Hibernate session and makes it available to classes in the data access layer. A similar pattern could easily be used to retain native JDBC connections should a JDBC persistence strategy be used.

Listing 10.1: Sample Transaction Management Filter Logic

```
public void doFilter(ServletRequest request,
   ServletResponse response,
      FilterChain chain) throws IOException, ServletException {

      Boolean transactionEstablished =
    transactionContextState.get();
        if (transactionEstablished != null) {
          chain.doFilter(request, response);
      }
      else {
          try {
              transactionContextState.set(Boolean.TRUE);
              new TransactionContext();

              chain.doFilter(request, response);
              TransactionContext.getCurrent().commit();
          }
          catch (Exception e) {
              TransactionContext.getCurrent().rollback();
          }
          finally {
              transactionContextState.remove();
              TransactionContext.getCurrent().close();
          }
      }

   }
```

Source: /src/j2ee/architect/handbook/chap10/TransactionManagementFilter.java

The AOP strategy uses aspect-oriented technologies, such as AspectJ (http://www.eclipse.org/aspectj/), to surround methods in data access classes with commit and rollback logic. Often, this approach is too granular to be useful. While one can address the granularity issue and take the time to plan which classes are targeted for transaction management, this can lead to confusion for developers. It is not obvious which class methods contain transaction management logic and which don't. The resulting confusion often takes more time and effort than the development time saved by using an AOP strategy.

The Autocommit strategy is the most convenient for initial development. It's possible, often at a JDBC driver configuration level, to set all connections to be "autocommit" by default. Using this strategy, the JDBC driver automatically issues a "commit" after successful SQL statements and a "rollback" after failed transactions. This strategy has the same issue as the AOP strategy in that it's too granular to be useful with most Java EE applications.

As you may have guessed, I trend toward using the Servlet Filter strategy for transaction management. It's simple. It alleviates the need for developers to concern themselves with transaction management issues. Should a given web transaction require multiple units of work, this strategy allows that where needed. It's easily reused in multiple applications.

You may notice that transaction state is actually retained in a `TransactionContext` class. This allows other classes to manage transaction state if needed. For example, batch jobs and JMS queue monitors require transaction management that cannot be addressed by a Servlet Filter.

Note that the Servlet Filter and AOP transaction strategies can be easily combined with other transaction management products such as Bitronix (http://docs.codehaus.org/display/BTM/Home), Atomikos (http://www.atomikos.com/), or JOTM (jotm.objectweb.org). Transaction management products facilitate commit and rollback strategies for applications using multiple data sources; some applications have such requirements.

DATA ACCESS OBJECT CODING GUIDELINES

As most use a JPA implementation such as Hibernate for database persistence these days, let's begin with a Hibernate example such as Listing 10.2.

Listing 10.2: Hibernate DAO Example

```
public class CustomerHibernateDAO extends BaseHibernateDAO
        implements
        CustomerDAO {

    public CustomerEntity findById(Long customerId) {
        Validate.notNull(customerId,
      "Null customerId not allowed.");
        return (CustomerEntity)this.getSession()
                .get(CustomerEntity.class, customerId);
    }

    public void saveOrUpdate(CustomerEntity customer) {
        Validate.notNull(customer,
      "Null customer not allowed.");
        this.getSession().saveOrUpdate(customer);
    }

    public void delete(Long customerId) {
        Validate.notNull(customerId,
      "Null customerId not allowed.");
        CustomerEntity customer = this.findById(customerId);

        if (customer != null) {
            this.getSession().delete(customer);
        }
    }

    @SuppressWarnings("unchecked")
    public List<CustomerEntity> findByPartialName(String name) {
        Validate.notEmpty(name,
      "Null or blank name not allowed.");
```

```
SQLQuery sql = this.getSession().createSQLQuery(
        "select * from Customer " +
        "where last_name like :name " +
"or first_name like :name");
sql.setParameter("name", "%" + name + "%");
sql.addEntity(CustomerEntity.class);

return sql.list();
    }


}
```

Source: /src/j2ee/architect/handbook/chap10/hibernate/CustomerHibernateDAO.java

Note that this DAO extends the class `BaseHibernateDAO` that exposes the current Hibernate session. This class is available in the source distribution.

DAO classes do not issue commits, rollbacks, or savepoints. The consistency makes DAO classes easier to reuse for multiple use cases. I can imagine several use cases that require a customer lookup by id, and it's possible that the lookup can occur in the middle of a larger unit of work. Were the DAO to issue a commit or rollback, it would effectively interfere with the larger unit of work. Furthermore, which DAOs issue commits or rollbacks isn't well documented. The inconsistency would cost developers time as it wouldn't be obvious where specific transactions began and ended.

DAO classes reference only entities, architectural components/utilities and other DAO classes. DAO classes do not reference classes in the business logic layer, presentation layer, or deployment layer. This enforces separation of concerns and is in keeping with a layered architecture.

Validate arguments for public and protected methods. The alternative is to allow the method to produce some type of derivative exception (such as a `NullPointerException`) that often takes more time to diagnose and fix. Furthermore, the validation is quick and rarely impacts performance noticeably. Note that the `Validate` utility from the Apache Commons Lang project is very effective for this purpose.

A JDBC EXAMPLE

In the early days, we all learned native JDBC. In fact, knowledge of native JDBC helps developers diagnose errors typically coming out of DAO classes. That said, the times where native JDBC coding is necessary these days are rare. It is more common to leverage JDBC helper utilities, such as those in the Apache Commons `DBUtils` (http://commons.apache.org/dbutils/) project for convenience. As an example, listing 10.3 presents a JDBC example that leverages `DBUtils` for convenience.

Listing 10.3: JDBC DAO example

```
public class CustomerJDBCDAO extends BaseJDBCDAO implements
        CustomerDAO {

    public CustomerEntity findById(Long customerId) {
        Validate.notNull(customerId, "Null customerId not
         allowed.");
        List<CustomerEntity> list = this.query(
                "select * from Customer where Customer_Id = ?",
                new Object[]{customerId},
         new CustomerResultSetHandler());
        if (list.size() > 0) {
            return list.get(0);
        }
        return null;
    }

    public void saveOrUpdate(CustomerEntity customer) {
        Validate.notNull(customer,
      "Null customer not allowed.");
        CustomerEntity readEntity = this.findById(
      customer.getCustomerId());
        String sqlText;
        Object[] params;

        if (readEntity == null) { // Insert
            sqlText = "insert into Customer " +
                    "(Customer_Id, Last_Name, First_Name, Middle_
         Initial ) " +
                    "values (?,?,?,?)";

            params = new Object[]{customer.getCustomerId()
                    , customer.getLastName()
                    , customer.getFirstName()
                    , customer.getMiddleInitial()};
        }
        else { // update
            sqlText = "update Customer " +
                    "set Last_Name = ? " +
                    ", First_Name = ? " +
                    ", Middle_Initial = ? " +
                    "where Customer_Id = ?";

            params = new Object[]{customer.getLastName()
                    , customer.getFirstName()
                    , customer.getMiddleInitial()
                    , customer.getCustomerId()};
        }

        this.update(sqlText, params);

    }
```

```
public void delete(Long customerId) {
    Validate.notNull(customerId,
"Null customerId not allowed.");
    this.update(
"delete from Customer where Customer_Id = ?",
            new Object[]{customerId});

}

public List<CustomerEntity> findByPartialName(String name) {
    Validate.notEmpty(name,
"Null or blank name not allowed.");
    return this.query(
            "select * from Customer where last_name like ?
    or first_name like ?",
            new Object[]{name,name},
    new CustomerResultSetHandler());
}

}
```

Source: /src/j2ee/architect/handbook/chap10/jdbc/CustomerJdbcDAO.java

Note that this DAO extends the class `BaseJDBCDAO` that exposes the current JDBC Connection as well as facilitates `DBUtils` usage for executing SQL statements. In addition, this example relies on class `CustomerResultSetHandler` which is an implementation of `ResultSetHandler` interface for select results. These classes are available in the source distribution.

JDBC objects created within a method should be closed within the same method. Examples of this kind of object include `PreparedStatement`, `Statement`, `ResultSet`, `CallableStatement` objects. For many database platforms to avoid resource leaks, it's necessary to close `ResultSet`, `PreparedStatement`, `CallableStatement`, and `Statement` objects when you're through with them. Some JDBC drivers close these objects automatically when the Connection is closed and some don't. It's easier to spot bugs involving resource leaks later if you adopt the convention of closing everything you create *at this layer*. Note that the `DBUtils` library provides utilities to do this.

Use host variables in SQL statements instead of hard-coding literals in SQL strings. `DBUtils` adopts this practice. As a convenience, many developers embed literals in SQL statements instead. Listing 10.4 is an example of the bad practice of embedding literals. Notice that this example places a customer ID directly in the SQL statement. Notice also that this example uses the + operator for string concatenation. Although using + is convenient, you can concatenate strings faster using `StringBuffer` and the `StringBuffer.append()` method.

Listing 10.4: Badly Written Update Statement

```
sqlText = "update Customer " +
   "set Last_Name = '" + customer.getLastName()
   "', First_Name = '" + customer.getFirstName()
   "', Middle_Initial = '" + customer.getMiddleInitial()
   "' where Customer_Id = " + customer.getCustomerId();

this.update(sqlText);
```

The problem with the code in listing 10.4 is that it circumvents database optimizations provided by Oracle, DB2/UDB, and many others. To get the benefit of database software optimizations, you need to use `PreparedStatement` objects instead of `Statement` objects for SQL that will be executed multiple times. Further, you need to use host variables instead of literals for literals that will change between executions. With listing 10.4, the SQL statement for Customer ID 1 will be different than for Customer ID 2 ("`where Customer_Id = 1`" is different from "`where Customer_Id = 2`"). The original version of the update statement in listing 10.3 is much better.

Notice that because listing 10.3 uses host variables instead of literals, the SQL statement is identical no matter what the qualifying user ID is. Further, a `PreparedStatement` is used instead of a `Statement`.

To better understand the database optimizations possible when using `PreparedStatement` objects, consider how Oracle processes SQL statements. When executing SQL statements, Oracle goes through the following steps:

1 Look up the statement in the shared pool to see if it has already been parsed or interpreted. If yes, go directly to step 4.

2 Parse (or interpret) the statement.

3 Figure out how to get the desired data and record the information in a portion of memory called the shared pool.

4 Get the data.

When Oracle looks up an SQL statement to see if it has already been executed (step 1), it attempts a character-by-character match of the SQL statement. If the program finds a match, it can use the parse information already in the shared pool and does not have to do steps 2 and 3 because it has done the work already. If you hard-code literals in SQL statements, the probability of finding a match is very low ("`where Customer_Id = 1`" is not the same as "`where Customer_Id = 2`"). This means that Oracle will have to reparse listing 10.4 for each portfolio selected. Had listing 10.4 used host variables and a `PreparedStatement`, the SQL statement (which would look something like "`where Customer_Id = :1`" in the shared pool) would have been parsed once and only once.

DB2/UDB uses different terminology but a similar algorithm for dynamic

SQL statements. Use of the `PreparedStatement` over the `Statement` is recommended for DB2/UDB as well.

Consolidate formation of SQL statement strings. As a former database administrator, I spend a substantial portion of my time reading the code others have written and suggesting ways to improve performance. As you might expect, I am particularly interested in the SQL statements. I find it especially hard to follow SQL statements constructed by string manipulation scattered over several methods. It greatly enhances readability if you consolidate the logic that forms the SQL statement.

Listing 10.5a is a good illustration of this point. Note that the string manipulation to form the SQL statement is located in one place. The SQL string is also defined statically to reduce the amount of string concatenation.

Listing 10.5a: Using a String Host Variable for a Date Field

```
Select sum(sale_price)
   From purchase_order
   Where to_char(sale_dt,'YYYY-MM-DD') >= ?
```

Limit use of column functions. Try to limit your use of column functions to the select lists of select statements. Moreover, use only aggregate functions (e.g., `count`, `sum`, and `average`) needed for select statements that use a "`group by`" clause. There are two reasons for this recommendation: performance and portability.

When you limit the use of a function to a select list (and keep it out of "where" clauses), you can use the function without blocking the use of an index. In the same way that the `to_char` function prohibited the database from using an index in listing 10.5a, column functions in "where" clauses very likely will prohibit the database from using an index. This results in slower query performance. Rewriting the SQL statement as shown in listing 10.5b allows most databases to use indices.

Listing 10.5b: Query with `java.sql.Timestamp` as a Host Variable

```
Select sum(sale_price)
   From purchase_order
   Where sale_dt >= ?
```

In addition, many of the operations for which developers use SQL column functions (data type conversion, value formatting, etc.) are faster in Java than if the database did them. I've had 5 to 20 percent performance improvement in many applications by avoiding some column functions and implementing the logic in Java instead. Another way to look at it is that you cannot tune column functions because you cannot control the source code. By implementing that logic in Java, you create code that you can tune if necessary.

Moreover, using non-ANSI standard column functions can also cause portability problems. Not all database vendors implement the same column functions. For instance, one of my favorite Oracle column functions, decode, which allows you to translate one set of values into another, is not implemented in many of the other major database platforms. In general, using column functions like decode has the potential to become a portability issue.

Always specify a column list with an insert statement. Many developers use the shortcut of omitting the column list in an insert statement to avoid having to type out a column list. By default, the column order is the same as physically defined in the table. Listing 10.6a illustrates this shortcut, and listing 10.6b illustrates the alternative of explicitly listing desired columns.

Listing 10.6a: Insert Statement without Column List

```
Insert into customer
   Values ('Ashmore','Derek','3023 N.Clark','Chicago',
'IL', 555555)
```

Listing 10.6b: Full Insert Statement with Column List

```
Insert into customer
   (last_nm, first_nm, address, city, state, customer_nbr)
   Values (?,?,?,?,?,?)
```

Explicitly listing columns in insert statements, as illustrated in listing 10.6b, is done for the same reason as explicitly listing columns in select statements. If someone reorders the columns in any of the tables in the insert or adds new columns, the insert could generate an exception, and you must modify the insert statement. For example, suppose that database administrator again changes the order of the columns, putting column CUSTOMER_NBR first, and adds a column called COUNTRY. The developer who used the shortcut will have to change code. The developer who explicitly listed all columns will be oblivious to the change because the code will still work. In addition, note that listing 10.6b uses host variables, so the same PreparedStatement can be used for all inserts if there are multiple inserts.

As in select statements, explicitly listing columns in an insert statement is a best practice because it can eliminate the need for maintenance. Further, allowing reuse of the PreparedStatement improves performance, especially for inserts of large numbers of rows.

Code test cases for all DAO methods and put them in the test suite. You should be able to run a regression test for all objects in the data access layer at any time. This improves product quality by automating a reasonable test process.

Define a standard method for managing data needed for DAO test cases. DAO test cases are dependent on the data used to develop the tests. Should that data change, tests may fail, but not because of a code defect. The test data and DAO test cases need to be kept in sync. One toolset I've used with success to assist with managing this issue is the open source product DbUnit (www. dbunit.org). There are also other toolsets that can be used to solve this issue.

XML ACCESS OBJECT CODING GUIDELINES

Data access objects are classes that read and write persistent data. XML manipulation, because it's really a data access operation, is part of the DAO layer. An XML access object (XAO) reads and writes data in an XML format and converts that format to value objects that other layers in the application can use. As an example, an XML access object found in the Admin4J product can be found in listing 10.7.

Listing 10.7: An Interface for an XML Access Object from Admin4J

```
public interface TaskTimerDAO {

    public Set<TaskTimer> findAll();
    public void saveAll(Set<TaskTimer> exceptionList);
}
```

Business objects use XAOs to interpret and produce XML data. Typically, XAOs should have little to do with implementing the business rules associated with processing the data. XML-related code is separated to limit and localize the impact that changes in the XML structure have on your application. If this logic were scattered in various places in the business logic layer, for example, it would be much harder to find and change.

As an application architect, you are responsible for forming coding standards and guidelines. This chapter provides implementation guidance and examples for structuring XAOs. In addition, I'll show you a way to generate code that XAOs can easily use, saving you development and maintenance time.

There are many XML products available to facilitate reading and creating XML. However, they generally fall into one of the following categories: DOM-based, reflection-based, or code generation-based. DOM-based technologies are based directly on the Document Object Model (package `org. w3c.dom`) that's now provided with the JDK. As native Dom code is verbose and awkward, using a complementary technology, such as JDom (http://www. jdom.org/) is preferable to using a DOM parser directly.

Reflection-based XML products use reflection to produce XML from Java objects and transform XML into Java for reading. An example of a reflection-based XML product is included with the JDK in classes `java. beans.XMLEncoder` and `java.beans.XMLDecoder`.

Another example of a reflection-based XML product is Castor XML (www.castor.org).

Code generation-based XML products use a schema or DTD and generate

Java classes that represent these XML constructs and also transform these Java classes into XML or transform XML into instances of these generated classes. The Apache XML Beans (http://xmlbeans.apache.org/) product is a good example of this type of technology.

Avoid direct use of the DOM to interpret XML data. It is faster to develop and easier to maintain applications using complementary technologies, such as XML Beans or JDOM, rather than using a DOM parser directly.

My preference is XML Beans, which generates Java source code that can read, interpret, and serialize XML documents conforming to a given schema. The advantages of XML Beans are that it maps XML documents to Java classes that are easy for developers to use, and the learning curve for XML Beans is very short.

Apply XML technologies consistently throughout the application. Whatever your technology choices are, there is a tremendous benefit to consistency. For instance, if the developers of your application prefer JDOM and are comfortable with that choice, you have little reason to use XML Beans. Consistency makes the application easier to maintain because it reduces the skill sets required for maintenance developers. Consistency also reduces the time it takes to investigate bugs because maintenance developers can begin with a base understanding as to how XAOs are structured.

Place XML-related code into separate classes. One reason for separating XML-related classes from those that implement business rules is to insulate your application from changes in XML document structure. Another reason is that separating XML document interpretation and business logic can lead to simpler code. Further, if multiple applications must read and interpret the same XML document formats, keeping XML-related code separate makes it easier to share that code across applications.

AN XAO EXAMPLE

Admin4J uses the reflection-based XMLEncoder and XMLDecoder that come with the JDK. The implementation for the interface in listing 10.7 is in a class named TaskTimerDAOXml, which is too large to reprint here in its entirety. The source is included in the download for Admin4J, which can be obtained at www.admin4j.net.

Listing 10.8 is an excerpt from TaskTimerDAOXml that illustrates how XML is read and converted into Java classes using the XMLDecoder.

Listing 10.8: An XMLDecoder Example

```
decoder = new XMLDecoder(
    new BufferedInputStream(
        new FileInputStream(xmlFileName)));
```

```
decoder.setExceptionListener(
    new DefaultExceptionListener(xmlFileName));
result = (Set<TaskTimer>)decoder.readObject();
```

Listing 10.9: An XMLEncoder Example

```
encoder = new XMLEncoder(
    new BufferedOutputStream(
        new FileOutputStream(tempFileName)));
encoder.setExceptionListener(
    new DefaultExceptionListener(xmlFileName));
encoder.setPersistenceDelegate(BasicTaskTimer.class,
    new DefaultPersistenceDelegate(
        new String[]{"label","dataMeasures"}));
encoder.setPersistenceDelegate(SummaryDataMeasure.class,
    new DefaultPersistenceDelegate(
        new String[]{"firstObservationTime"}));

encoder.writeObject(exceptionList);
encoder.close();
```

FURTHER READING

Alur, Deepak, John Crupi, and Dan Malks. 2001. *Core J2EE Patterns: Best Practices and Design Strategies.* New York: Prentice Hall.

Horstmann, Cay S., and Gary Cornell. 2008. *Core Java 2, Volume II: Advanced Features,* 8th ed. Essex, UK: Pearson Higher Education.

Johnson, Rod. 2002. *Expert One-on-One: J2EE Design and Development.* Indianapolis, IN: Wrox Press.

CHAPTER 11

BUILDING
BUSINESS OBJECTS

The business logic layer for Java EE applications combines data with application logic, business rules, constraints, and activities. I usually package business objects separately to maximize the possibility of reuse. It's common for business objects to use and coordinate the activities of multiple data access objects. Figure 11.1 illustrates how business objects function in a layered architecture.

Figure 11.1: Using Business Objects within a Layered Architecture

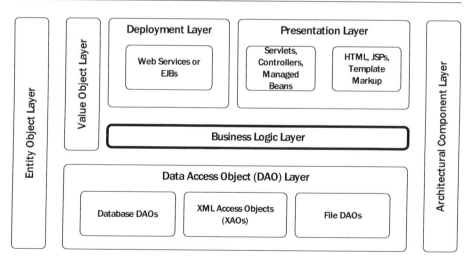

Business objects are used by other business objects or classes in the presentation or deployment layers, such as enterprise beans or web services.

They often instantiate and use classes in the data access layer, such as those discussed in the previous two chapters.

BUSINESS OBJECT CODING PATTERNS

The first and simplest coding pattern commonly used in the business logic layer is the Transaction Script pattern, as described by [Fowler]. This pattern organizes application code into a series of discreet transactions. For example, consider normal banking transactions you might conduct at an ATM machine. Behind the entering of my passcode, there very well might be a transaction script that verifies that the passcode I entered belongs to the card I presented. Behind my cash withdrawal, there might be a transaction script to verify my account balance, record the withdrawal transaction, and tell the ATM machine to dispense the cash. In fact, every action I can take at an ATM machine could be divided into a series of discreet transactions. Beyond this banking example, it is possible to look at all applications as a series of transactions that accept input and do a predetermined set of work activities.

The Transaction Script pattern is frowned upon by many as being too simple. Having seen more arbitrarily complex code (e.g., spaghetti code) than I would like, I see simplicity as a good attribute, not as a disadvantage. For simple to moderately complex tasks, the Transaction Script pattern is completely appropriate. All business applications, regardless of size, have features that fall into the simple to moderately complex category. In fact, most features for most business applications fall into this category.

Because of its simplicity, the Transaction Script pattern is easy to teach, even to very junior developers. Code following this pattern is usually easy to understand.

However, the Transaction Script pattern is also disliked by many, as it isn't truly object oriented. That is, it doesn't comingle state with a set of related actions. Transaction script classes do not have state (e.g., fields). They accept inputs, often in the form of entity or value object form, and they utilize DAO layer classes to perform needed reads or writes. Object-oriented code tends to combine application data with the actions on it in the same class or set of classes. In this light, the Transaction Script pattern can be seen as a throwback to procedural programming.

Classes implementing the transaction pattern serve as classification categories. For example, a collection of transaction scripts to manage bank account transactions might be called `AccountScripts` or `AccountManager`. These classes do not have state. In fact, most often methods on these classes can be declared as `static`.

It is possible to reuse code using the Transaction Script pattern. In large business applications, some transactions will be composite transactions. That is, they will make use of other existing transactions. To return to the ATM example, a script to "record a transaction" may very well be leveraged for a "deposit" transaction script as well as a "withdrawal" transaction script.

While complex tasks can be written as a large and complex series of transaction scripts, these scripts become fragile and more difficult to maintain. Yes, you can mitigate this somewhat with unit testing support. But the pundits who frown upon the Transaction Script pattern are correct in pointing out that it has limitations. It is common for large business applications to have some features that are really too complex for the Transaction Script pattern and need a more object-oriented approach. The beauty of a layered architecture is that transaction script code and object-oriented code can co-exist. That is, feel free to utilize more advanced patterns for features that truly need it and transaction scripts for simpler features. There's no objective algorithm for deciding which features are too complex for transaction scripts and which need more advanced coding patterns.

BUSINESS OBJECT CODING GUIDELINES

Never put anything deployment specific in an object in the business logic layer. Business objects should be reusable in any context (e.g., web transaction, web service, or batch job) without changes. This insulates business logic from changes and developments in the deployment or presentation layers, which change more rapidly than anything else.

To keep business objects independent, business objects don't reference presentation tier classes or make any assumptions (save for transaction management) about the context in which they will be called. They can assume that they are executed within the context of a transaction, as transaction management typically occurs at the point of deployment.

Many Java EE books guide you toward incorporating business logic directly into enterprise beans. I don't subscribe to that view because of the rapid pace at which deployment methodologies have changed over the years. Secondly, enterprise bean usage has diminished over the past few years and is recognized as unneeded complexity in many cases.

All public methods should explicitly validate the arguments. If they don't, you run a significant risk of generating a derivative exception, such as a `NullPointerException`, which can take longer to debug and fix. If you generate an `IllegalArgumentException` with a clear message, programming errors in the deployment layer or within business objects that call you will have a better chance at being caught in unit testing.

Always have a consistent strategy for instantiating business layer and data access layer classes. Common strategies include autowiring with the help of Inversion of Control (IOC) software or by using the Factory pattern.

The Factory pattern consists of using factory classes to instantiate classes as illustrated in figure11.2.

Figure 11.2: Using Business Object within a Layered Architecture

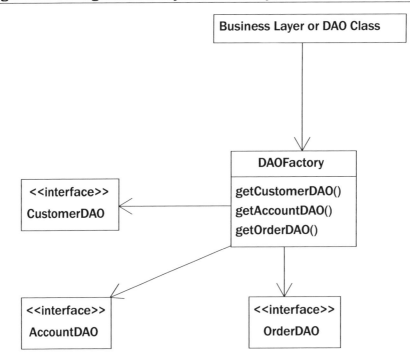

The Factory pattern consolidates responsibility for instantiation and configuration, and it alleviates that concern from the rest of the application. In the simplest case, the Factory pattern merely instantiates a class, e.g., via the new keyword. With more complicated applications, it may need to interrogate the application's configuration to make a decision as to which concrete class is produced.

IOC software products, such as Guice (http://code.google.com/p/google-guice/) or Spring (http://www.springsource.org/), provide you with ways to configure applications by controlling which concrete class implementations are used with a particular installation of the application. IOC software products alleviate the amount of custom code needed to manage your application configuration. IOC software products also simplify some unit testing code as they allow you to easily stub classes that aren't currently under test. It is possible to combine IOC software product use with the Factory pattern.

The use of IOC products forces rigorous use of interfaces to decouple class dependencies. This has advantages and disadvantages. The decoupling does tend to make classes more reusable; however, it also reduces the ability for development environments to provide call hierarchy information (i.e., information about which classes call a given method on a concrete class). This is information that is extremely useful to developers and shouldn't be sacrificed lightly.

Many consider the use of IOC software products essential and use them consistently with every project they undertake. I don't subscribe to this view. IOC software products introduce complexity that needs to have a corresponding benefit to offset that cost. Applications that have configuration options that require using different implementation classes might benefit from the use of IOC software products. An example of this would be: applications that support multiple database platforms might require different DAO implementation classes. Similarly, if you stub data access layer classes or business layer classes for unit testing purposes, you might benefit from IOC software product usage. Another thing to consider is that IOC configuration bugs are not always straightforward to find and fix.

Whichever strategy you use, it's important to use it consistently throughout the application. Having multiple methods for business or data access layer classes causes confusion among developers and introduces unnecessary complexity.

Trend toward stateless classes in the business layer. That is, trend toward use of the Transaction Script pattern. State (e.g., knowledge of the users' work in progress beyond local variables needed for currently executing code) for web applications is more appropriately kept on the session in the form of entity or value object classes. Keeping additional copies of state in the business layer or other layers adds unneeded complexity in that keeping those additional copies up-to-date requires additional code and violates the DRY principle. Instead, pass information to the business layer, as needed, to perform specific tasks.

A BUSINESS LAYER CLASS EXAMPLE

Listing 11.1 contains a code excerpt from an example business layer class. It manages deletion of a customer. In this example:

Listing 11.1: Business Layer Class Excerpt

```
public void delete(CustomerEntity customer)
      throws BusinessProcessingException {
   Validate.notNull(customer, "Null customer not allowed");
   Validate.notNull(customer.getCustomerId(),
     "Null customer Id not allowed");

   BusinessProcessingException busException =
     new BusinessProcessingException(
                "Customer cannot be deleted");

   // Business level validation performed here.
   if (DAOFactory.getOrderDAO().findByCustomerId(
     customer.getCustomerId()).size() > 0) {
      busException.addContextValue("deleteError",
   "Customers with purchase orders can't be deleted;" +
        " they must be inactivated instead.");
```

```
    }

    List<AccountEntity> accountList =
      DAOFactory.getAccountDAO().findByCustomerId(
        customer.getCustomerId());
    for (AccountEntity account: accountList) {
        if (account.isActive()) {
      busException.addContextValue("deleteError",
    "Customers with active accounts can't be deleted;" +
        " they must be inactivated instead.");
      break;
        }
    }

    // throw Business Exception if any discovered.
    checkForBusinessException(busException);
    DAOFactory.getCustomerDAO().delete(
          customer.getCustomerId());

}
```
Source: src/j2ee/architect/handbook/chap11/Customer.java

Note that this example follows all of the guidelines described in this chapter. It doesn't make any assumptions about its execution context. This method is stateless and could be executed from a web transaction, a web service, a batch job, or any other context.

This method validates its arguments and throws an unchecked exception if the method arguments aren't valid due to some kind of programming error. This method then goes further to validate that this customer could actually be deleted from a business perspective. In this example, the business processing exception is a checked exception that the caller must handle. At this level, validations that need to occur regardless of execution context are put here. If this were used in a web transaction, the application might display the errors to the user so they could be addressed. If this were used in a web service, these errors would likely be passed on in the response to the caller.

This class delegates all data access class instantiation to a factory class (DAOFactory). This factory class could use IOC technologies or some other way to instantiate the data access class requested. What's used for configuring the data access layer doesn't affect this business layer method or impact how it operates in any way.

AN ADMIN4J BUSINESS LAYER EXAMPLE

In a previous chapter, a class diagram for the exception summary features of Admin4J was presented. This diagram is reprinted in figure 11.3. Class ExceptionTracker is the central business layer class providing these features. We'll focus on this class as another example of business layer code.

Figure 11.3: Using Business Object within a Layered Architecture

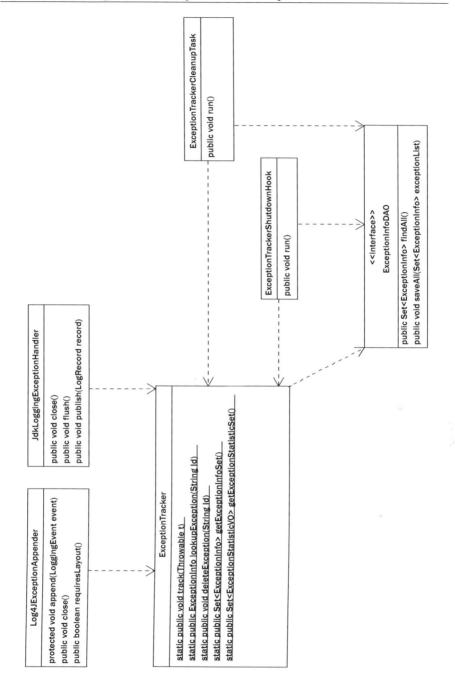

The first example from Admin4J is the business layer method that tracks an exception generated by an application. This method is presented in listing 11.2.

Listing 11.2: Business Layer Class Excerpt from Admin4J

```
public static void track(Throwable t) {
   Validate.notNull(t,
     "Null exception not allowed.");

   Throwable rootCause =
     ExceptionUtils.getRootCause(t);
   if (rootCause == null) {
      rootCause = t;
   }

   if (exemptedExceptionClassNames.containsKey(
     rootCause.getClass().getName()))
   {
      logger.debug(
     "Exception bypassed: {} - {}",
     rootCause.getClass().getName(),
     rootCause.getMessage());
      return;
   }

   ExceptionInfo eInfo =
     findExceptionInfo(rootCause);
   eInfo.setLastOccurrenceMessage(
     rootCause.getMessage());
   eInfo.postOccurance(
     System.identityHashCode(rootCause));

   logger.debug("Exception tracked: {} - {}",
     rootCause.getClass().getName(),
     rootCause.getMessage());
}
```

Note that this example follows all of the guidelines described in this chapter. This method validates its arguments. This method, and in fact the entire class, is stateless. Furthermore, there is nothing deployment-specific about anything in this class.

This method is used by two classes: `Log4JExceptionAppender` and `Jdk-LoggingExceptionHandler`, which capture exceptions logged via Log4J and the native JDK logging that's part of Java itself respectively. Listing 11.3a illustrates usage of this business layer class within a Log4J appender. This example does take great care to not throw an exception in order to avoid accidentally covering up logging of a root exception. This care is normal for log appenders, but not normal for most presentation layer code using business logic classes. Listing 11.3b provides a similar example for a JDK Logging Exception Handler.

Listing 11.3a: Example Usage for Business Layer Class from Admin4J Log4J Appender

```
@Override
protected void append(LoggingEvent event) {
    /*
     * It's important that this logger not even throw a
     * RuntimeException. Throwing any exception will mask
     * the underlying error and do users a great
     * disservice by masking the root issue.
     * D. Ashmore -- Aug, 2010.
     */
    try {
        if (event != null
          && event.getThrowableInformation() != null
          && event.getThrowableInformation()
          .getThrowable() != null)
            {
        ExceptionTracker.track(
        event.getThrowableInformation()
         .getThrowable());
            }
    }
    catch (Throwable t) {
        if (logger != null) {
      logger.error(
        "Error tracking logged exception", t);
        }
        else t.printStackTrace();
    }

}
```

Listing 11.3b: Example Usage for Business Layer Class from Admin4J JDK Logging Exception Handler

```
@Override
public void publish(LogRecord record) {
    /*
     * It's important that this logger not
     * even throw a RuntimeException. Throwing
     * any exception will mask the underlying
     * error and do users a great disservice
     * by masking the root issue.
     * D. Ashmore -- Aug, 2010.
     */
    try {
        if (record != null
          && record.getThrown() != null) {
      ExceptionTracker.track(record.getThrown());
        }
    }
    catch (Throwable t) {
        logger.error("Error tracking logged exception"
```

```
        , t);
    }
}
```

FURTHER READING

Alur, Deepak, John Crupi, and Dan Malks. 2003. *Core J2EE Patterns: Best Practices and Design Strategies*, 2nd ed. New York: Prentice Hall.

Fowler, Martin. 2002. *Patterns of Enterprise Application Architecture*. Reading, MA: Addison-Wesley.

Gamma, Erich, Richard Helm, Ralph Johnson, and John Vlissides. 1995. *Design Patterns*. Reading, MA: Addison-Wesley.

BUILDING THE DEPLOYMENT AND PRESENTATION LAYERS

The deployment and presentation layers of Java EE applications are used directly by users.

Objects in the presentation layer produce the pages or screens that users physically see and use. There are several aspects to the presentation side: static content, dynamic content, and navigation. For Java EE applications, HTML pages typically provide static content; and a combination of JSPs and servlets usually provide dynamic content. For applications that require special effects (e.g., mouse-overs), Javascript can be used in combination with either static or dynamically produced HTML. Users navigate pages using controls (e.g., push buttons) on the page.

Objects in the deployment layer (which I call deployment wrappers) "publish" the content of the business logic layer to other applications. Examples of deployment layer constructs include web services and enterprise beans. I was tempted to call this layer the "service" layer, but that would lead to confusion as to why this layer contains enterprise beans. The deployment layer provides remote calling capability for other applications. For instance, it is not uncommon to support mobile applications by publishing Restful web services; those services would be part of the deployment layer.

Deployment wrappers such as web services and enterprise beans are purposely kept relatively simple and thin because they are more difficult and time consuming to develop and maintain than normal Java classes. Simple, thin deployment wrappers are less likely to have bugs.

Figure 12.1 depicts the role of the presentation and deployment layers.

Figure 12.1: The Presentation and Deployment Layers within a Java EE Application

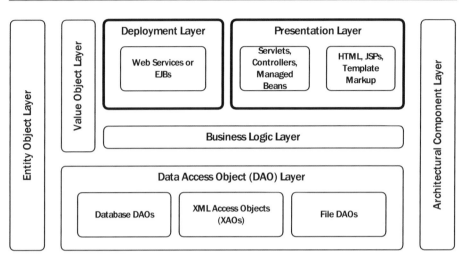

WEB APPLICATION FRAMEWORK CONSIDERATIONS

Most architects leverage third-party frameworks to assist development for web services and user interfaces. Without such frameworks, the amount and complexity of code within these layers would be extremely high. Consequently, the largest deliverable for application architects with respect to these software layers is determining which frameworks will be used.

Some organizations make framework choices for these layers at an enterprise level. There are good reasons for doing this. Most frameworks have significant learning curves. Leveraging the same framework set across the organization optimizes the time spent learning these frameworks. It also makes transferring developers between applications easier and less costly. Furthermore, by consolidating the frameworks in use, it becomes easier to share common code across applications and get greater reuse.

Some organizations leave framework choice up to individual application teams. In these types of organizations, application architects either decide which frameworks will be used or they facilitate the decision. Examples of presentation frameworks commonly used include Spring MVC, Apache Struts (or Struts 2), Java Server Faces, Google Web Toolkit, Freemarker, Apache Velocity, and many others. Examples of web service frameworks commonly used include Apache Axis (2), Apache CXF, Glassfish Metro, and many others.

Once framework decisions are made, application architects usually provide usage guidance. This guidance should address cross-cutting concerns such as error handling, transaction logging, configuration, and build/deployment methodologies. Furthermore, I typically will provide a couple of working examples.

There are several considerations common to the deployment and presentation layers. One of the most important considerations is effectively reusing presentation code. Every website has graphics that are consistently reused throughout the site. Having an ability to reuse visual "components" can greatly optimize development time. The web framework choice for the application will largely dictate strategies for creating visual components and effectively reusing code in the presentation layer. Some web frameworks provide better support for creating and reusing visual components than others. The choice of web framework makes such an excellent example for illustrating a process for selecting a technical product that I use it as an example in the chapter entitled "Making Technology Product Selections." Material on how to code using specific web frameworks, such as Spring-MVC, Java Server Faces, or Struts, is out of scope for this book.

SECURITY CONSIDERATIONS

Another important consideration is security. Most organizations will provide a security architecture for the enterprise along with processes for defining users and authorizing those users for specific web applications and assigning them security roles and security groups. Most developers can assume that users have already been authenticated and are authorized to use the application being called. Developers can assume that the Java EE container will provide them the identity of the authenticated user and the security roles to which they've been assigned.

The Java EE container will enforce security constraints defined within the web.xml configuration file for your application. Security constraints will specify secured URLs and indicate which roles are allowed access to them. For instance, if all URLs in your application require the assignment of the Manager role, you might add a security constraint like the following to the web.xml file of the application:

```
<security-constraint>
  <display-name>Restrict to those with Manager authority.</
      display-name>
  <web-resource-collection>
   <web-resource-name>Protected Area</web-resource-name>
   <url-pattern>*.jsp</url-pattern>
   <url-pattern>*.html</url-pattern>
  </web-resource-collection>
  <auth-constraint>
   <role-name>Manager</role-name>
  </auth-constraint>
 </security-constraint>
```

If your application has URLs that are publicly available, it's common to make all secured URLs have a common pattern so they can be specified in a security constraint (e.g., /secure/*). Many applications, however, have additional security requirements beyond merely protecting specific URL patterns.

While the Java EE container will provide the credential or user id for the logged in user from the HttpServletRequest, it's common for applications to require additional information about the user (e.g., full name, e-mail address, etc.). For example, some applications display the name of the logged in user. Some applications have need to initiate e-mail where the user's full name and e-mail address are used. Additionally, other layers besides the presentation layer may need this information. For example, business logic that needs to keep an audit trail of a user's actions will also need the user id for the logged in user.

As knowledge about the current logged in user is required in most applications, I usually incorporate a User context into the application architecture and populate it using a servlet filter. This idea is similar to the Transaction Management filter introduced in chapter 10 that maintained a `Transaction-Context`. Classes in the presentation layer that needed information about the logged in user would leverage the user context. For example:

```
String userId = UserContext.getCurrent().getUser().getUserId();
```

An example of a filter that maintains the user context for the application can be found in listing 12.1. Note that needed user information is contained within a value object created for that purpose.

Listing 12.1: Sample User Context Management Filter Logic

```
public void doFilter(ServletRequest request, ServletResponse
        response,
      FilterChain filterChain) throws IOException,
        ServletException {
    HttpServletRequest httpRequest = (HttpServletRequest)
        request;
    UserContext.UserVO currentUser =
  (UserContext.UserVO)httpRequest.getSession().getAttribute(USER_
        VO_LABEL);

    if (currentUser != null) {
      new UserContext(currentUser);
    }
    else if (httpRequest.getUserPrincipal() != null
 && httpRequest.getUserPrincipal().getName() != null) {
        currentUser = new UserContext.UserVO();
        // TODO Put logic in to lookup user information,
        populate currentUser

        new UserContext(currentUser);
        httpRequest.getSession().setAttribute(USER_VO_LABEL,
         currentUser);
```

```
        }
        else {UserContext.clear();}

        try {filterChain.doFilter(request, response);}
        finally {UserContext.clear();}

    }
```
Source: /src/j2ee/architect/handbook/chap12/UserContextManagementFilter.java

If your application has logic that presents different options for users with different security roles, then as a practical matter you need to be able to emulate different users for testing purposes. As an example, additional menu options might appear for managers that aren't available for staff. We can extend the user context paradigm to handle emulating other users as well. Listing 12.2 provides an example of how the user context concept could be extended to allow user emulation. For testing purposes, merely set the emulated user value object to values you want to test with.

Listing 12.2: Sample User Emulation Logic

```
public class UserContext {
public UserVO getUser() {
    if (this.emulatedUser != null) {
      return this.emulatedUser;
    }
    return this.currentUser;
  }

  public void setEmulatedUser(UserVO emulatedUser) {
    this.emulatedUser = emulatedUser;
  }
}
```
Source: /src/j2ee/architect/handbook/common/user/UserContext.java

ERROR-HANDLING CONSIDERATIONS

One topic that always comes up in presentation layer coding is error handling for exceptions that a user could correct. For example, many sites allow you to register as a user. Most of these sites have requirements for the user name you select. For example, many will require at least eight characters. If the user were to enter a user name that's too short, the user could easily correct their input and resubmit their registration. In correctable errors like this, we don't want to throw a runtime exception. Instead, we'll want to display a message telling the user what field is incorrect and what the correct answer requirements are.

Most web frameworks have a strategy for handling correctable errors and user messages. However, generic strategies for user messages tend to not be aesthetically pleasing. Furthermore, it's likely that the business logic layer would identify the correctable errors. To make the business logic layer aware of the specific web framework in use, so that the framework strategy could be used, is undesirable because it violates the separation of concerns principle. The business logic layer should not be aware of its execution context. One strategy is to create a custom checked exception (e.g., `CorrectionsRequired-Exception`) that contains information about the error and an appropriate message. The presentation layer would be forced to catch the exception and properly format the error message for the user. This is a little more work, but it does allow flexibility for handling correctable errors.

SUPPORTING MOBILE DEVICES

As mobile device support is a requirement for larger Java EE applications these days, it deserves focus. Mobile devices can be supported in largely two ways: through the mobile browser as a website specifically designed to display on smaller screens; and as a collection of services that support native mobile device applications. Providing a Java EE site catering to smaller screens is usually the easiest, as it only affects the presentation layer. For simple sites, it is possible for the same markup to be used for large and small display sizes by using different CSS style sheets for different types of displays. For those that aren't familiar, this can be accomplished using the `media` attribute. A couple of simple examples follow:

```
<link rel="stylesheet" type="text/css" href="stylesheet.css"
      media="screen" />
<link rel="stylesheet" type="text/css" href="stylesheet-small.
css" media="handheld" />
```

The media attribute also supports attributes for assigning style sheets based on display height and width and a variety of more specific characteristics than `screen` and `handheld`.

As a practical matter, this technique only works on simple sites. For complex sites with a large number of controls, it is common to slim down the site (provide less content and fewer features) for devices with smaller screens. For these sites, there will be two or more sets of markup. The device is redirected to the markup that will best display on the size of the screen it has. There are several ways to accomplish this redirection. The simplest I've seen is through Javascript.

```
<script type="text/javascript">
 <!--
  if (screen.width <= 700) {
  window.location = "http://mobile.mysite.com";
  }
 //-->
</script>
```

Another alternative is to provide web services that allow a native mobile device application to obtain data and post transactions. This option can be used to provide a more robust end-user experience, but it requires more work and is more expensive. Providing a Java EE site that supports native mobile applications will largely affect the deployment layer. Most mobile developers consider Restful web services easier to consume than SOAP. Furthermore, most mobile developers consider JSON format data easier to use than XML.

There are several products that support reading and formatting JSON data. This product selection should be treated just like any other product selection; I provide guidance on making technology product decisions in the next chapter. Two popular open source products in this space are Jackson (http://jackson.codehaus.org/) and GSON (https://code.google.com/p/google-gson/). Likewise, there are multiple products that provide Restful web service support. Two popular open source products in this space are Apache CXF (http://cxf.apache.org/) and Restlet (http://restlet.org/).

It is not uncommon for native applications to require users to authenticate. How the mobile application manages authenticating the user depends on the security product chosen. It is not unusual for the mobile application to maintain cookies with security tokens that the server can interrogate or provide credentials. Regardless, all communication with mobile devices should be encrypted (https) at the very least.

CODING GUIDELINES

Keep every web service, EJB, or presentation layer class thin. Testing these classes requires a container. While environments in which to test these classes are generally available and unit tests can be written against these classes, deploying changes to these classes is generally more time consuming. If you want to optimize development time, delegating work performed at this level to classes that are locally debugable and don't require container services is advised.

Keep HTML markup (e.g., JSP page) embedded logic thin. While tag libraries, EL expressions, and other features make it possible to embed complicated logic in HTML markup, writing unit tests for these pages that ensure they behave correctly for users is difficult and time consuming. Anything in markup that increases the number of test cases increases ongoing maintenance costs much more than adding those test cases in classes where comprehensive unit tests are easier to write and maintain. Of course, some of this will be unavoidable for many applications. In places where you have the option of delegating complicated logic to more easily tested classes, do it.

COMMON MISTAKES

Putting business logic in presentation layer or deployment layer classes. Business logic tends to make JSPs and servlets more complex and difficult to maintain. Furthermore, this logic isn't easily reusable in other contexts. Consequently, business logic incorporated in this layer has a higher chance of being copied and violating the Don't Repeat Yourself (DRY) principle.

Not taking advantage of templating technologies. Most presentation products have templating features that make it easier to reuse HTML markup and violating DRY. This will keep the presentation less verbose and often easier to maintain. For example, I can't imagine implementing a JSF application without using Facelets' templating features (which were formally incorporated into the JSF specification in version 2.0). Struts, another popular presentation product, also provides templating features. Not utilizing templating technology often leads to large repeated sections of HTML markup.

CHAPTER 13

MAKING TECHNOLOGY PRODUCT SELECTIONS

It is common for architects to guide the selection process for technology products. Sometimes the products selected are directly utilized by end-users. Sometimes the products selected are libraries incorporated into applications to save development time and support resources. My experience is that most organizations don't approach technology selection in a very structured or organized way. In this chapter, I present strategies for making technology product decisions. As the choice of which of the many web frameworks to use is a common technology product choice, I use it as an example.

The choice of a web framework is one of the most important product selections made for Java EE applications. Framework choice is not an easy decision, and the potential effect of these choices on development and maintenance costs is large. Given the importance of these decisions and product choices in general, let's spend some time detailing strategies for making these types of decisions.

PRODUCT DECISION CRITERIA

With regard to web service or web presentation frameworks, there are many product choices available. We need a way to rate these products and hopefully differentiate them to the point where a logical choice will develop. The "attributes" on which we rate these frameworks in essence become decision criteria.

Common decision criteria that normally make the list in one way or another are as follows:

- Fitness for Objective
- Ease of Use
- Market Share
- Switching Costs
- Expected Cost Savings (over a custom solution)
- Level of Community Activity
- Performance
- Dependency Requirements
- Licensing

Not all of these criteria are equally weighted; some may be more important than others. I usually weight each of these criteria with a high, medium, or low. Furthermore, I usually rank each product choice with respect to these criteria from 1 to 10, with 10 being the best rating.

Fitness for Objective. Is the product choice designed to be used for your intended purpose? Are others using it for a similar purpose? This criterion supports the principle "Swim with the stream." By using products as they are designed, you increase the likelihood that the resulting application will benefit from future product improvements. For example, relational database products are optimized for third-normal form. In the early days of relational databases, performance of joins was a frequent issue. However, over time, database products have solved these performance issues as relational database theory incents normalized designs. Users who used normalized designs benefited the most from these improvements.

These types of criteria are most often phrased as a list of specific features. For example, when choosing a Content Management System, the list of features measuring "fitness for objective" might include spell checking, audit/change history, WYSIWYG editing capabilities, etc. This feature list is designed to help you determine if the product choice is consistent with how you wish to use the product.

Drawing an example using a web presentation framework, let's suppose the business objective is to delegate presentation design to HTML-literate specialists (which typically cost less and are more plentiful). With that objective, any presentation product that leveraged HTML skill sets would be advantageous. A choice of Apache's Wicket (http://wicket.apache.org/), which relies heavily on Java coding skill sets, would not fit the business objectives as well as frameworks that were HTML-based.

You also have the best chance of capitalizing on the experience of others.

Frequently, problems—and hopefully their solutions—are reported in blogs on the Internet. The chance that a problem you encounter has been previously reported and solved increases if your use is consistent with how the product was designed to be used.

Ease of Use. Choosing products that are easy to use optimizes training costs, lowers development and support time, and potentially reduces the mean time from defect reporting to fix. Ease of use also makes the product more accessible to a wide variety of developers and provides management with greater flexibility.

Let's consider examples at both ends of the spectrum. To a development team that receives detailed HTML page designs for the applications they build, web presentation frameworks that rely on HTML templating, such as JSP, Freemarker, Velocity and Java Server Faces, will be easier to use than Wicket, which consists of Java code exclusively.

Market Share. Choosing products that are more widely used makes it easier to acquire developers with previous experience with that product. It also increases the chances that solutions will be posted on the Internet for problems encountered in development. Also, products with low market shares are at risk for being abandoned and, consequently, will no longer be enhanced. Yes, if the product is open source, you can enhance it internally, but rarely will organizations fund projects like that. In that case, it's usually better to switch products.

Market share numbers are usually hard to come by. I've found two proxies for market share: search engine keyword search data and job posting data. Search engine keyword search data can be obtained from Google Trends (http://www.google.com/trends/explore). A good source for job posting data is available at www.indeed.com trending page (http://www.indeed.com/job-trends). As an example, let's look at the popularity of several web presentation frameworks as presented in figure13.1.

As you might expect, Apache Struts is the market leader followed by Java Server Faces (JSF) and Spring MVC. Note that job posting data, which I can't present due to licensing restrictions, show Spring MVC in second place with JSF in third. There are sometimes differences between trends noted by job posting data and keyword search data; you'll have to make a judgment as to which results more closely represent market share. All other web presentation frameworks included in my search had small market shares compared to those three.

Figure 13.1: Search Engine Keyword Trend Data for Web Presentation Frameworks

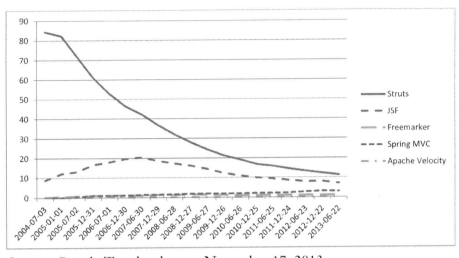

Source: Google Trends taken on November 17, 2013.

My purpose isn't to advertise for Struts, Spring MVC, or JSF. My purpose is to illustrate how easily you can get an estimate of market share of a particular framework or product; and that information should be a factor in the decision being made. If you use a web presentation framework not listed here, I invite you to do your own comparisons, including that framework.

As another example, I've run a similar comparison for several web services frameworks commonly used with Java EE applications. I present it in figure 13.2.

Figure 13.2: Search Engine Keyword Trend Data for Web Services Frameworks

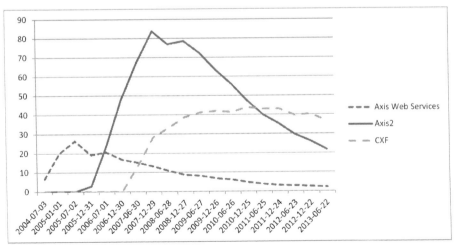

It is surprising, but Apache Axis is still the market leader, despite the fact that the product was rewritten and released as Axis2. The Axis product was last released in 2006, and all development effort has shifted to Axis2. Another Apache product, CXF, appears in second place, but may in fact be the market leader relatively soon. This information should be a factor in making a web service framework decision.

Switching Costs. No matter what your product choice is today, it's always possible that your requirements will change or that the product you chose will be depreciated in the future or become obsolete. In that case, any applications using that product will need to be changed to use a competing product instead. Because of this, products that can more easily be switched out to use a competitor should receive a higher rating than those that can't.

There's no objective measurement for switching costs. I usually assign a high, medium, or low rating based on a brief survey of product documentation examples. In the case of web services frameworks and web presentation frameworks, switching costs for all products are high and cause products to receive a low rating. Because this factor doesn't differentiate any of the products, it's not important when discussing web presentation or web services frameworks. I mention it because it does differentiate other types of products and should be considered.

Expected Cost Savings (over a custom solution). A custom solution is always an option, but not always an attractive one. In order to estimate expected savings of choosing one product or another, you need a comparison base. That is, choosing product 1 over product 2 will save us 200 hours of work. But, to provide such an estimate, you need to have a product to compare to. I usually choose a custom/homegrown solution as that comparison product.

Having said that, the custom solution—let's say for publishing a web service—doesn't mean replicating all functionality in the Apache Axis2 product, per se. It means producing a publishing method just good enough to publish only what's needed for your project.

If you choose the same comparison base product (e.g., a custom solution) for all products in consideration, then expected savings becomes comparable. The product with the most savings will be rated the highest, and the product with the least savings rated the least.

As an example, at a recent client, we needed to implement a single sign-on (SSO) product. During the course of the evaluation, we estimated that it would take approximately 1200 hours of development to custom build an SSO solution. We did similar estimates of implementation costs for each of the open source product candidates. We eventually chose JOSSO (www.josso.org), with which we could make slight customizations and implement it enterprise-wide for a combined cost of approximately 200 hours.

Level of Community Activity. If some of your product choices are open source projects, it's less risky to choose projects that are actively maintained than those projects that are not. The chance of a product becoming obsolete is much greater for projects that aren't maintained. Furthermore, you have little hope that bugs encountered with the product will ever be fixed or that the product features will be enhanced.

One of the easiest ways to measure community activity is to average the number of releases per year for the past three years. This information is available for most open source projects. Another way is to measure the mean time between releases for the past three years. My choice of three years is an arbitrary choice. What's important is that you measure each product identically.

If you're concerned that one project might be skewing the statistics by releasing more quickly with fewer features, you can always measure the number of defects and improvements in those releases for the same time period. However, gathering this information, while available, takes more effort. Furthermore, it misses the point.

What's important is to detect projects that have very little or no activity and rate them lower. As an example, the Apache Axis2 web services product has had nine releases in the past three years. The Apache CXF web services product has had thirteen releases in the past three years. From these statistics, it's clear that both projects are very actively maintained. I would rate them equal with regard to community activity, despite the slight number difference in the number of releases.

Performance. Yes, performance is a consideration. However, you might not need to go to the expense of constructing and running performance comparisons for these products yourself. Often for mainstream frameworks and products, you can find published performance comparisons. Even if those comparisons are on old versions of the product, the time and expense of constructing and running your own performance benchmarks often isn't worth the effort if published accounts are available.

For example, surveying the Internet for performance benchmarks of web services Axis2 and CXF, I found four separate accounts that judged performance of both products favorable, with minor differences noted for different data binding strategies. I don't indicate those sources as this text will be dated by the time you read it; you can do your own research. My point is that it's possible to gather information about performance comparisons between products without going to the expense of constructing a rigorous set of tests yourself.

Dependency Requirements. The fewer the dependency requirements, the less chance of library version conflicts. A library version conflict is when one product requires version x of a library while another product requires version y. As an example, say one product requires Apache Commons Logging V1.0 while another requires V1.1. As there are API differences between the two, one of the two products using it has a chance of running into a "method not found" error at runtime.

An open source product called JarAnalyzer (http://www.kirkk.com/main/ Main/JarAnalyzer) will let you know about jar file dependencies. However, its analysis doesn't go far enough to tell you about method signature issues that can cause runtime linkage issues like what I described above.

With respect to web service and web presentation frameworks, most choices have large numbers of dependencies. The only exception I know of is the Freemarker (http://freemarker.sourceforge.net/) template engine, which is used by some to produce dynamic HTML instead of JSPs. Having said that, Freemarker has other limitations as a web presentation framework and might not be your best choice when some of the other decision criteria are considered as well.

Licensing. Many organizations have guidelines over what types of open source licenses are acceptable. This is particularly true for software that will be sold as a product as some open source licenses have restrictions. Most organizations will have a standard list of open source licenses they will accept and a process for evaluating new licenses as needed.

MAKING A PRODUCT DECISION

When doing research for a particular product, it usually involves multiple people. Typically, it's the application architect that facilitates these kinds of decisions. In the first meeting, I usually suggest a set of features/decision criteria (patterned after the concepts described above) and get general consensus as to what criteria these products will be judged on. It's possible that additional criteria might be proposed and discussed after this meeting, and that's okay.

Additionally, I suggest a list of products that should be considered and get general consensus for that list. At this stage, if a product remotely appears to have a chance at fulfilling the business requirements for your project, it should be added to the list. Bad suggestions will get eliminated down the line as different features are identified and measured. You also don't want to appear to be gaming the selection process by unilaterally eliminating somebody's product suggestion upfront.

The next topic of discussion is the weight that should be given each criterion. As I stated in the previous section, some criteria are less important than others. For example, fitness of purpose is much more important than dependency requirements for most product decisions.

Many developers will over-rate the importance of performance in making framework decisions. Slight differences in performance aren't material to most organizations. Just because one web service framework has a slight edge over another in a given test, doesn't mean that you should necessarily choose the highest performing product; other criteria need to be considered.

As an example, I participated in a process to evaluate Content Management System (CMS) products for use with one of my client's public sites. This selection was conducted in the summer of 2010. The reader should note that a CMS product was already in use by this client but had significant limitations. In the first meeting of the people conducting this research, we decided upon an initial list of products to evaluate, a list of features and characteristics that would be examined and evaluated, and weights that would be assigned to individual features and characteristics. That list did include the CMS product currently used since status quo is always an option.

The project scope was limited by management to open source products, as there was no funding for proprietary software purchases. Furthermore, management established the task force personnel and time frame limits for the evaluation. With those guidelines in mind, the list of products included in the evaluation was determined by group consensus to be as in table 13.1:

Table 13.1: Products Included in a CMS Product Decision

Product	Version
OpenCms	7.5
Drupal	6.17
Joomla	1.5.318
WordPress	2.9.2
Alfresco	3.3
DotNetNuke	5.4.2
Typo3	4.3

The versions of the products evaluated were the current stable releases for those products at the time of the *start* of the evaluation. There are many more products that could have been considered, but including every product in the CMS space would have been too labor intensive, given the number of people on the task force and the time limit imposed. Therefore, this narrowed-down list was determined by a consensus of members in that task force.

Additionally, a list of product features and characteristics were determined, as well as an initial weight that would be assigned to those features. This list of features and weights are listed in table 13.2. In addition, I've listed the type of decision criteria supported by each individual feature listing.

Table 13.2: Features Evaluated in a CMS Product Decision

Decision Criteria Type	Feature (1–10)	Priority (High/Medium/Low)
Dependency Requirements	Single Sign-on Compatability	High
Dependency Requirements	Supported Databases	Medium
Dependency Requirements	Supported Platforms	Medium
Ease of Use	Content Organization Support	High
Ease of Use	Friendly URL Support	Low
Ease of Use	Image Resizing Support	Low
Ease of Use	Macro Language	Medium
Ease of Use	Menu Support	High
Ease of Use	Site Map Support	Medium
Ease of Use	Spell/Grammar Checking	Medium
Ease of Use	Templating Support	High
Ease of Use	Wysiwyg Editing Support	High
Fitness for Objective	Advertising Management	Low
Fitness for Objective	Content Approval	High
Fitness for Objective	Content Scheduling	Low
Fitness for Objective	Dead-link Detection	Low
Fitness for Objective	Import/Export Support	High
Fitness for Objective	International Character Support	Medium
Fitness for Objective	Online Administration	High
Fitness for Objective	RSS Support	High
Fitness for Objective	Search Support	High
Fitness for Objective	Version Control	High
Fitness for Objective	Workflow Support	Medium
Level of Community Activity	Number of Releases Since Jan. 1, 2008	Medium
Market Share	Market Share (percent Job Postings as proxy)	Medium
Ownership Impact	Commercial Training Options	Medium
Ownership Impact	Custom Add-on/Plug-in Support	High
Ownership Impact	Documentation	Medium
Ownership Impact	Usage License	Medium
Ownership Impact	Vendor Support Availability	High
Ownership Impact	Windows Support	High

Performance	Multi-User Concurrent Editing Support	High
Performance	Support 3x the Current Number of Pages	High
Performance	Support the Current Public Site Transaction Volume (pages/sec)	High
Security	Audit Trail	Medium
Switching Costs	Dynamic Content	High
Switching Costs	Static Content	Medium

The next topic of discussion for that initial meeting is dividing the work for evaluating products with respect to the criteria that's been chosen. Usually, I suggest rating each product for each criterion using a rating of 10 to 1, with 10 being the best rating and 1 being the worst. As to dividing the work, there are a couple of strategies, each with advantages and disadvantages.

The first strategy is to assign each person to completely rank one or more products with respect for each of the criteria. Considering a web services example, have one person rate the Apache Axis2 product for all decision criteria decided upon. This has the advantage of minimizing the learning curve for the team member and highly leveraging the learning they experience. It has the disadvantage that rating standard differences will occur between products. That is, the person who rated switching costs for Axis2 will be different than the person who rated CXF. The ratings for these products might differ because they have different evaluators; not because of product differences.

Another strategy is to assign all decision criteria to the team (all members). Their responsibility is to evaluate all products against each criterion. This increases the likelihood that different products are rated in a consistent way. It also guarantees that any one reviewer can't materially bias the group for or against a particular product due to private concerns. The disadvantage here is that each team member has to learn about each product, which costs more in terms of time spent. However, I personally prefer this approach. Usually, with these types of decisions, they are important enough that it's worth the additional time spent. It also provides the opportunity to question another team member's ratings if there is disagreement.

Once product decisions for presentation and deployment wrappers such as web services are made, the products need to be integrated into your project(s), and usage and coding guidelines established for their use.

CHAPTER 14

BUILDING ARCHITECTURAL COMPONENTS

Architectural components are classes and static utilities generic enough to be used for many applications. After you've identified a need for an architectural component, your first step should usually be looking in the marketplace for a component that meets that need. I recommend starting your marketplace search by checking out open source alternatives. If you have the necessary budget, commercial alternatives should be included. Open source alternatives, which can be just as good as commercial software, are usually much easier to acquire and a lot easier on the budget. At the end of the chapter, I highlight some of my favorite open source websites.

Open source projects that routinely appear in my projects are the following:

- Apache Commons (http://commons.apache.org)
- Lang—General Java language utilities
- IO—Common Utilities for classes in java.io
- BeanUtils—Utilities for manipulating Java bean and POJO classes
- Collections—Utilities for manipulating Collection classes such as Maps and Sets
- DbUtils—Utilities for simplifying JDBC code
- Apache Log4J (http://logging.apache.org/log4j/)

One issue with component software, both open source and commercial, is the extreme variance in quality. Some components are easy to understand and use; others are inscrutable and impractical. In this chapter, I list the capabilities that developers generally associate with quality components. You can use this list to evaluate open source or commercial component software. I also present a series of tips and techniques for creating your own architectural components with those capabilities considered the marks of quality.

The role of architectural components is illustrated in figure14.1.

Figure 14.1: Using Architectural Components within a Layered Architecture

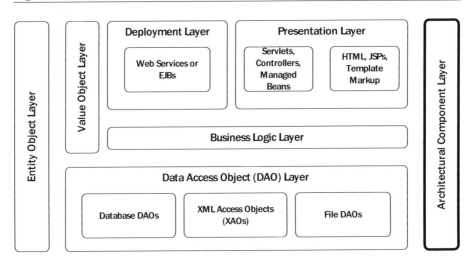

COMPONENT QUALITY

High-quality architectural components have the following capabilities:

- Shorten development time and effort
- Shorten expected maintenance time and effort
- Work in many applications because they are generic
- Work as advertised

These traits are desirable for any component software, whether components are commercial, open source, or authored by you.

A common guideline people use when judging software is: if they have to consult a manual to do basic tasks, they judge the software "too hard to use." You can use much the same standard when assessing component software. I consider component software difficult to use if either of the following is true:

- You have to read more than two pages of material to install and configure the component.
- It takes more than an hour from installing to using the component for a basic task.

A common mistake people use when designing architectural components is choosing a scope that is too large. A large scope usually results in a complex component that will take a long time to become available and will have a long learning curve. I use the 80/20 rule when selecting features to implement in an architectural component. Component designers shouldn't get bogged down with features people will rarely use.

MAKING COMPONENTS EASY TO USE

If you're evaluating component software, ease of use should be one of the deciding criteria. If you're creating an architectural component, there are a number of things you can do (that many component developers don't do) to make your component easy to use.

Limit the instructions for basic tasks to a one-page cheat sheet. You can have a more detailed document for sophisticated, unusual tasks. The longer the material developers need to read to get going, the higher the percentage of developers who will give up in the process and look for something else.

Minimize the number of statements necessary to perform basic tasks. One of the chief benefits to using a component is eliminating code in the application. A one-line call is ideal because it eliminates typing and reduces the number of classes and methods you need to learn.

One way to achieve a one-line call is to rely on a static method. This eliminates having to instantiate anything. The choice to make that call static is more than just a tactical choice. As examples, consider any of the `Utils` classes (e.g., `StringUtils`, `NumberUtils`, `ExceptionUtils` from Apache Commons Lang). These classes are replete with convenient static methods that accomplish much with one line of code.

Minimize the number of arguments necessary to perform basic tasks. You can accomplish this by providing multiple overloads. Some of those overloads have small numbers of arguments with sensible defaults for the rest.

As an example, let's consider the `reflectionEquals` methods in the `Equals-Builder` for Apache Commons Lang. This class makes it easy to implement `equals()` in any class. `ReflectionEquals` at a minimum requires two arguments; the values being compared. However, more sophisticated overloads optionally provide you control over which fields are considered and how much of the inheritance hierarchy is considered. As most don't need the additional control, these additional arguments are optional.

Separate the classes meant for public consumption from those needed internally by the API. The more classes a component has, the longer it takes to find the class with the functionality you want. Keeping all these classes together just adds to the time required to learn the API.

One way to solve this problem is to move classes not meant for public consumption to a separate package that's documented as "for internal use only." Users don't have to wade through low-level classes they don't need yet to find the functionality they want.

As examples of this, Apache Commons Logging separates internal classes into a separate package (`org.apache.commons.logging.impl`). The Quartz scheduling package (http://quartz-scheduler.org) uses the same technique by placing internally used classes into package `org.quartz.impl`. This technique concisely informs users that they need not bother with the documentation for these classes as they are unlikely to need it.

Provide samples that are easy to copy and include an index. Make it easy to find a sample that is close to what the user wants. Most of us learn by example and don't type very quickly; having something to copy from saves users time. A good place for short samples is within the JavaDoc.

As examples, both `EqualsBuilder` and `HashcodeBuilder` from Apache Commons Lang provide usage examples in their JavaDoc that can easily be copied into your code and quickly be changed to suit your needs. As another example, the Primefaces project, which is a library of Java Server Faces (JSF) components, provides a demo site (http://www.primefaces.org/showcase-labs/ui/home.jsf) that includes easy-to-access source code for easy copying into your own project.

Limit dependencies on other APIs. I once was forced to implement a poorly written scheduling component for a client (I wasn't given a choice). This component used two internal components that were hard to use and complex to configure. I've since learned how to avoid inflicting the same kind of pain on users of my open source components: use interfaces to decouple.

Check all arguments on all methods meant for public consumption and produce clear error messages for invalid inputs. Rather than degenerating into derivative exceptions (e.g., null pointer exceptions), put information on how to correct problems in the exceptions. For example, the error message "Invalid format type argument" isn't as useful as an error message like "Invalid format type 'foo.' Valid types are the following constants in this class: PDF, HTML, XLS, and DOC." Simply displaying the erroneous value passed to a method in the error message might shorten the time it takes to debug and correct the issue.

Avoid throwing "checked" exceptions. Throwing "unchecked" exceptions, which extend `RuntimeException`, is preferred, because it doesn't force the user into as much `try/catch` logic. Not needing as much code to use a component definitely makes it easier to use. The only exception (no pun intended) to this is if the caller can reasonably provide alternative business logic in response to the exception; however, this is rare. For a more detailed discussion of this rather controversial concept, see chapter 9.

MAKING COMPONENTS EASY TO CONFIGURE AND CONTROL

Minimize the number of properties a user must configure. Some components use a properties file, which is a file of key and value pairs, to manage configuration settings. These files are often used in conjunction with the `java.util.Properties` object.

The more properties users need in order to choose values for running your component, the longer and harder your component is to configure. You can alleviate this problem by choosing sensible defaults for as many configuration properties as possible. In addition, clear error messages for incorrect configurations can make your components easy to use.

Minimize the required complexity of any needed XML documents. The more complex the document structure, the harder the component is to configure and control. Jakarta's Ant project is an excellent example of using XML files effectively. Ant is an XML scripting utility commonly used for application builds. Its scripting language is XML based, and its structure is simple and intuitive. Although Ant has an extensive array of options, it also has sensible defaults and good documentation. This open source project is available at http://ant.apache.org/.

Produce clear error messages on invalid configurations. Components must have clear error messages. Nothing is more aggravating than trying to figure out why code you didn't write is degenerating into a `NullPointerException`. Clear error messages can make the difference in a developer's perception of your component.

Provide numerous configuration file examples that are easy to copy. This is especially important if the component is capable of complex configurations. I suggest providing basic examples as well as complex ones.

Limit installation and configuration instructions to a one-page cheat sheet. If the instructions are too long and complex, it reduces the benefit of using the component in the first place. Having an expanded document for complete functionality is fine, but users doing basic tasks shouldn't have to read more than a page or two.

OPEN SOURCE ALTERNATIVES

Open source alternatives have blossomed, so much so that searching for open source alternatives for a given need has become a complicated task.

Most organizations accept open source usage with guidelines. Many companies will define open source licenses that may be used (e.g., Apache License, Version 2.x and others). Should a desired product not adopt a standard license verbatim, most companies provide an approval path so that licenses can be evaluated by their legal department.

Some organizations are wary of using open source products. The perception is that these products are essentially unsupported. And while the price of open source technologies will fit into any corporate budget, many organizations like the security of having a technical support number to call when problems come up. There are really two issues here. The first is the practical issue of being able to solve technical problems with an open source product to get your applications working, and keep them working. The second is having someone else to blame (or potentially sue) if your product selection decision turns out to be a bad one. Usually, companies with anti-open-source policies are more worried about blame assignment. Thankfully, resistance to open source usage appears to be declining.

Resolving Technical Issues

The following are some steps I've gone through to solve problems with open source component software. Step 1 is the simplest solution. If that doesn't work, you'll need to perform step 2 before trying any of the remaining steps, which are listed in order of simplicity.

- **Step 1:** Search the product's bug list. True, many open source products don't have formal support organizations. However, many products provide access to a bug list and provide a way to report identified bugs. Often, the problem you are having has been discovered and reported by someone else. Perhaps a workaround or solution has been posted.

- **Step 2:** Search the Internet. Often generic Internet searches will reveal postings of others who have encountered the same problem. Often, solutions will be posted in the same news groups or blogs.

- **Step 3:** Upgrade to the latest version. If a newer version of the product is available, a good time to try it out is when you're trying to resolve a technical issue. Maybe the problem is the result of a bug that someone caught and fixed. Often, the work involved in upgrading is just including a more recent jar(s) in your classpath.

- **Step 4:** Evaluate competing products. I look for competing open source products that do the same thing. If I can easily switch products, I'll try that. I once had an issue with an open source Java FTP client API that had a memory leak. When a news group search didn't reveal an answer to my problem, I switched to another open source FTP client API.

- **Step 5:** Debug your test scenario. Although this isn't a pleasant task, it invariably enables you to determine the root issue. Once you know what the problem is, you can start looking for a workaround.

- **Step 6:** Modify component code to fix the problem. This should be treated as an option of last resort. If you use an altered version of an open source product, you'll be on your own for problem investigations after that. You'll never know if the problem you're experiencing was a result of a product bug or the result of your change. If you have to modify the code, take the trouble to report the bug and solution to the developers that produced the component. Most developers of open source products would release a new version with a bug fix. As soon as you can get to an unaltered version of the component that works for your application, you should use it.

Mitigating Political Risk

The second issue surrounding the use of open source component software is the corporate need to have someone to blame if the choice of open source product doesn't work out as well as intended. I can't think of a way to completely solve the issue, but I can think of many ways to mitigate the risk.

Suggest a commercial software component along with open source alternatives and keep any documentation of the decision. This tactic effectively makes the component decision a group effort. If an open source decision is ever questioned, you can frame the issue as a group decision and point to budgetary advantages.

Track which open source products you use and keep source as well as binary distributions. You won't want to find out at the time you're having trouble that the source for the version you're using is no longer available. As a last resort, you can try to fix the problem yourself.

Identify competitors to the open source product. This shortens the time it takes to switch components should you need to do so. It also helps document due diligence in the product search.

COMPONENT USAGE GUIDELINES

Whether a third-party component is open source or not, one of your goals should be minimizing business risk. A large part of that is keeping switching costs small so that if a mistake is made, it will be easier to correct.

Minimize the classes directly using third-party components with direct competitors. Products with direct competitors are products that have a focused feature set offered by multiple products. For example, logging products fall into this category. Developers have conflicting opinions about which logging package should be adopted. While the main players are Apache Log4J, Slf4J, and the logging framework within the JDK itself, there's no consensus as to which package should be utilized. Given this, I usually have application code use a logging proxy that leverages one of these logging frameworks underneath. Should there be a need to change logging packages, the use of third-party specific code doesn't pervade the applications.

You can isolate dependence on a particular product by creating a proxy class. Continuing with the logging product example, I often create an application `Logger` class that serves as a proxy for an underlying logger provided by one of the logging products. As application code relies solely on the proxy class, it's fairly easy to change logging products if need be as it's only the proxy that would need to be changed.

Another example of this concept is scheduling packages. Quartz (http://quartz-scheduler.org) is the product I usually leverage, but there are several competing products available. If enterprise scheduling considerations arise, it's possible that the scheduling product might be changed. Usually, I provide a base class that implements any needed interfaces required by the scheduling package. Hence, this base class is the only class that directly interfaces with the scheduling package and can easily be changed to use a different package instead.

Some third-party products have too broad a scope for a proxy technique to be effective. For example, Apache Commons Lang, Collections, and BeanUtils packages provide utility libraries. The work involved to create proxy classes for all the utilities would be extensive, as the scope of these libraries is very broad and would provide very little benefit since these products have no direct competitors.

You can use this technique with virtually any software component. Remember that you also limit reliance on any third-party component exception classes so that your application relies on internal classes, not external ones. To accomplish this, have the proxy surround usage of the underlying product with a `try/catch` block. Any component-based exceptions generated can be converted to application-based exceptions and prevent unwanted reliance on third-party exception classes.

CHAPTER 15

APPLICATION ARCHITECTURE STRATEGIES

To ensure that your applications have internal consistency, you need to establish strategies from the outset for logging, exception handling, threading, and configuration management. Most developers have preferences for each of these areas. If your team has many developers and you let them use their preferences, you will create an application that is internally inconsistent and harder to maintain. This chapter offers strategies for each aspect of application architecture. In this section, I've articulated examples of strategies I've used in the past. Once you establish the strategy, don't be afraid to refine it with additional detail to suit the needs and comfort level of your developers.

LOGGING STRATEGIES

Application classes should not depend on a specific logger. General-use components should be able to use any logging package an application adopts. This can be done by having one class in the application acting as a log proxy, delegating the log write to Log4J, JDK Logging, or one of the other logging packages. Listing 15.1 is an example of an application logger proxy implementation.

Listing 15.1: Sample Log Proxy Using SLF4J

```java
public class Logger implements java.io.Serializable
{

    public Logger (String loggerName) {
        this.loggerName = loggerName;
        initLogger();
    }

    public void error(String messageFormat, Object ...argArray)
        {
        getLogger().error(messageFormat,argArray);
    }

        public void info(String messageFormat, Object ...argArray)
            {
        getLogger().info(messageFormat, argArray);
    }

        public void warn(String messageFormat, Object ...argArray)
            {
        getLogger().warn(messageFormat, argArray);
    }

        public void debug(String messageFormat, Object ...argArray
        )    {
        getLogger().debug(messageFormat, argArray);
    }
}
```

The Apache open source component software Commons has a package called Commons Logging designed to fill this need. Unfortunately, it is rather heavy (despite being billed as intentionally "lightweight") and not very easy to use. It requires an XML parser and has a more complicated configuration scheme. I consider Commons Logging more hassle than it's worth.

The open source product Simple Logging Facade for Java (SLF4J) is an excellent product that meets this need. This product is a generic proxy for Log4J, JDK Logging, Commons Logging, and other logging products. It's easy to install and use. I've started using SLF4J in my own open source projects. I still, however, use a logger proxy class, such as listing 15.1, for business applications as this space is still changing and evolving. Many popular open source products, such as Hibernate, ActiveMQ, and others have adopted it.

Limit coding for logging methods to one line. Logging is done so frequently that you'll save a lot of time by reducing the code it takes to log. SLF4J introduced a nice feature that assisted developers in reducing logging code by providing basic message formatting features. For instance, consider the following log example:

Listing 15.2: Sample Log Illustrating Formatting Feature

```
logger.debug("Application id set to {}", applicationId);
```

This feature accomplishes code reduction by formatting the message for the developer. It also reduces risk as the developer code contains fewer operators and doesn't have to check for null values in formatting the message.

Also, for performance purposes, it is not uncommon to check if logging is set to debug before issuing a debug log message to improve performance. SLF4J provides this check automatically without developers having to code the additional conditional.

Note that the logger proxy in listing 15.1 supports SLF4J message formatting capabilities. Were I to switch from SLF4J to another logging package, the logger proxy would have to provide similar message formatting abilities to keep from impacting the application code that uses it. Message formatting capabilities reduce risk by eliminating custom logic to format logging messages. Message formatting also provides performance improvement by only formatting messages meeting the current log level setting. For instance, if your logger is configured to provide info level output, debug messages will not be formatted as they aren't needed. The benefits of message format support are large enough that I assume the risk of a slightly higher switching cost, should the need to switch logging packages arise.

Bundle needed information with exceptions that you throw. One of the main reasons for logging is to provide information needed to resolve a bug resulting in an exception. This additional logging code adds additional risk since exception code isn't typically tested as thoroughly. Hence, there's usually a larger chance of excepting (e.g., from a `NullPointerException`) during exception message formatting than with non-exception code.

Apache Commons Lang provides a contexted exception ability starting with V3.0 that reduces this risk by making it easy and less risky to include additional information with the exception itself (see classes `ContextedException` and `ContextedRuntimeException` from Commons Lang). This additional information will be present when this exception is logged. Consider the example in listing 15.3.

Listing 15.3: Sample Contexted Exception Example

```
    throw new ContextedRuntimeException("Error creating
        application"
, exception)
.addContextValue("application id", applicationId)
.addContextValue("customer id", customerId);
```

When the exception in listing 15.3 is logged, the context labels and values will automatically appear in the log, along with the error message and stack trace. Note that application code doesn't increase risk of a derivative exception by adding conditional logging logic or formatting logic. Note that if it weren't for the contexted exception ability, developers would have to add logging code to supply the information needed to resolve the bug.

Log transaction exceptions only once. Logging exceptions multiple times will greatly inflate your logs and make a specific exception pertaining to a reported defect much harder to find. You can avoid the problem of repeating log messages by logging exceptions at the entry points only. For example, it's easy to implement a servlet filter that will log exceptions for any web transactions. This ensures that exceptions are logged only once. This advice assumes that you've bundled any additional information needed to resolve the error with the exception itself, as described earlier in this chapter. Listing 15.4 illustrates a servlet filter of this type.

Listing 15.4: Logging Servlet Filter Example

```
public void doFilter(ServletRequest request, ServletResponse
        response,
            FilterChain chain) throws IOException,
        ServletException {
        try {chain.doFilter(request, response);}
        catch (Throwable t) {
            logger.error("Web Transaction Error", t);
            ServletUtils.reThrowServletFilterException(t);
        }

    }
```

Source: Class net.admin4j.ui.filters.ErrorLoggingFilter from Admin4J (http://www.admin4J. net)

This technique reduces application code and increases the chance that generated exceptions are logged. Furthermore, if you leverage the Admin4J product, which has an error handling filter, you'll get the request URI and a dump of any request and session attributes at the time of the exception. In other words, you can leverage an open source product to accomplish this, rather than creating your own servlet filter for this purpose.

Incidentally, you'll need to provide similar architectural support for batch job classes, EJB classes, and message-driven beans. Leaving exception logging to application code increases the probability that an exception doesn't get properly logged.

Do not commingle transaction logs with normal application logging. Transaction logs (e.g., user Fred changed the address of customer Acme) have a different purpose. Often, transaction logs are needed by normal business processes and really aren't directed at product support. Most logging products will allow you to direct transaction logs to a separate output for this purpose.

Note that log retention and storage concerns are a completely separate topic. Most logging products support storing logs in a variety of formats, including file or database formats. Application code should only be concerned with issuing log messages, not with the specifics of how they are stored or for how long they are retained.

Application architects need to clearly articulate the logging strategy for developers. Below is a simple example of such a strategy:

Sample Logging Strategy

- Use `myapp.util.Logger` for all logging. Do not use `System.out.println()`.

- Do not log error messages directly in application code. Rely on the application architecture (e.g., error handling servlet filter) to log for you.

- Warnings, informational, and debug messages (i.e., errors not severe enough to warrant the throwing of an exception but that would be useful to a developer fixing bugs) can be logged anywhere from any layer.

- When using logging to output information, use logger message formatting features, instead of employing custom formatting logic, to reduce application code and the risk of producing derivative exceptions.

- Do not use the general logging facility as a transaction log.

EXCEPTION-HANDLING STRATEGIES

Validate all arguments explicitly in all public methods and constructors in all public classes. Validating all arguments for publicly consumed methods prevents derivative exceptions. Derivative exceptions are those reported well after the error occurred. It's an all-too-common error to pass a null argument to a method accidentally, only to find that a `NullPointerException` was generated when the class that was called (directly or indirectly) tries to use the argument and isn't expecting the null value.

While it's possible to get the class, method, and line number where the `NullPointerException` occurred, the actual error occurred well before, at the point where the null value originated. This often is in an entirely separate method and class from what's reported in the stack trace and can take significant time to track down, especially if the code is complex and multiple variables could have generated the exception. Typically, derivative exceptions like this take more time and effort to fix because the error message and information don't make the problem clear. Had the method generated an exception message like "The name argument may not be null." the error would be easier to find and fix.

Argument validation enables you to report an error with a clearer message than you would otherwise get. Null arguments are commonly validated. If an argument has to conform to a specific value set (for example, a docType argument that allows only "pdf," "xls," and"txt" values), the value should be validated as well. I typically leverage the Validate class from Apache Commons Lang for this purpose, as illustrated in listing 15.5.

Listing 15.5: Argument Validation Example

```
public BasicTaskTimer(String label, Collection<DataMeasure>
        dataMeasures) {
      Validate.notNull(dataMeasures,
    "Null data measure collection not allowed.");
      Validate.notEmpty(label, "Null or blank label not
        allowed.");
      this.dataMeasures = dataMeasures;
      this.label = label;
   }
```

Source: Class net.admin4j.timer.BasicTaskTimer from Admin4J (http://www.admin4J.net)

Trend toward unchecked exceptions. This reduces application code by eliminating try-catch logic required by checked exceptions. Several commonly used open source projects, such as Hibernate and Spring, have adopted this approach. At the time the first edition to this book was released, this was a controversial idea with zealots on both sides. This idea is much more accepted and utilized today.

Include general catches for thrown exceptions at all entry points. The reason for this is so that these exceptions can be logged. This advice is related to the logging advice given earlier in this chapter; I won't repeat that material here.

Use native JDK exceptions before creating your own. There's no need to reinvent the wheel. Many developers won't even check if there is an appropriate JDK-defined exception that they could use in lieu of creating an application-specific exception. As a real-world example, I've seen a developer create an exception called `NullValueException` that was thrown when a method was provided a null argument instead of a valid value. `IllegalArgumentException` (from `java.lang`) would have been a better choice.

Limit the nesting depth of a `try/catch` block to two. (Many of you, I know, would campaign for one.) If you need more, remove the inner blocks of code to separate private methods for readability. In addition, fixing bugs in nested `try/catch` scenarios can be difficult. As an aside, the need for deeply nested `try/catch` logic usually indicates a need to refactor this section of code.

Don't catch exceptions and do nothing with them. For programmatic convenience, some developers catch exceptions but fail to code the catch block. This practice eliminates a compiler error but makes the code harder to maintain. Many times, swallowing exceptions leads to derivative exceptions later on that are harder to find and fix. If you catch an exception, do something with it (e.g., convert it to a contexted runtime exception and include information needed to fix the underlying bug).

Never put a return statement in a `finally` block. If something throws an exception within a try block, the `finally` block is executed before the exception is thrown. If you issue a return statement within the `finally` or something excepts within the `finally`, the original exception will never be thrown and never be seen. This will increase the time and effort needed to debug a problem.

The architect and project manager should establish an exception-handling and logging strategy before coding begins. Developers often have personal preferences for exception handling and logging. If you don't define a strategy for exception handling and logging, developers will choose their own, and you'll have no consistency across the application. Eventually, when different sections of the application are integrated, conflicts will arise. In addition, it will be more difficult for an outsider to maintain the application.

For example, suppose one developer adopts the philosophy of logging exceptions when they're instantiated, while another expects logging to occur at the deployment level. When all code is integrated, some errors will go unreported, which will greatly increase testing and maintenance time.

One of the most valuable pieces of information generated by an exception is the stack trace of the root exception. The stack trace indicates where the exception was thrown definitively. In some cases, you will even get an exact line number. Ideally, you should see the stack trace of the root exception combined with more descriptive context information. Leveraging the contexted exception feature of Apache Commons Lang V3.0 and above is great for this.

You also need to enforce your exception-handling strategy. I use group code reviews as a mechanism for enforcement and education. Code reviews, if conducted properly, are very constructive. Developers can learn a lot by reviewing the code of other developers. Reviews also make it more difficult to skirt established policy, like an exception-handling strategy. Additionally, code reviews allow you to identify any shortcomings in the exception-handling strategy and make adjustments, if necessary.

Sample Exception-handling Strategy

- Use `Validate` from Apache Commons Lang to check all method arguments on public methods and constructors.
- Always include enough information in the message of the exception to duplicate the condition in a testing environment.
- All application exceptions should extend

`ContextedRuntimeException` from Apache Commons Lang. New application exception proposals should be reviewed by the application architect.

■ All `try/catch` blocks in the business logic layer or the data access layer should not interfere with the throwing of unchecked exceptions. Throw the exception to the caller instead and rely on the application architecture to catch and properly handle the exception.

ASYNCHRONOUS TASK STRATEGIES

Most applications have tasks that run asynchronously (e.g., doesn't force a user to wait). These tasks can include scheduled "batch" work and long-running tasks. Java EE applications are no exception. Fortunately, there are several open source products that provide batch job capabilities for Java applications. I usually leverage the Quartz Job scheduler (http://quartz-scheduler. org/) for this purpose.

It's generally preferable to leverage a product to manage asynchronously running tasks rather than write threading code yourself. This area of Java programming typically takes the most senior developers and is very difficult to get right. Bugs from multi-threaded code can be the most difficult to find and fix. It's also not an area of programming where you want junior developers involved as the risk potential is high.

As with other third-party components, I usually provide a proxy batch job that can be used by a scheduling package. This will reduce switching costs should changing the scheduling product used become necessary. Listing 15.6 is an example of a Quartz batch job base class. The idea is that application extends this class filling in the `execute()` method that contains logic for the batch work to be done. Note that the base class provides a way for the application to schedule the batch job for immediate execution. Should switching schedulers be needed, it's only the batch job base class that would need to change.

Listing 15.6: Sample Base Job Class Designed to Use the Quartz Scheduler

```
public abstract class AbstractBatchJob implements StatefulJob {
      public final void execute(JobExecutionContext context)
    throws JobExecutionException {
    this.execute(context.getMergedJobDataMap());
  }

  @SuppressWarnings("rawtypes")
   public final void execute(Map jobParmMap)
  throws JobExecutionException {

    try {
      logger.info("Batch job successfully started.  class={}",
```

```
                this.getClass().getName());

        this.stateMap = jobParmMap;

        new TransactionContext();
        this.execute();
        TransactionContext.getCurrent().commit();
        logger.info("Batch job successfully completed.
         class={}",
                this.getClass().getName());
    }
    catch (Exception caughtException) {
        TransactionContext.getCurrent().rollback();

        SampleAppRuntimeException sampleException = null;
        if (caughtException instanceof SampleAppRuntimeException
         ) {
         sampleException = (SampleAppRuntimeException)
            caughtException;
        }
        else if (caughtException instanceof
         JobExecutionException
         && caughtException.getCause() instanceof
                SampleAppRuntimeException ) {
         sampleException = (SampleAppRuntimeException)
            caughtException.getCause();
        }
        else sampleException = new SampleAppRuntimeException(
             "Batch Job failure", caughtException)

        .addContextValue("Batch class", this.getClass().
         getName());
        this.addContextValues(sampleException, jobParmMap);
        logger.error("Batch Job failure", sampleException);

    }

    }
    }
```

Source: /src/j2ee/architect/handbook/chap14.AbstractBatchJob.java

As with logging and exception handling strategies, application architects need to provide guidance for asynchronous tasks. A sample strategy similar to what I use in business applications follows:

Sample Asynchronous Task Strategy

▣ Extend `myapp.util.AbstractBatchJob` for all asynchronous tasks. Do not spawn asynchronous threads individually.

▣ Do not log your own exceptions; the architecture will ensure that any exceptions you throw are properly logged, along with specifics about the job and any execution parameters used.

■ Do not manage your own transactions; a commit will be executed on successful completion and a rollback will be issued should an exception be generated.

CONFIGURATION MANAGEMENT STRATEGIES

Most Java EE applications have some configurable properties, such as connection pool names, group e-mail addresses, and much more. Regarding configuration, there are several topics to address for most Java EE applications:

■ Determining values for configuration items from the environment or some data source (e.g., properties file).

■ Making values for configuration items available to application classes.

■ Documenting configurable items for developers.

Making configuration values available to application classes can be as simple as declaring a configuration class with static accessors and mutators representing individual application properties. An example of such a configuration class can be seen in the Admin4J product and its `Admin4JConfiguration` class excerpted in listing 15.7.

Listing 15.7: Example Configuration Class from Admin4J

```
public class Admin4JConfiguration {

    private static StorageFormat
        exceptionInformationStorageFormat = null;
    private static String exceptionInformationXmlFileName =
        null;
    private static StorageFormat
        performanceInformationStorageFormat = null;
    private static String performanceInformationXmlFileName =
        null;
    private static Notifier defaultNotifier = null;
    // Numerous fields omitted for brevity.

    static {
        PropertyConfigurator.configure();
    }

    public static StorageFormat
        getExceptionInformationStorageFormat() {
        return exceptionInformationStorageFormat;
    }

    static void setExceptionInformationStorageFormat(
            StorageFormat exceptionInformationStorageFormat) {
        Admin4JConfiguration.exceptionInformationStorageFormat =
                exceptionInformationStorageFormat;
```

```
    }

    // Numerous accessors and mutators omitted for brevity

}
```

Source: Admin4J product class net.admin4j.config.admin4JConfiguration

Application classes use the configuration accessors to retrieve configuration values. A class responsible for interrogating the environment and reading the configuration from some external source will use the mutators to set configuration values at start up. Note the static block in listing 15.7 that relies on class `PropertyConfigurator` to interrogate the environment and set configuration values. As this is a static block, it will execute when this class is first referenced by the application.

Javadoc in the configuration class can describe the list of configuration items and the purpose of each for developers. Some developers prefer to retrieve configuration values from the environment directly. The largest disadvantage to this is that it leaves no discrete place where all possible configuration items for the application are documented.

The fact that the act of configuring the application is separate makes it possible to support multiple forms of configuration at some point without increasing complexity now. An example of this is the Apache Log4J product, which will allow configuration through either a properties file or an XML configuration document.

Some developers like to put application configuration items in the application database as that's more easily changed at runtime in most organizations. While I understand the appeal, given the bureaucracy in most organizations, I usually avoid storing configuration items in the applications database as it complicates backloads (copying a production database for development or testing purposes). It's common to backload application data from production to a testing environment periodically so developers are working with current data. If configuration items are stored in the application database, production values might be used by mistake. This can cause problems in production if those configuration items identify production files or resources.

There are configuration products that will provide support for gathering configuration information. One such product is Apache Commons Configuration (http://commons.apache.org/configuration). For most Java EE applications, the list of configuration properties is small; involving a separate product to read configuration information is usually overkill.

Sample Configuration Guidelines

■ Define all configuration values as properties in class `com.myorg.myapp.Configuration.`

- Ensure that logic to set the configuration value is present in class `com.myorg.myapp.Configurator`.

- If possible, ensure that the configurator assigns a default value for the property in case it's not specified in a particular runtime environment.

- Throw an exception in the configurator should the configuration value not be set to an allowed value. Please include the invalid value and a blurb about what valid values are in the error message.

Another example of establishing strategies for exception handling, logging, and coding conventions drawn from the open source community can be found at http://commons.apache.org/lang/developerguide.html.

This example is the coding conventions established for the open source product Apache Commons Lang. The URL above is an excellent example of formally establishing the architectural policies discussed in this chapter and communicating them. While the advice may differ from what I provide here, I still provide it as an example because establishing clear guidelines for developers to follow is more important than the minor disagreements I have with some of the line items.

CACHING STRATEGIES

Caching, keeping frequently used data in memory, is a common tactic for performance benefit. Basically, caching trades memory for CPU and disk utilization and speed. As with all strategies, caching has risks as well as benefits, so it should only be used in cases where you get material performance improvement. Low volume applications may not need to implement caching at all, but it's common enough that it deserves focus.

For caching in application code, the algorithm is usually simple. I'll use a primitive `ExpiringCache` class as a usage example; `ExpiringCache` source is included in the source bundle. Lest you think I custom-coded a cache, `ExpiringCache` wraps caching functionality in Guava (https://code.google.com/p/guava-libraries/). Consider the usage example in listing 15.8.

Listing 15.8: Example Cache Use

```
private static ExpiringCache<Long, String> cache = new
        ExpiringCache<Long, String>();
…..
String value = cache.get(key);
if (value == null) {
   //  Put code to look up the value
   cache.put(key, value);
}
```

Note that some JPA implementations provide caching abilities. For example, Hibernate provides caching abilities that you can use instead of custom coding use of a cache as I've done above.

As caching works by avoiding I/O, it carries a stale data risk. That is, data in the cache might have been changed at the source and that stale data is being used by the application for processing. For example, if you cache data from a remote web service call, it's possible that the data may have changed since the last read. In that case, your application will be using stale data. That is also possible if you cache the result of a database read.

As caching trades memory for speed, the additional memory requirements for caches you configure need to be considered. Guava and another popular caching package Ehcache (http://ehcache.org/) provide ways to limit the number of cache entries to mitigate the risk of caching causing a memory shortage.

Since I mentioned using caching features of JPA implementations (e.g., Hibernate), I should point out that implementing a Java cache for database reads is usually redundant. Relational databases have built-in caching ability and if properly configured will cache frequently used data. I've had occasion to test Hibernate caching extensively, and I've discovered that unless your database is poorly configured or your network between the application server and database server has bad performance, Hibernate caching doesn't make any difference. If you have a poorly configured database or a poorly running network, it's better to fix them, if possible, as they would be the root cause.

FURTHER READING

Johnson, Rod. 2002. *Expert One-on-One: J2EE Design and Development.* Indianapolis, IN: Wrox Press.

Lea, Doug. 2000. *Concurrent Programming in Java Second Edition: Design Principles and Patterns.* Boston, MA: Addison-Wesley.

SECTION IV

TESTING AND MAINTAINING JAVA EE APPLICATIONS

Once the work of building the application is finished, the technical architect is often asked to lead performance-testing activities and ensure that the application is production ready. At this stage, the architect's primary objective is improving application performance, stability, and operational readiness. To achieve this goal, the architect needs to conduct performance tests and make performance improvements, recommend changes to make applications easier to monitor and support, and identify candidates for code refactoring.

This section guides you through these activities. In it, you will learn how to:

- Establish coding guidelines for functional test cases.
- Conduct effective performance tests.
- Effectively profile your application to improve its use of memory and CPU.
- Improve supportability for your applications.
- Recognize when code needs refactoring.
- Adapt software architecture principles to new technologies.

CHAPTER 16

TESTING GUIDELINES AND STRATEGY

There are several different layers of testing:

- Unit testing: tests that verify the correctness of a public or protected method or constructor of a specific class.

- Integration testing: tests that verify that an individual software feature or function works as intended.

- System integration testing: tests that verify that the software product as a whole functions as intended and interfaces correctly with external applications or software components.

- User acceptance testing: tests conducted by end users or end-user representatives to ensure that delivered software works correctly and delivers on its intended business purpose.

- Performance testing: tests that the software product scales and that performance is acceptable when operating under a full workload (e.g., expected number of users).

As an application architect, you need to ensure that testing guidelines exist for the project at each of these levels. Typically, the application architect's recommendations on these items will be sought. While management might overrule parts of the recommendations, given that they require resources to be implemented, it is often the case that the architect's recommendations are accepted outright. In this chapter, I will elaborate on my views regarding each form of testing.

UNIT TESTING GUIDELINES

Unit testing operates on the principle that finding defects earlier in the project is usually cheaper, in that fewer people are impacted by the defect before it's identified and fixed. Once in place, it helps prevent future defects by allowing developers to make changes with a reasonable degree of confidence that their changes won't break anything.

Damage from bugs occurs in many forms. A bug discovered late in the testing process can impact a project timeline. A bug discovered after deployment can damage users' faith in the system and the development team. And fixing bugs late in the process involves more manpower. At that point, the fix can involve not only the developer but an entire testing team (if your project has them, and many do).

By contrast, news of a bug caught early in the project passes no further than the development team. The testing team and end users won't be directly involved in verifying a fix to a bug they have never experienced.

Unit testing guidelines need to answer the following questions:

- What level of code unit test code coverage is considered adequate? Which classes and methods require unit tests?

- Where do I put my unit tests so that they can be easily found and used by other developers?

- How often are my unit tests expected to be run? Who fixes them when they break?

- If my unit tests require external resources (e.g., relational databases or external applications), what environment are they expected to run in?

- What unit testing tools are in the technical stack and are available for use?

This is where most pundits make the sales pitch for Test Driven Development (TDD); that is, write unit tests before writing the code itself. In this way, developers ensure a high level of unit test coverage and ensure that they understand the requirements of what they are about to code. This practice also guides developers toward writing code in such a way that it can be unit tested. Most pundits make the claim that anything less than 100 percent unit test coverage (that is, all lines of code are tested at least once by a unit test) is unacceptable.

On the other side of the argument, if you write unit tests after writing the underlying functionality, your tests are more likely to address the higher-risk areas of your code, as you'll write them at a point when you understand the most about the problem you're trying to solve.

I think it's more important to specify what *level* of code coverage is required than to micromanage exactly when in the development process a developer writes the code.

What level of unit test code coverage is adequate? Most organizations won't fund 100 percent unit test coverage. In any case, it doesn't completely eliminate bugs as it only tests the inputs that are scripted in the unit tests. While unit tests allow developers to refactor code more safely, it also means that more code is involved for each change (you need to change the expectations in the unit tests along with changing the behavior of the application), thus leading to a longer development time for that change. Pundits would argue that additional time spent maintaining the unit test cases will be made up, because less time will be needed to fix bugs, given that there will be fewer bugs to fix.

If you're curious as to the code coverage percentage experienced by other applications, check out Nemo (http://nemo.sonarsource.org/). Nemo is sponsored by Sonar and presents Sonar statistics, including code coverage, for several popular open source projects. You'll quickly see that the code coverage percentage varies widely from project to project. If you're skeptical that less than 100 percent code coverage might be acceptable, visit Nemo; you'll find that most projects (including some very successful projects) operate with well under 100 percent unit test coverage.

There are products that will measure unit test coverage for you. One such product, Sonar (http://www.sonarsource.org/), is open source and freely available. Sonar also provides a wide variety of software metrics to help you measure the quality of your applications. Another product that will measure unit test coverage is Crap4J (http://www.crap4j.org/).

I usually recommend requiring at least one positive and one negative unit test case per public and protected method—for data access and business logic layer classes and for all utility classes. A positive test case is one where the method completes normally. A negative test case is where the method issues an exception (e.g., for invalid input).

This is far from 100 percent coverage, but it's simple to follow. Simple to follow means that it's more likely to be followed. While it is possible to express this requirement in terms of a code coverage percent and arrange for automated testing to measure this percentage, that takes more time and shifts management work onto the developer. In all honesty, utility classes probably should have a higher test coverage as they are often more widely used than business logic or data access classes.

At a management level, I try to ensure that unit tests exist for the most commonly executed code and the most complex code. Both Sonar and Crap4J will also provide code complexity metrics in addition to code coverage metrics. Also, if a section of code continues to appear in defect reports, ensuring that this code has an adequate test harness is a way to reduce its defect rate.

Where do I put my unit tests? This should be established by the application architect with input from all developers. I usually define a "test" source folder for every application where the unit tests reside. Most Integrated Development Environments (IDEs) have rich unit testing support for Junit. For example, in Eclipse, you can right click on a source folder and run all Junit tests contained in it. The package structure of the test folder should mimic the package structure of the main source folder. I usually specify that test classes contain the name of the class under test (e.g., CustomerDAOTest) and exist in the same package as the class under test (so protected methods can be tested as well).

How often are unit tests expected to be run? Who fixes them when they break? Ideally, these unit tests are run in some automated fashion at least once a day. The trouble really comes when a unit test breaks. The conventional thinking is that the developer who checked in the code responsible for the breakage should fix it. However, in an active project, it's not always obvious who checked in the mistake that broke the unit test. For example, there might not be an offending check-in; a developer could have changed the input data that the particular test relies on. Also, in an active project with looming deadlines, fixing the test cases often gets lower priority.

Often, the application architect advises the project manager on this topic but doesn't unilaterally decide the answer, as managing which tasks are assigned to which people is really the project manager's responsibility.

One option is to rotate the responsibility for fixing unit test breakage. This is often easier to manage as the project manager can expect less from that person when they are on unit test patrol. It also punishes developers who check in code that breaks the unit tests by embarrassing them (e.g., calling attention to their mistakes by calling the attention of others to them). Therefore, it provides an incentive for developers to *not* check in code that breaks unit tests. Unfortunately, it also provides an incentive for developers to "comment out" unit tests so they aren't embarrassed.

What environment are my unit tests expected to run in? Most applications require external resources, such as databases. Usually, I maintain a development database that services development tasks and unit tests and a separate database for automated integration tests. Some organizations have developers maintain their own databases for development, but that's an inefficient use of time. Developers by definition aren't database administrators and can't solve database environment issues as quickly. It's more efficient to have one person with these skills maintain that environment for everyone.

What unit testing tools are in the technical stack and are available for use? Some additional tools are needed to support unit tests. The Junit testing framework (http://www.junit.org/) appears to be the most popular and is the framework my projects use. In addition to the testing framework, it's normal to need a mocking framework to provide implementations for interface class dependencies that aren't the subject of a particular unit test. I typically use EasyMock (http://easymock.org/), but there are other tools available.

It's important that libraries and tools needed for unit testing aren't used by production code. Toward that end, I usually define a `dev-lib` folder in my projects; `dev-lib` contains jars that are needed for development and unit tests but won't be included in the production deployment. The build process usually enforces that developers don't accidentally code a reliance on Easy-Mock or some other testing product in production code.

In addition to selecting and making unit testing tools available in your projects, it's often necessary to provide a base testing framework to make creating unit tests easy. For instance, I frequently have a base unit test that performs all Hibernate configuration tasks and a test JNDI factory. This way, all a developer needs to do to create a new Junit test is extend the base test class. Frequently, this base will provide common mocks as well, e.g., `HttpServletRequest, HttpServletResponse`).

Automated Testing

As applications mature and gain complexity, automated testing becomes preventative medicine. With complex code comes the likelihood that a developer will fix one problem and inadvertently cause another. Some would say that this is a red flag indicating a need for code refactoring, as discussed in a later chapter. Automated testing decreases the possibility that a fix to one problem causes another problem and then goes unnoticed until after production.

Automated testing is better because it's consistent and easier to run. It doesn't slack off at the end of a hard day, and it's easily repeatable. As a result, automated regression testing for even small changes in the application is more cost-effective. I've seen projects that go so far as to incorporate the test suite in the build script. If one of the regression tests fails, the build fails and the developers are forced to fix the bug.

Automated testing is as complete as you want it to be. If you subscribe to the view that test cases should be created as the application is developed, then you also feel that developers should initially create test cases. But these test cases are usually not complete. If you adopt the recommendation that the first step in fixing a bug is writing a test case that reproduces it, your regression test is enhanced as you find more bugs. Over time, you get a robust set of regression tests that increases the probability of finding bugs before deployment.

Automated testing isn't free. Creating and maintaining tests consumes manpower, so it's important to use the 80/20 rule. Initially, code test cases for the 80 percent of the application that is most complex and most prone to error. You can fill out the remaining 20 percent over time. If you stop to create automated tests that are 100 percent comprehensive, you'll end up adding many hours to the timeline, to the extent that the costs will outweigh the benefits.

Unit Testing Best Practices

Keep test cases and supporting classes in a separate folder, but in an identical package structure. Although test cases are developed in conjunction with the application, they are not truly a part of it. Typically, you have no need to deploy them to anything but your testing environments.

I usually organize the package structure of my test cases and supporting classes after the application package structure. Keeping a consistent package structure will save developers time.

Adopt a naming convention for test classes that makes them easy to find. This is another suggestion that can save developers time. For instance, I name all of my test classes `TestXxx`, where `Xxx` is the name of the class being tested. For example, class `TestValueObject` is the test class for `ValueObject`. I prefer to combine all unit tests for the same class into one test class, but this is not a technical requirement or suggestion.

Make each test case self-sufficient and independent. A test case should not rely on other test cases having to execute before it. If you write the test cases so that test case #1 has to be run before test case #2 will work, it's not obvious to other developers what the prerequisites are, should they want to use a test case for unit testing and debugging. However, there may be some isolated cases where implementing this suggestion isn't practical.

INTEGRATION TESTING

Integration testing (sometimes known as acceptance testing) verifies that an individual software feature or function works as intended. Typically, I consolidate the environments for integration testing and system integration testing as their requirements are similar enough. One component of integration testing certainly can be Junit tests executing presentation layer support class methods that support major features of the application. It is difficult, however, to completely automate integration tests for GUI features. While testing frameworks can verify that a feature works without exception, it can't verify that the GUI aesthetics are correct. For this reason, I usually maintain a manual regression test plan for my projects. At this stage, developers should be making any needed modifications to that regression test plan so that it accommodates the new feature(s) being added.

SYSTEM INTEGRATION TESTING

System integration testing is a process that ensures that the software product as a whole works as intended. This process is usually executed in preparation for the User Acceptance Testing period. During this phase, developers (or a subset of test team members) execute the manual regression test. Developers are responsible for fixing any defects found.

The responsibility of the application architect for this process is usually to ensure that the environment supports this type of testing activity. Developers typically need an easy way to initiate the build and deployment to this environment. I find it helpful to standardize the build and deployment procedures across environments and projects. Not only does this streamline maintenance for your build and deployment scripts; it also makes life easier for developers, who are often transferred between projects in many organizations. This consistency allows developers to concentrate on the testing activity itself and the required defect fixes, rather than spending unnecessary time with unique build and deployment procedures for a particular project.

USER ACCEPTANCE TESTING

User acceptance testing usually requires a separate environment. This ensures some stability for the testing team (or user side representatives in some organizations). Usually, the application architect or a senior developer manages needed changes to this environment so that those changes can be made in production when the project is eventually deployed to production.

Once again, the application architect's role with this process is to ensure that an environment exists to support this activity. Usually, I manage changes to this environment so I can ensure that needed changes will also be made in the production environment when the time comes. If change management for this environment is decentralized (i.e., changes managed by several people), the chance that a needed change is missed when the project deploys to production increases dramatically.

For my projects, I usually review defect tickets and check-ins during the UAT testing period. This provides feedback as to how well I did with design tasks earlier in the project. Defects at this stage of the project should not require major architectural changes. If they do, this needs to be analyzed so that those kinds of mistakes are not made with future projects.

PERFORMANCE TESTING

Performance testing is a process that verifies if the project meets scalability requirements in terms of the number of users and transactions it supports. This process requires direct involvement of the application architect or a very senior developer. To be honest, I take it upon myself to participate in this exercise. Developers know when they screw up when unit tests fail or defects appear in testing. Architects need similar feedback. Performance testing is a good way to find out if the application architecture meets (or can be tuned to meet) performance specifications.

When constructing a performance test plan, the following questions need to be answered:

- What metrics will be measured?
- What measurements are required to "pass" the performance test?
- What products and tools will be used to conduct the test?
- What features will be included in performance tests?

The application architect is responsible for ensuring that these questions are answered and often will facilitate needed discussions with other team members and end-user representatives to answer these questions.

While application architects often don't execute performance testing, they are often called on to contribute should problems be discovered. It is possible for performance testing to be managed by senior developers rather than application architects. However, I closely monitor this process for my projects, even if it's performed by developers, as it is valuable feedback on the quality of the initial design. How easy or difficult it is to tune the application reflects directly on the quality of the underlying application architecture. If there are indeed difficulties in tuning one of my applications per requirements, I want to understand those difficulties so I can avoid them with other applications.

What metrics will be measured? Measurements must be completely objective. I usually measure throughput (e.g., 20 hits per second) and average client response time (e.g., three seconds per hit). Most tools that support performance testing will provide these metrics.

You might wonder why I don't pay attention to the "number of virtual users" and state the objective in terms of the maximum number of virtual users the application can support. After all, most end users would relate to the number of supported users better than throughput. The reason is that by controlling the lag time between hits (something that most load test tools allow you to configure), I can make any software product achieve almost any number of concurrent users. By increasing the lag time, I can achieve a higher number of concurrent users (in fact, any number required by the business). While this initially placates users, measuring the supported number of virtual users allows me to rig the test. Throughput cannot be rigged in this way, which is why I use it.

What measurements are required to "pass" the performance test? This is an arbitrary decision and often discussed with end-user representatives. I usually recommend aiming to support twice the throughput needed to support the application in production. For example, if the production application typically supports 5 hits per second in production, I usually ensure that the application supports 10 hits per second in performance tests. This provides headroom should an unexpected usage surge be encountered in production.

Although there are always opportunities for performance improvement, performance tuning has diminishing returns over time. When you start tuning, the changes you make will result in larger performance improvements. But over time, your improvements will get smaller and smaller with most applications. Because most of the benefit you get from tuning will occur in the first 20 percent of the work, the 80/20 rule applies once again.

What products and tools will be used to conduct the test? I usually rely on Admin4J (http://admin4j.net/) for server-side performance metrics and Jmeter (http://jmeter.apache.org/) to script and run the performance test itself. Jmeter will optionally provide client response time statistics and throughput statistics as well.

While Admin4J might appear to be redundant, it is not. Statistics Admin4J reports are server-side. That is, they don't include web server, firewall, and network latency time. Jmeter statistics are client-side and do include time taken by the web server, firewall, and network. If a performance or scalability problem surfaces, it's important to be able to distinguish between problems with the application and problems with the environment it runs in as the tactics you use to solve those problems are different.

What features will be included in performance tests? It is often not possible or even necessary to include every product feature in the performance test. The content of the performance test is usually the result of a discussion with end-user representatives. I usually recommend scripting the most commonly used features. Typically, you can figure out what these features are from an examination of the production access logs.

I try to keep this feature set and the performance test script consistent between releases as much as possible. This makes comparisons of performance between releases more meaningful. For example, if a common function tested out at 5 hits per second in the last release, but only supports 3 hits per second in the current release, something changed in the application or the environment to negatively impact performance.

Performance tests are not functional tests. Many managers make this mistake. Often, the performance test scripts are not comprehensive enough to substitute for functional tests. However, it is important to validate that each request in the performance test is working without error; measuring the speed of your error page isn't all that useful, even though it can produce some impressive performance numbers.

I often monitor performance test runs personally to ensure that I capture metrics needed for analysis should performance tests fail. Often, if performance isn't meeting requirements, I'll capture the following information during a performance test:

■ Thread dump

- O/S Disk usage measurements

- O/S CPU usage measurements

- O/S Network usage measurements

- Database disk, memory, and lock contention measurements

Thread dumps will tell me if there is any Java-level synchronization issues that need to be addressed. The O/S measurements will tell me if resource constraints are an issue. Database measurements will often tell me if database tuning is needed.

Performance Testing Tips and Guidelines

Don't start tuning until after the application is in user acceptance testing. Many developers have a desire to tune every piece of code they write. I admire their desire for completeness, but it hurts the timeline of the project. Chances are high that a good percentage of the code being tuned at this level will not result in good performance enhancement to the application as a whole. Although I've met many developers that are not comfortable with this concept, experience has taught me that at some places in the application, the cost of tuning doesn't reap enough benefit for anyone to care about it.

Most performance problems originate in application code. Developers tend to ferret out performance problems by examining container configurations, JVM options, operating system performance, network performance, and the like, rather than looking at code. This is usually wishful thinking on the part of developers.

Measure performance before tuning to establish a baseline. The next section discusses how to measure performance. The numbers that result from performance measuring will be the basis for judging the effectiveness of performance improvements. I also keep a log of changes I make to an application between performance tests. This way I know if the tuning effort is helping or hurting and to what degree.

Always run load tests under the same conditions multiple times. You need to make sure that nothing is interfering with the test that you're not aware of. I've seen load tests accidentally contending for batch runs or server backups. If you run each test at least twice and get similar results each time, then you'll have a higher degree of trust in the information JMeter gives you.

Document and limit changes between each test. If you make several changes between load tests, you won't know which of the changes helped or hurt performance. For example, let's say you changed four things. It's possible that one of the changes helped performance, one of the changes hurt performance, and two didn't make any material difference whatsoever. Because you combined the changes, however, you'll never really know what helped performance and what hurt it.

Monitor and record CPU and memory usage during the test. The simplest way to do this is at the operating system level. Most UNIX operating systems provide a top utility, which provides CPU and memory usage for each process as well as usage for the entire server. You're obviously interested in what's happening for the container process during the load test. Listing 16.1 is an extract from a top utility output. If your application runs on a Windows platform, you'll need to use the perfmon utility.

Listing 16.1: Sample Top Utility Output

PID	USER	PRI	NI	SIZE	RSS	SHARE	STAT	percentCPU
	percentMEM	TIMECOMMAND						
21886	dashmore	15	0	1012	1012	776	R	0.1	0.1
	0:00java							
1	root	15	0	480	480	428	S	0.0	0.0	0:04
	init							
2	root	15	0	0	0	0	SW	0.0	0.0	0:00
	keventd							
3	root	15	0	0	0	0	SW	0.0	0.0	0:00
	kapmd							

It's more convenient to limit `top` utility output to the process running the container. Unfortunately, the options to the `top` utility are different for each platform. For instance, on Solaris, using the `-U` option will limit output to a specific user.

```
top -U username
```

On Linux, you would limit output by specifying the process ID with the –p option.

```
top -p pid
```

If you're using a UNIX other then Linux, you'll have to consult the man page for the top utility for your specific UNIX platform. By the way, Loukides (2002) is an excellent reference for interpreting CPU and memory utilization statistics that UNIX utilities provide.

You expect to see both CPU and memory usage increase during the test and decrease after the test. If you don't see memory allocation diminish after the test (e.g., within fifteen to thirty minutes), it's likely that you have a memory leak. You should profile your load test both for CPU usage and memory usage.

As discussed previously, I usually monitor heap memory via a JMX console such as VisualVM or Jconsole. Memory at an operating system level includes memory that isn't directly controlled by application code.

Use load tests to detect memory leaks in addition to performance. Yes, even though Java has a garbage collector for memory, it's still possible to have a leak. It's fairly easy to determine if you have a memory leak; it's much harder to find where it is. There will be more on identifying memory leaks in the next chapter.

Measuring Performance under Load

Most load generators (such as Jmeter) operate by running a test script (or a set of them) several times concurrently, simulating a configurable number of virtual users. By measuring the performance each virtual user gets, the load generator enables you to examine the performance averages over all virtual users. Sometimes this information is presented graphically.

As an example, I've written a Jmeter load test for the Admin4J product. The results of the load test are in figure16.1. The two most important numbers in the output are the 10.5 hits per second (hps) throughput rate and the average 29 millisecond client response time. As you would expect, the throughput requirements are quite low (e.g., 2 hps with a response time of less than 2 seconds is reasonable) as these are pages accessed infrequently by support developers investigating problems; 10.5 hps should be more than adequate. The general rule is that users don't like to wait more than two seconds for a response; the 29 ms average response time meets requirements.

Figure 16.1: Sample JMeter Load Test Example

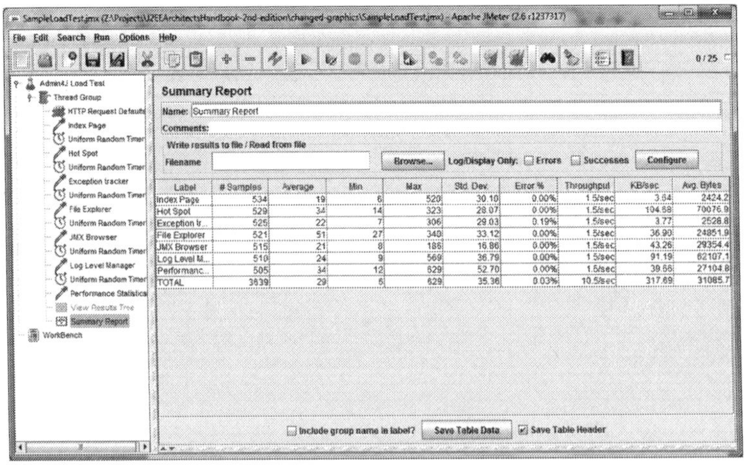

Load tests are usually written in the form of URL sequences. I prefer not to set up tests for other classes unless the application has significant back-end processing that needs to be tested under load. This can happen if your application processes JMS messages from other applications, for example.

Although a load generator can tell you if you're meeting performance targets, it can't tell you why your performance is what it is. If you meet your performance targets, you should stop the tuning effort. If you don't meet your targets, you'll need to apply additional techniques to diagnose the causes of the performance problem.

Should you identify a performance problem and need to tune an application, there's material on improving performance in the next chapter.

It should be noted that there are a wide variety of browser-based tools that can be used to measure and improve performance (e.g., PageSpeed, SpeedTracer, and YSlow). Measurements you get from these tools do, however, include much more than application performance; they also include network performance and performance of the device running the browser. Two people measuring performance of the same page using the same test script from different parts of the world on different computers may get drastically different results.

Memory Leaks Defined

With Java, memory leaks occur in code that retains references to objects that are no longer needed. A reference is a variable declaration and assignment. Java's garbage collector periodically frees memory associated with non-referenceable variables. If a variable is referenceable, its memory will not be freed.

For instance, the variable account in the following code is a reference for a value object:

```
AccountVO account = new AccountVO();
```

If this line of code appears as a local variable declaration within a method, the reference ends when the method completes. After the method completes, the garbage collector frees memory associated with the account declaration.

If the declaration is an instance-level field, the reference ends when the enclosing object is no longer referenced. For example, if the variable account is declared as an instance-level field for CustomerVO, the reference to account ends when the reference to an instantiated CustomerVO object ends, as shown here:

```
public class CustomerVO
{
  private AccountVO account = new AccountVO();
}
```

A variable defined as static can easily cause a memory leak because the reference ends when the JVM stops or the reference is specifically nulled out.

Memory leaks in Java EE applications are frequently caused by statically defined `Collection` objects. For instance, it's common to statically define an application Properties object to store configuration details, as in the following:

```
public class Environment
{
    private static Properties _configurationProps =
new Properties();
}
```

Any value stored in this statically defined `Properties` object can be referenced. `Collection` objects, such as `Properties` or `HashMaps`, often produce memory leaks because it's easy to put values into them and forget to remove them later.

Identifying Memory Leaks

To identify memory leaks, note how much memory the container is using before, during, and after the test. You should see memory at a low level to start, then ramp up during the test, and slowly decrease within a few minutes to an hour after the test. For example, a container might initially start at 128MB of memory and grow to 180MB during the performance test. After the test, memory allocation should trend back toward 128MB. I usually run this test for twenty-four hours (long enough to reveal slower memory leaks).

Load testing will not find all memory leaks. Note that even if no memory leaks are identified with your load test suite, there still might be a memory leak in the application. Most load test scripts aren't comprehensive; that is, they don't execute all features of an application. It is possible that there's a memory leak in your application that isn't a part of your load test suite. Most of the time, the amount of resources it takes to create and maintain comprehensive load test suites is much more than most organizations are willing to fund. Because of this, it's important to instrument your applications and configure your Java EE containers so you get enough information should memory shortages occur in production. More information on how to accomplish this will be presented in chapter 16.

Memory leaks are most likely discovered in production. While I encourage you to check for memory leaks by running a load test for twenty-four hours or more, the load test will only execute what's scripted. If the load test script doesn't create the conditions for the memory leak to occur, then running the load test for a long period of time will not uncover the leak.

I use VisualVM (http://visualvm.java.net/) to monitor memory during performance tests. VisualVM is a JMX console and requires that you open a JMX port for the container being tested. You can also use Jconsole utility that comes with the JDK. I prefer VisualVM as it has a wider selection of plugins and has many other uses in addition to measuring memory. While you can measure memory at the operating system level, you can separate heap memory (where memory leaks typically occur) from the various other memory pools typically allocated in a JVM.

It's not realistic for memory to return to its pretest level, but most of the memory allocated during the test should be freed. To investigate memory leaks, I start taking a memory dump once the leak has been confirmed. While you can use the `jhat` utility to read the content of a memory dump, this is laborious and time consuming. I usually use the commercial profiler YourKit to investigate memory leaks. The result of this should be that you've identified which transaction(s) are generating the leak and you can construct a load test script or unit test that will produce the memory leak. Given a reproducible leak, you can use the profiler to verify the fix after you've fixed the leak.

Configure the Java EE container to produce a memory dump when the first `OutOfMemoryError` is thrown. This can be accomplished by specifying the `XX:+HeapDumpOnOutOfMemoryError` option on the container if you're using the Oracle JVM. You can then use either the `jhat` utility that comes with the JVM or a commercial profiler to investigate where the memory is being allocated. I use this configuration option for all Java EE containers in all environments; and this isn't just for load testing. Should a memory leak occur in production, the information in the dump will be very valuable.

Additionally, I use Admin4J to generate alerts for abnormally high memory usage. These alerts come with a configurable amount of memory allocation history and a thread dump. The tool doesn't automatically generate a memory dump as that is very resource intensive. The thread dump may be useful in identifying transaction types that are potential targets for a memory tuning exercise.

Investigating Performance Problems

At some point, a load test will identify performance problems and issues that need to be solved. Performance tuning follows the 80/20 rule; you get 80 percent of the benefit from the first 20 percent of the work. After identifying the problem, the next information you need is where in your code you're spending the most time. Profilers do this nicely. However, before even profiling the process, take a thread dump during the load test that failed.

One output of load testing is knowing which transactions are not performing to requirements. In the layered application architecture discussed in this book, the business layer and the data access layer are the most likely places for performance problems to occur. Beans and web services usually only publish functionality in business objects anyway. It should be relatively quick to construct a test case (or modify an existing one) specifically for the underlying business objects that produce the performance problem. Constructing these test cases gives you something that's easier to profile.

Take a thread dump during a load test. Believe it or not, a thread dump taken during a failing load test will have the same information as what a profiler gives you; it's just not as easy to interpret. Let me explain why that's a true statement.

A profiler works by taking a copy of all thread stacks every defined interval (usually five milliseconds or ten milliseconds). When method `CustomerDAO.findCustomerByState()` is encountered, metrics associated with that method are tallied. The more time you spend in `CustomerDAO.findCustomerByState()`, the higher those tallies and the more your profiler considers that method a hot spot. A *hot spot* is a section of code that appears as a larger number of observations than other sections of code. This can be either because it's executed more often or because it takes longer to execute.

When you take a thread dump on a load test where all threads are at a random place in the test script, you're effectively taking many profiler-type observations at once. If `CustomerDAO.findCustomerByState()` shows up in most active threads, it's a hot spot and may yield performance improvement if tuned.

There are tools like the Thread Dump Analyzer (http://java.net/projects/tda/) that make interpreting a thread dump a bit easier. I check thread dumps for lock contention (threads marked as `BLOCKED` and waiting on a resource). Profiling one thread will not tell you anything about lock contention.

Tuning methods that aren't hot spots isn't a wise use of time. For example, say you can tune a section of code and get a 10 percent performance improvement on it. Tuning a hot spot consuming 50 percent of your time will get you a 5 percent throughput improvement overall (50 percent times 10 percent). Tuning some other method that only consumes 5 percent of your time will generate only a 0.5 percent throughput improvement (5 percent times 10 percent) overall.

Use profiler tools to tune hot spots with a specific unit test script. A profiler reports the activity of a JVM at a configurable interval (typically every five milliseconds) and reports the call stack in use for every thread. The methods taking the most time will most likely show up in more observations and provide leads as to where you should tune. My first preference is to construct a Junit test that executes the nonperforming code.

If your container uses one JVM, you can profile the entire container and run your JMeter test script against it. I profile a Java EE container as a whole as a last resort as profiling individual unit tests usually take less time.

Some Java EE containers use multiple JVMs, making it difficult to profile the entire container. Instead, you'll want to directly profile test cases that use the underlying business objects. You'll skip profiling the deployment and presentation layers in their entirety, but performance tuning is most likely to be at the business logic layer or lower anyway. In a layered architecture, the deployment and presentation layers don't perform much of the processing.

Do not attempt to profile in a clustered environment. For those of you in a clustered architecture, I recommend profiling in one instance only, not in clustered mode. Your goal is to tune your application, not wade through the work your container does to implement clustering.

Profilers tell you where (in which class or method) CPU time is being spent and where (in which classes) memory is being allocated. The default profiler that comes with the JVM (HPROF) produces output that's not intuitive and is hard to read, but that output contains much the same information as commercial profilers. The advantage of commercial profilers is that they make performance information easier to read and interpret. If your organization has a license for a commercial profiler, use it instead of HPROF.

If you don't have access to a commercial profiler, you'll probably have to spend a few more minutes interpreting the output than your colleagues with commercial profilers. The default profiler measures both CPU time and memory allocation, but I recommend measuring these separately to avoid contaminating the test. Methods for debugging memory leaks are also included in the next chapter.

MAKING JAVA EE APPLICATIONS SUPPORTABLE

Java EE applications require support to varying degrees just like other types of applications. In previous chapters, we've discussed at length error handling strategies, logging strategies, unit testing strategies, and other techniques to improve the quality of your Java EE applications and make them easier to support. Those techniques are a beginning to making Java EE applications supportable, but they are not comprehensive. To start, exception logs and notifications, while important, aren't a complete source of information when it comes to diagnosing many types of outages, such as memory shortages or locking issues. Furthermore, administrators also need to assist with capacity planning efforts and help management effectively direct resources to improve quality and affect bug fixes. This chapter will detail typical support issues that arise with Java EE applications and suggest ways to instrument your applications to address those issues.

While application architects in many organizations aren't directly involved with providing application support, they should be concerned with the resources required to support the applications they design. Having architects' support for the applications they design is extremely constructive as it provides valuable feedback that they can use on future designs.

APPLICATION SUPPORT OBJECTIVES

Most organizations seek to maximize the end-user experience with their applications while minimizing the costs associated with providing that experience. Java EE applications are no different than applications built on other technical stacks.

These two objectives are extremes in the same continuum. That is, providing better end-user experiences often costs more in terms of labor costs. Conversely, cutting labor costs often lowers the end-user experience as it takes longer to address problems and defects. Most organizations strike a subjective balance between these two extremes.

Maximizing the end-user experience with an application means minimizing unplanned outages, minimizing defects, providing acceptable performance, and resolving user issues with the application quickly and efficiently, among other things.

Minimizing costs associated with providing a desired end-user experience means minimizing the costs and time associated with addressing outages and defects. Yes, part of this cost is the various testing procedures and frameworks supporting the application as these prevent defects in the first place. However, no matter how robust your testing procedures and frameworks, defects will surface in production. Minimizing costs for defects at this point means minimizing investigation time and the time involved in diagnosing, fixing, and testing the fix for the issue.

STREAMLINING INVESTIGATIONS FOR APPLICATION DEFECTS

Defects are reported by users and in many cases by the application itself through generating exceptions. If logging and notifications are put in place, it's possible for application support personnel to be alerted to a system-generated exception before it is reported by end users. Furthermore, not all defects are reported by end users. There are many reasons for this: it takes time they may not have, they may incorrectly assume somebody else has reported the defect, or it may be that the response time on reported defects is less than desired so they don't bother reporting them. The point is that some defects will only be reported via system exception.

User-reported defects can be accompanied by system-generated exceptions. While system-generated exceptions are more detailed and can provide more reliable information to developers, it's not always easy to infer from an exception exactly how the user is being affected. It's important to note that not all application defects will produce an exception. Having the ability to increase the logging level (e.g., to debug) in production at runtime is valuable.

Prioritize defects using the number of system-generated exceptions produced by that defect. The number of exceptions is usually a good indicator of how often users are experiencing the defect. By prioritizing defects producing the larger number of system-generated exceptions, you help the most people the soonest. Admin4J can help you summarize logged exceptions and let you know which exception type/defect is happening most often.

Prioritize defects indicating the lack of needed resources first. An example of this is database unavailability. Resource outages, such as database unavailability, usually affect a large number of transaction types and user activities within the application.

System-generated exceptions usually precede corresponding user-reported defects. Consequently, if a system-generated exception is fixed quickly enough, it's possible that a user will never notice or report it. I generally monitor system-generated exceptions closely after a new release. This gives me an early indication if we've accidentally released a new bug and gives me a chance to start addressing the issue even before it's reported by users.

Follow best practices for generating exceptions. Ideally, enough information should be present in the exception report to diagnose the bug and formulate a strategy for a repair. Use `ContextedException` and `ContextedRuntimeException` to safely include useful information with your exceptions. The reason for this is to save developer time in investigating the defect. If the exception report doesn't provide enough information to diagnose the bug, then you have two changes to make: correct the bug and enhance the error report to save developers time investigating future defect reports.

STREAMLINING INVESTIGATIONS FOR UNPLANNED OUTAGES

Common causes for unplanned outages in Java EE applications include memory shortages, java locking or race condition issues, or unexpected heavy user load. For these types of outages, the time it takes to investigate is typically greater than what's required to actually fix them. This section will show you ways to instrument Java EE applications to help reduce the investigation time associated with these events.

Additionally, low-level bugs with the Java Virtual Machine (JVM) can cause Java EE container crashes; thankfully, crashes due to JVM bugs are rare these days.

Investigating Memory Shortages

Heap memory shortages come in two categories: leaks and usage spikes. Leaks typically come from memory that is accidentally referenced longer than needed. Memory that is referenced cannot be garbage collected and occupies memory that could be better used for normal application activities. When leaks are large enough, there's no longer enough memory to service user requests and the container becomes inoperative. Usage spikes are memory used to satisfy user activities. Usage spikes can be initiated by unexpectedly heavy user volume or unexpectedly large user requests for information. Please note that Java allocates memory for purposes other than the heap, but non-heap shortages are rare and are noted by very specific exceptions; plus they are easy to solve. Consequently, this section concentrates on heap memory issues, which are the most common by far and the most difficult to solve.

The first and most important question with any memory shortage investigation: Is it a memory leak or a usage spike? The answer to this question is important as it dictates activities for the rest of the investigation and your options for fixing the issue. Memory leaks, once identified, are usually addressed with a code fix if you control the code causing the leak. Usage spikes can often be reduced by tuning memory consumption and finding ways to satisfy user needs using less memory. Usage spikes can sometimes be addressed by placing limits on user capabilities within an application. For example, limiting the amount of information that can be retrieved for display can often reduce the size of usage spikes. An example of this would be writing an application so that if a user initiates a search that returns a large result set, the first five hundred rows (or whatever size is chosen) would be provided, along with a user message informing them that more results are available, if required. Once these options are exhausted, you can allocate additional memory to the JVM to accommodate the load.

Often, memory shortage problems are difficult to investigate as there may be little information as to what memory was allocated at the time of the crash. That is, if investigators happened to be on hand during a run-up to a memory shortage and somehow knew about the impending crash, they could initiate a memory dump and thread dump of the container, identify memory allocations that are unexpectedly large, and also identify a list of user activities in process at the time of the crash. Unfortunately, imminent memory shortages are almost never known to support personnel in advance. For those using the Oracle (formerly Sun) JVM, memory dumps are taken with the `jmap` utility. Thread dumps can be taken with the `jstack` utility or programmatically within the container.

There are a large number of monitoring tools that alert administrators to memory shortages. Open source examples of such tools include Zabbix and Nagios. In addition, there are a plethora of commercial alternatives available. These tools are often implemented and configured at an enterprise level, and most of them can be configured to initiate a thread and memory dump in addition to alerting administrators. Note that taking memory dumps is resource intensive, so trigger automatic memory dumps with care. Most of these tools rely on the Java Management Extensions (JMX) and monitor from outside the container. For those developers supporting applications for organizations that have not implemented enterprise monitoring tools, Admin4J provides memory monitoring services from within the container and can be deployed with your application.

Memory can be measured at the container-level only. For organizations that deploy multiple applications per Java EE container, identifying the offending application within a container is much more difficult, as you can't reliably measure memory allocated to individual applications within that container. For this reason and others, I recommend deploying one application per container. Yes, this practice does consume additional memory as each container has some amount of overhead. However, on most platforms, memory is cheap these days.

Memory leaks can be detected from memory dumps, but it requires detailed knowledge of application code running within the container. Without such knowledge of the monitored applications, the person investigating the memory incident won't be able to tell what's normal and expected allocation from the memory referenced by accident. If thread dumps taken during the incident are also available and show no active user requests, then memory allocated is either from a leak or is yet to be garbage collected. Memory dumps will distinguish between referenced and non-referenced (available to be garbage collected) memory.

Memory leaks can also be detected by analyzing memory allocation patterns over time. Minimum memory allocation (memory consumed immediately after garbage collection) for an application with memory leaks will always grow and never shrink. For example, if a leaking application's minimum memory allocation one day is 100MB and that minimum perpetually grows and never shrinks, then an application within that container leaks.

Java locking or race condition issues can cause memory shortages. This is because locking issues keep user activities active for longer than they would otherwise be. While those activities are active, memory allocated to service them cannot be garbage collected and reused. In this case, the memory shortage is derivative. That is, it's not the root problem as it wouldn't exist if it weren't for the Java locking issues that caused it. In these cases, solve the Java locking issue first; the memory shortage issue will often disappear when the locking issue is solved. As an example, JDBC drivers synchronize the ability to create database connections. That is, only one database connection can be created by the container at a time. Normally, with a properly configured connection pool, this isn't a problem. However, should there be unexpectedly large user demand, the container may have an unusually large number of threads waiting for database connections to work with. As each of these active threads consume memory, this can lead to a memory shortage.

It is possible for a Java EE container to be unstable after an `OutOfMemoryEx-ception`. On the other hand, it's also possible for the container to operate normally and completely recover. It depends on exactly what thread(s) were impacted by the memory shortage. It's possible that a thread working with memory tracking sessions, database connections, or some other needed resource was impacted, leaving that tracking memory in a corrupted state.

Other threads attempting to use that memory may encounter unexpected conditions and error out. For this reason, I usually schedule a container recycle for the next normal maintenance window.

Resource limits can cause memory shortages. A common example of such an event is a database connection pool with a connection limit that's too small. Many containers will hold incoming user requests for database connections until a connection is available to service the request. If you have an unplanned large number of requests, each request "held" for lack of an available database connection consumes memory. I've seen this issue manifest as a memory shortage issue many a time. In these cases, a thread dump taken during or shortly before the event reveals this issue rather quickly.

I concentrate on investigating memory issues rather than fixing them, as the investigation is what usually consumes the most time and resources. Once the root cause of the memory issue is found, whether it be the source of a leak or a spike due to a specific user activity, fixing the issue is often comparatively easy. Memory leaks usually require a code change. They usually involve statically defined collections that are added to but never purged. Memory spikes can become the focus of a memory tuning effort. Once the activity producing a spike has been tuned, the only alternative left is allocating additional memory to the container. The activity of fixing memory issues usually falls to senior developers rather than the architect, but I find memory investigations and their resolutions informative for architects. Should the cause of a memory issue be a design issue, knowledge of that defect can be used to avoid similar defects in future applications.

Investigating Java Contention Issues

Code that uses the `synchronized` keyword is potentially a creator of contention issues. That is because use of the `synchronized` keyword forces that section of code to be executed by one and only one thread at a time. There are cases where synchronization is necessary; however, it should be used with care. The `synchronized` keyword can be declared on individual methods or it can be used to guard access to all synchronized methods in a specific object. Entire books have been written on the subject of multi-threaded programming. That topic is really out of scope for this book.

Contention issues often appear to users as performance issues. The bottlenecks that occur as a result of contention issues increase clock time consumed by all threads involved. Hence, contention limits throughput. Load tests revealing contention issues will often display a throughput limit as a symptom. As an example, a contention issue in one of my Java EE applications limited throughput of a load test to just under 5 hits per second (hps). No matter how we changed settings on the load test, we couldn't exceed 5 hps.

A thread dump during the test revealed the contention issue, which we were able to tune around and raise our resulting throughput.

Contention does not consume CPU resources. That is, CPU utilization will often show a significant CPU percent idle. During the load test example in the previous paragraph, there were significant CPU resources available when load testing my applications with the 5 hps throughput limit. Those CPU resources decreased when the contention issue was removed.

Contention issues must be caught red-handed with a thread dump to be diagnosed and resolved. Thread dumps indicate which threads are BLOCKED (waiting on exclusive use of an object or method) and which resource that thread is waiting on. For more detail on thread states like BLOCKED, see Java documentation on the subject here. As with memory issues, having an administrator on hand to take a thread dump at the time of the event is often not possible. It is far better to install a monitoring tool to detect such conditions and take a thread dump automatically.

Monitor Java contention and automatically take thread dumps in response to contention events. This provides administrators with real-time information when contention events are encountered. I don't see this feature natively in Nagios or Zabbix, but both products are extensible enough that I'm sure it's possible. Admin4J will monitor thread contention and include thread dumps in the notification.

Database connection pools are a common cause for contention issues with Java EE applications. This is primarily due to synchronization that occurs when creating database connections. Contention involving database connection pools is less of an issue with JDK 1.6 and later, but it still can cause problems. Often, tuning the connection pool (e.g., the maximum number of connections and the number of allowed idle connections) can alleviate contention issues due to connection pooling.

Investigating Performance Issues

Measure performance for all HTTP traffic, batch jobs, and JMS message handling in production. Knowing current performance runtimes often isn't enough; you need some amount of history to understand if performance is slower than normal. It's important to measure server-side performance of the application. I realize that users experience client-side performance, and that is more important to them. However, poor client-side performance could be the result of poor network performance instead of poor application performance. Measuring performance on the server side is the only way to distinguish between the two. How you improve network performance is far different than how you improve application performance.

I've successfully used both the JAMon API and Admin4J for measuring server-side performance. Both products run from within the container, and both products are fast enough to use in production. Typically, HTTP traffic monitoring is achieved through a servlet filter, and both products provide such a filter out of the box.

Establish performance targets for common application features. Performance tuning is an activity that doesn't have to end. Furthermore, all tuning efforts have diminishing returns over time. Tuning only activities that are not meeting performance targets is a good way to make the resources devoted to tuning cost effective.

Performance tuning benefits follow the 80/20 rule. That is, the first 20 percent of a performance tuning effort provides 80 percent of the benefit. As a performance tuning effort progresses, incremental performance improvements get smaller and smaller. For example, at the beginning of a tuning effort, identifying tuning opportunities that increase throughput 5 percent or more is common. At the end of such an effort, identifying opportunities that increase throughput more than 1 percent can be a challenge.

Performance tuning activities should be planned for the UAT testing phase of the project. A common mistake developers make is to performance tune as they develop. Tuning during development often results in tuning code that is insignificant or doesn't represent a large enough target to provide cost-effective benefit to the performance tuning exercise.

Thread dumps taken at high load can be used to identify hot spots within your application. Hot spots are sections of code that are executed most frequently. Consequently, tuning hot spots often provides more benefit than tuning code executed less often.

For those who may not immediately see how thread dumps help identify hot spots, consider how a profiler works. A profiler works by taking a thread dump at a regular interval (say every 5 milliseconds) and recording what classes/methods are currently being called within that dump. If `Foo.doWork()` is executing in an active thread in one of these intervals, the time allocated to `Foo.doWork()` is incremented and the percentage of time spent in `Foo.doWork()` is computed from that allocated time. The more intervals in which `Foo.doWork()` appears, the higher percentage your profiler assigns it and the more it appears to be a hot spot your profiler identifies as a tuning opportunity. The same concept can be applied to taking a thread dump in production at high load. The more threads in which `Foo.doWork()` appears, the higher percentage of time spent in that method and the more benefit will be realized by tuning it. Thread dumps taken at high load will not replace your profiler, but they can often identify performance tuning activities worth pursuing.

Measure resource utilization on all application, database, and web servers in production. Measure CPU and memory utilization as well as I/O throughput rates. Performance issues will often show up as a resource shortage. It is important to keep some amount of history as developers are often notified of performance issues after they've occurred.

Deploy one application per Java EE container. It's much easier to investigate unplanned outages as the amount of application code that could have caused the outage is smaller.

Take a thread and memory dump as standard procedure before recycling an inoperative Java EE container. It may provide some clue as to what made the container inoperative.

ASSESSING APPLICATION QUALITY

I'll discuss some metrics that are used to measure application code quality. As there are limitations to each of these metrics, it is advisable to evaluate several metrics in making an overall assessment of quality.

The number of application defects that made it into production is often viewed as an indicator of application quality. The fewer number of defects, the higher the perceived quality. The trouble with this measurement is that more heavily used applications tend to have more reported defects than rarely used applications. This issue can be mitigated by scaling the number of defects with the number of transactions or page loads per unit time for the application.

The quantity of resources needed to address user issues and complaints with the application can be viewed as an indicator of application quality. Usually, this is measured in terms of the number of full-time developers that are needed to support the application. This is often called Full-time Equivalents (FTEs). Applications are not of the same size or complexity; the fact that one application consumes twice as many FTEs for support as another application might be due to the size and breadth of features provided by that application. Hence, to effectively compare the quantity of support FTEs for one application with another, you must weight the FTEs by some independent metric (e.g., lines of code, code length, cyclomatic complexity).

Automated test coverage can be taken as one indicator of quality. The higher the coverage, the less risk of unintended consequences when that application is changed. We have already discussed the fact that few applications have 100 percent coverage and that higher levels of automated test coverage have diminishing returns. I usually look for a test coverage percentage of at least 60 percent.

Simpler code is perceived as higher quality code, and many tools exist to measure code complexity (e.g., JavaNCSS). Very complex code tends to be more difficult to change without experiencing unintended consequences.

IDENTIFYING REFACTORING OPPORTUNITIES

Refactoring is rewriting selected code to make it easier to understand and maintain. Fowler (2000) provides an extensive list of conditions that indicate the need to refactor—conditions he calls "Bad Smells in Code." Although his list is so comprehensive I wouldn't presume to add to it, it is very code centric. For readers who may not have the intimate understanding of code required to apply Fowler's advice, I describe some observable symptoms that may indicate a need to refactor but don't require a full audit of the application's source.

Classes that you can't change without inadvertently creating other bugs may need to be refactored. This symptom is reminiscent of the movie *Night of the Living Dead*. Some programming bugs don't die; they just come back in different forms. Various circumstances can cause a bug to undergo such a metamorphosis.

Sometimes this happens when code within a class behaves differently, depending on context. For example, I had one client that used a central API to provide reports for multiple applications. For political reasons, the API interpreted some of the argument values differently, depending on which application was calling it (not a good idea, I know). Eventually, this service needed to be refactored because we couldn't change it without inadvertently causing bugs in some of the applications calling it.

Sometimes bugs morph when code within a single class is doing too much and should be separated into multiple classes. For example, one application I worked on had to be able to accept data from multiple data sources. Some of the data sources were relational databases and some weren't. At first, we had only two data sources. The programmer took a shortcut and put conditional logic in the class managing input to handle either data source. When we had to add data sources, the class had to be refactored.

Enhancements or bug fixes requiring identical changes in multiple classes may indicate a need to refactor. Some developers are almost too fond of copy-and-paste technology. In most cases, identical code in multiple classes should become common code "called" by multiple classes. Given a tight time frame, the developer who discovers a case of copied code might not have the time to make the code common. The architect or manager can assist by providing a mechanism to track these cases so they can be fixed when time permits.

Abnormally complicated methods or classes that developers fear changing may need to be refactored. Sometimes this symptom occurs in combination with the morphing-bug symptom described earlier. It is another indication that the code is too complex and needs to be refactored. Of course, the validity of this symptom depends on the assumption that developers are rational and their "fear" justified, which might not always be the case.

CHAPTER 18

FINDING YOUR WAY WHEN TECHNOLOGIES CHANGE

One of the challenges of being an application architect in the Java EE space is keeping up with the sheer number of third-party frameworks, tools, and libraries available, and the speed at which they change. Because of this, published works on computer technology topics become out-of-date soon after they are published. Many of the best practices and advice presented in this book, and any other published work, rely on features and toolsets available in the Java EE space today. As technologies advance, the practices and advice presented in any published work in the computer technology space will at some point need revision and updating.

It's time to take the conversation up a level and look at how that advice and list of best practices were derived; best practices and good advice are not arbitrarily created.

Application architecture, including the best practices and advice presented in this book, is guided by an underlying set of fundamental principles. These principles can be used to help you make architecture and design decisions not only now but also down the road, as new frameworks, tools, and libraries become available and existing technologies advance. I'm not the first by any means to attempt to document application architecture principles. I also don't claim that my list of principles is comprehensive; I have purposefully reduced the set of principles to those that are the most important and the most commonly used.

A principle is a primary law or truth that can be used to derive other principles.

Numerous examples of principles can be found in the worlds of physics and mathematics. Every young math student learns about the commutative properties for addition in mathematics; namely that 2 + 3 is the same as 3 + 2. That property is used abundantly in mathematics to prove more complex theories. Application architecture operates in a similar fashion in that it's guided by a base set of fundamental principles that are used to derive many accepted best practices common today. One example of a frequently referenced software development principle is DRY or Don't Repeat Yourself.

I distinguish between architectural principles and best practices because the two are often confused. Best practices are principles applied to a specific technology, product, or development condition. For example, the best practice of designing relational databases using 3rd normal form applies the DRY principle and avoids recording the same data in multiple places. The best practice of writing unit tests along with your production code applies the principle that catching errors earlier is better than catching them later. The best practice of checking arguments for all public and protected methods applies the principle that catching errors earlier is better than catching them later. In essence, the "best practice" is a rule of thumb written in terms that can be directly applied to a set of specific situations and technologies. By contrast, the "principle" is the underlying truth that makes best practices useful and beneficial to follow.

Architectural principles worth discussing have several qualities or attributes. Architecture principles are product generic; that is, they do not reference specific products, frameworks or technologies. As illustrated above, principles are often combined with specific frameworks and products to form best practices. Architecture principles are simple; complex principles will never be remembered or applied. Architecture principles are applicable; that is, they are worded in a way that can be easily applied to new situations. Architecture principles are independent; that is, they are unrelated to other principles. Architecture principles are logically consistent; they don't contradict other principles.

Without further ado, architectural principles I follow are:

- Simpler is better.
- Reuse, don't reinvent.
- Enforce separation of concerns.
- Swim with the stream.
- Catch errors earlier rather than later.
- Functional requirements are the highest priority.

Note that these principles are applicable for all applications, not just Java EE applications.

SIMPLER IS BETTER

Simpler solutions are always better than complex solutions. This applies to application code, it applies to business processes serviced by the application, and it applies to IT support procedures needed to keep the application functioning properly. Simpler solutions in application code are easier to understand and maintain. They have fewer defects. They are easier to teach to new members of the team and are quicker for new members to learn. Simpler application support procedures greatly increase the chance that they will be understood and followed, and it's easier to bring new support developers on to the team. Furthermore, the simpler the application is for users, the fewer questions users will have regarding how to accomplish their work.

Tolerate only enough complexity to satisfy known business requirements. Some problems are naturally complex. For example, air traffic control (e.g., keeping track of the position of all airplanes with the intent of avoiding collisions) is a naturally complex business problem. Consequently, some complexity will be necessary in all applications. But we distinguish between complexity that is required by the business problem and complexity that is unnecessary. Examples of unnecessary complexity are components that are introduced by developer mistake or poor design decisions. Complexity required by the business problem can't be avoided.

Sometimes it's not easy to distinguish between the two types of complexity. Sometimes, a little added complexity will make planned future changes easier. The problem is that if those plans are changed, then the complexity previously added becomes unnecessary, and potentially harder to maintain while providing no benefit. For example, we often make a choice whether to hardcode a value, make a needed value a constant, or make the value configurable (i.e., pass as an argument or obtain the value from the environment). The additional complexity needed to make the hardcoded value a descriptively named constant is low, and it doesn't add to the number of needed test cases as there's no conditional logic involved. It communicates to future developers what the value describes and very possibly saves developers time in making changes down the road. Most developers would be comfortable with the small amount of additional complexity needed to support the constant as opposed to the hardcoded value.

It's often tempting to make that value configurable and make that section of code more flexible, and perhaps more easily usable, in other use cases. However, making that decision adds conditional logic (i.e., you need to test the configured value and produce a descriptive error message if the value is invalid). Using the "simpler is better" principle, making the value configurable should *not* be done until it's needed since it adds conditional logic. Applying the "simpler is better" principle to deciding whether to hardcode the value or make it a constant is more difficult. Strictly speaking, making the value a constant isn't required to produce working software. However, making code easy to read (and consequently easier to change) is an implicit business requirement that we live with most of the time. Most of us would go ahead and declare the constant for code readability reasons.

Consistency is a form of simplicity. This can apply to coding conventions as well as product choices. Consistency in coding conventions optimizes developer time and reduces the amount of needed documentation. For example, if your package structure is consistent in all your applications (e.g., data access objects in the `.dao.` package, user interface related classes in the `.ui.` package, etc.), then it's much easier for new developers to find code they seek, even if they have limited experience in a particular application. An alternative package structure may have small incremental improvements, but those differences will cause at least some amount of confusion among developers. This confusion will slow them down. Granted, a different package structure may not slow down a developer all that much for all that long, but other examples of differences are more invasive.

As an example of consistency with product choices, consider user interface (UI) frameworks. Most UI frameworks are complex and require a significant learning curve. Consider Struts, Struts II, Java Server Faces, or any of the other user interface frameworks. Standardizing on one UI framework (i.e., being consistent with your product choice) throughout the enterprise allows developers to more easily transition between applications. The same concept can be applied to persistence frameworks and other included products.

Standardize solutions to common problems across the enterprise. For example, if some applications need to programmatically transfer data from one host to another, adopting a common library with FTP capabilities is a simpler solution. Once developers understand how to use that library, it's easier for developers to enhance or fix FTP logic in any of the applications in the enterprise. As another example, some applications require batch processing; that is, processing not initiated by a user but occurring on a defined schedule. If you choose one scheduler and standardize it across the enterprise, developers only have to learn one scheduler product and that knowledge is easily transferable.

REUSE—DON'T REINVENT

Trend toward reusing components that exist rather than inventing new versions of existing components. This principle applies to application and unit test code. It also applies to stored data (e.g., relational database designs should be 3rd normal form to avoid multiple copies of the same information). This principle is sometimes known by the acronym Don't Repeat Yourself (DRY).

Code reuse, by definition, reduces the size of the code base as measured by the number of lines of code. Code reuse optimizes development time;

it's often faster to reuse than reinvent. Code reuse also consolidates maintenance; a bug fix with commonly used code potentially fixes a wide array of bugs as the same code is used in multiple places. For example, consider a utility function used across the enterprise that forms a full name from the first, middle, and last names of a person (i.e., turns values "Derek," "Clark," and "Ashmore" into the string "Ashmore, Derek Clark"). Suppose this utility function produces a null pointer exception for people without recorded middle names. This bug may well surface in multiple applications but could be fixed in one centralized section of code.

A corollary to the reuse principle is Don't Repeat Others. Don't rebuild/rewrite what's already in the JDK or available in vended or open source products. To this end, Apache Commons Lang, Commons IO, Commons Collections, and Commons BeanUtils are frequent additions to my applications. Not only does this practice save development time; it saves testing time and reduces the likelihood of bugs. To illustrate the point, consider any of the products mentioned above. All of them have extensive unit test suites that have been developed over a period of years. Furthermore, these products have been field tested in thousands of products and applications throughout the world. This level of test coverage far exceeds what you will be able to provide with code you reinvent.

Centralize domain or architecture specific utility code across the enterprise. Organizations with several development teams often have similar if not identical needs. As I examine one of my current clients, I see sets of commonly used Hibernate entity classes that are shared/included in applications across that organization. I also see classes common for the specific technical product stack they've adopted: base classes for data access objects (DAO) classes, entity classes, web service server classes, user interface converter classes, for example. I also see interface classes for interfacing vended products they use. All of these are located separately in source control and are easily included in multiple applications.

Centralized code needs stricter code management. One model that effectively polices common code is to appoint a small group of senior developers as administrators for the centralized code. This ensures that code added to the centralized library adheres to code quality and design standards and has unit tests. You can view this group as the "committer" group for an internal product. While centralizing code at this level does take additional work, the benefits in terms of saving development time across the enterprise can be large. If your organization adopts the same technical product set for multiple applications, you can address cross-cutting concerns at an architecture level. Error handling and logging should not be a concern for application developers for a specific application; the architecture should take care of that for you. Likewise, transaction management and security concerns can also be addressed at an architecture level.

The reuse principle can also be applied to database designs. Database designs should be strict 3rd normal form to avoid recording the same fact multiple times. Often, developers are tempted to break this paradigm under the label "denormalization"; I've discussed in a previous chapter the fact that this isn't needed as much as it was in the days when relational database technology was new. Essentially, recording the same data multiple times means that those additional copies need to be maintained. The extra code needed for maintaining those additional copies of data is only necessary because multiple copies are maintained. By centralizing facts and only recording them once, you reduce the amount of maintenance code needed overall.

ENFORCE SEPARATION OF CONCERNS

Software components should have a narrow focus and be concerned only with what they need to accomplish their objective; nothing more. Software "components" are defined loosely. They could be individual classes or a separate library.

The "separation of concerns" principle promotes simplicity since code to handle unneeded information dependencies isn't present. Components that are narrowly focused promote reuse; they are easier to use as their purpose is clearer to developers and more versatile and useful in a wider variety of contexts. This principle makes software components easier to test as they reduce the dependencies the test code must manage. This principle effectively breaks down complex problems into a series of simpler problems; it promotes writing code with a clear and concise mission. There are several practical implications to this principle, as follows:

Applying the separation of concerns principle will produce a large number of software components or classes. However, these classes will be much simpler and more versatile. Software layering, which is the practice of separating applications into tiers, is an example of applying the separation of concerns principle. As you have seen in previous chapters, software layering produces more classes, but each class has a more clearly defined role and purpose. For example, a data access class or DAO handles all reading and writing for a specific entity or database table. Its purpose is clear, and it can easily be used and reused in a variety of contexts and sometimes in a variety of applications.

Software components should have a clearly defined mission. Anything else will lead to developer confusion and unnecessary code complexity. Components that have multiple missions or uses are often more complex and contain more conditional logic than those classes with a single purpose. This mission focus makes the component easier to use and more versatile. It also reduces the need to change the software component as it has less responsibility. For example, embedding business logic in DAO classes (a common mistake I see) makes the DAO more complex and also less versatile as it now must assume a call context. Had that business logic been separated out, it would be much easier to reuse that DAO class for other features in the application.

Only give software components information they "need" to accomplish their task. Providing unnecessary information makes the software component harder to use because what's important is hard to distinguish from what's needed. For instance, if you provide a class method a full customer entity class when it only really needs the customer's first, middle, and last name, it's unclear to developers which portion of the customer entity the component actually needs. When changing the customer entity, that component would have to be examined for possible impact. On the other hand, if the three strings were the arguments for that component method, changes to the customer entity class could not possibly affect that component's behavior. Avoid unnecessary parameters in methods. Avoid unnecessary class-level fields. Expressed another way, components are like spies; they should operate on a "need-to-know" basis.

Individual classes and methods should not make assumptions about execution context. In other words, classes and methods should be independent and shouldn't assume they are a part of a larger call sequence. For example, I've seen developers hardcode commits in DAO classes, assuming that the particular DAO will only be used in a specific use case. This limits use of that DAO class since it really can't then be used in other use cases which have additional database writes to perform in the same unit of work. It would have been better to handle the commit or rollback separately; as it's a cross-cutting concern, I often handle commits and rollbacks using a servlet filter instead. Often, developers have a hard time with this concept. They have a hard time visualizing uses for a particular section of code other than the use case they're currently concerned with.

Don't expose more fields and methods than are necessary. That is, protected methods should be references by at least two extended classes. Public methods should be references by at least one external class. This is a continuation of the need-to-know concept. Exposed fields and methods open the possibility that a class is used in a way that wasn't expected or tested. Put another way, if you expose fields or methods, you need additional unit tests to cover the additional functionality. One exception that is commonly made for complex methods that would ordinarily be made private is to make them protected, so that unit tests can be written to test them specifically. This happens rarely, but it does happen, and there is a benefit to promoting complex methods to protected status for testing purposes.

Don't introduce dependencies that aren't needed. This is a continuation of the need-to-know concept. Unnecessary dependencies make components harder to use and test, as these dependencies need to be provided and any requirements they have in order to function need to be met. For example, only DAO classes should be dependent on Hibernate or JPA classes. For code in the business logic layer to have a Hibernate dependency means that Hibernate needs to be at least present and possibly configured for that logic to run. This places an extra burden on unit test cases for these business logic classes. Additionally, it widens the possibility of impact should Hibernate be upgraded or switched to another JPA implementation. You can see this concept illustrated more clearly by looking at the work you go through to introduce different third-party products into your application. Introducing dependency-heavy products like Spring or Hibernate involve a lot more work as you typically need to examine potential version conflicts for those dependencies. Conversely, introducing products without dependencies (e.g., Apache Commons Lang) is very easy as there is much less possibility of version conflicts.

Insulate all application interfaces using proxies. That is, create a proxy class for all external applications used by your application. For example, if your purchasing application utilizes functionality in a customer management application via web services, create a proxy class or classes for that activity. This limits the effects of changes within the external application; changes to that external application will affect the proxy class only. Also, this makes unit testing easier as you can effectively stub the external application. Utilizing proxies also makes it easy to log all requests/responses with external applications to make problem diagnoses easier.

SWIM WITH THE STREAM

Use products and technologies as they were intended to be used. Using products in the way they were intended to be used increases the likelihood that your use of the product has been tested. Should you require assistance, that assistance and code examples will be easier to obtain for mainstream uses of a product than for nonstandard or nonsanctioned uses of the product. This is true whether it's a vended product or an open source product. It's just that with open source products, your "support" isn't provided by a vendor and usually consists of Internet searches or searches of the product's bug lists.

Using the product as it was meant to be used increases the probability that you will benefit from product advances. For example, users of relational databases that used designs in 3rd normal form (as relational databases are meant to be used) require frequent joins. In the early days, this was cause for concerns about performance. Now, due to product advances, joins using primary and foreign keys usually present no performance issues whatsoever. Users who normalized their database designs benefitted from technological advancements made to the relational database products they were using.

Don't use internal product classes that were not meant to be used outside the product. This is an example of inappropriate usage. It is common for API products to have classes used internally that were never meant for published consumption. For example, the web service product Apache Axis has internal string manipulation classes used internally within the product. It is technically possible for you to utilize those string manipulation classes and methods. However, they were never really meant to be exposed to users of the product. Those classes are public so that they can be used by several packages within the product and for no other reason. Your use of those internal classes might work for the current version of the product you're using, but those internal classes are subject to change when you upgrade. As they were never meant to be consumed by users, little or no effort will be made to ensure that they still work in the same way. In other words, your risk of introducing bugs during an upgrade increases if you have been using classes and methods that were never meant to be consumed. While published interfaces of products can change (e.g., Hibernate seems to change its publically consumed APIs quite often), there is usually documentation provided for the change, with advice on how to modify your applications on upgrade. This assistance usually doesn't exist with internal classes that were never intended for publication.

CATCH ERRORS EARLIER RATHER THAN LATER

It is always better to catch coding errors as early in the development process as possible. By "'better" we mean that errors caught earlier are generally cheaper to fix and usually cause less damage. If a bug is detected by end users, then the bug at the very least negatively impacts end-user productivity and consequently has a labor cost. Depending on the nature of the bug, the enterprise may incur other costs associated with the bug, such as inconveniencing and potentially losing customers. Costs associated with tracking, documenting, and eventually fixing the bug are also present. On the other hand, had that bug been detected before deployment to production, the bug would have cost development time to fix, but potentially none of the other costs to the enterprise would have been incurred. The practices of Test Driven Development (TDD) and Continuous Integration (CI) are based on this principle. If nobody notices the error before you fix it, did the error really occur?

The recommended practice of checking arguments to all public or protected methods applies this principle. By catching and explicitly labeling the error, we save development time fixing the bug. As you know, derivative errors are often harder and more time consuming to diagnose and fix. The recommended practice of trending toward runtime exceptions applies this principle by making it much easier and safer to throw and descriptively label errors without incurring the cost of verbose try/catch logic. The recommended practice of providing an error notification method to support developers applies this principle by reporting the error before an end user does.

A corollary to this principle is to adopt practices that prevent bugs in the first place. The practice of paired programming, in which all code is written by a team of two coders, is an example of applying this principle. The idea is that the observing coder will catch errors that the typing coder misses and thus prevent bugs. Tools such as PMD for Find Bugs can scan your code and highlight places in your code prone to causing known types of defects, such as null pointer exceptions.

Automated error reporting and notification of support personnel is essential. Users don't report all errors. It takes work to fill out a help desk ticket or explain the problem to a technician in enough detail to reproduce. Often, if users can find a workaround, they'll take the lazy way out and not report it. However, even though they don't report the error, their perception of the software application lowers. Consequently, automated error reporting is the only way you'll get notified of some errors. Further, automated error reporting can give you a clearer vision of how frequently users encounter the error. In addition, automated reports will arrive more quickly, giving you the opportunity to resolve issues earlier.

Code the most technically risky portions of a project first. Tasks that have the largest technical risk are generally those involving new or unfamiliar technologies or containing complex logic. Errors are more likely to be generated from these aspects of the project than from any other. Consequently, coding these sections first tends to increase the amount of testing time these sections receive and increases the chance that errors are caught before release.

FUNCTIONAL REQUIREMENTS ARE THE HIGHEST PRIORITY

A functional requirement is a business need; it is something that your application must provide for its end users. A "need" is a feature essential to the operation of the business. Building applications that don't meet business needs is pointless. Without a successful business side, there is no reason to sustain and fund business applications and the architecture supporting them. The importance of identifying functional requirements can't be understated. This is why I have spent entire chapters guiding you in how to identify and document those requirements. One way to document business needs is by use case, and there are certainly other methodologies. I list this as an architectural principle as I've seen developers sacrifice satisfying business requirements to preserve technical design ideals. If an application architecture or technical design doesn't support a new business requirement, it's time to enhance or replace that design. We don't get to selectively ignore business requirements simply because they are inconvenient to program or they introduce additional complexity. The complexity introduced by a new business requirement frequently adds to the cost of developing and maintaining the applications supporting that requirement. Once users understand the costs of the requirements they express, they may express those needs differently.

It's true that sometimes end-user representatives don't clearly understand what those needs are or can't express them effectively. Worded another way, sometimes clients don't initially *say* what they really mean. Sometimes, users confuse a "need" with a "want." A "need" is a feature essential to the operation of the business. A "want" is something that optimizes one portion of that business (e.g., reduces manual labor for someone) but isn't essential to the operation of the business. For example, a user may "want" a new report detailing information needed to make business decisions. If the user has other ways to obtain that information, the new report is a "want" (e.g., it makes gathering the information more convenient) but it is not a "need." Ferreting out and documenting true business needs in detailed enough terms for software developers to implement is a separate and important skill.

Nonfunctional requirements are requirements that specify the conditions under which the application is to operate, but don't define specific behaviors like functional requirements do. As an example of nonfunctional requirements, an application may require the presence of the Microsoft Windows operating system with at least 100MB of disk space and 2GB of memory. Another example of a nonfunctional requirement is to be accessible by the user over the Internet. These requirements do not state what the application is used for or even what business requirements are satisfied. Ideally, nonfunctional requirements should never disrupt satisfying business needs.

Index

About the Author

Derek Ashmore is a senior technology expert with more than twenty-five years of experience in a wide variety of technologies and industries. His past roles include application architect, enterprise architect, project manager, application developer, and database administrator. He has extensive experience with custom application development as well as integrating applications with commercial products such as Great Plains, Sales Force, Microsoft Dynamics, and more. Derek has been designing and leading Java-related projects since 1999.

If you need a project assessment for your Java-related project, Derek can be retained by contacting sales@dvtconsulting.com.

Derek can be contacted the following ways:

- E-mail: derek.ashmore@dvtconsulting.com
- LinkedIn: http://www.linkedin.com/in/derekashmore
- Facebook: https://www.facebook.com/JavaEEArchitectHandbook